TESTING IT

An Off-the-Shelf Software Testing Process, 2nd Edition

JOHN WATKINS

IBM Software Group, U.K.

SIMON MILLS

Ingenuity System Testing Services Ltd., U.K.

CAMBRIDGE
UNIVERSITY PRESS

CAMBRIDGE UNIVERSITY PRESS
Cambridge, New York, Melbourne, Madrid, Cape Town, Singapore,
São Paulo, Delhi, Dubai, Tokyo, Mexico City

Cambridge University Press
32 Avenue of the Americas, New York, NY 10013-2473, USA

www.cambridge.org
Information on this title: www.cambridge.org/9780521148016

First published 2001
Second edition 2011

Printed in the United States of America

A catalog record for this publication is available from the British Library.

Library of Congress Cataloging in Publication data

Watkins, John (John Edward)
Testing IT : an off-the-shelf software testing process / John Watkins, Simon Mills. – 2nd ed.
   p.   cm.
Includes index.
ISBN 978-0-521-14801-6 (pbk.)
1. Computer software – Testing.   I. Mills, Simon.   II. Title.
QA76.76.T48W38   2010
005.1′4–dc22   2010041956

ISBN 978-0-521-14801-6 Paperback

Additional resources for this publication at www.cambridge.org/9780521148016

To Francesca, Julie, and Valerie

Contents

Foreword to the Second Edition

Geoff Thompson

So what is this testing thing then?

A question that I and many other aspiring software testing professionals get asked frequently. We try to explain, and watch the questioner's eyes glaze over as he or she furtively starts looking around to find a reason to step away or change the subject.

Isn't it strange that this happens? Is it that the explanation is simply incomprehensible by any sane person, or is it that software testers themselves need to understand in simple terms what it is they do?

I can add my own personal perspective on this issue; I help organize the British Computer Society Specialist Group in Software Testing (BCS SIGiST), and I am regularly surprised by two things: first, 70% of the attendees have never attended any form of networking meeting before, and second (and perhaps more important), none of the attendees read any of the many software testing books that exist.

Having had the opportunity to discuss this with many of the attendees, it is clear that the reason for this is the content of the typical testing book – it's just too complex for them to get their teeth into and understand. What is needed is a straightforward, simple-to-read, and simple-to-use testing book.

When the first edition of *Testing IT* was released in 2001, this changed. For once there was a book that provided a simple overview of what testing was, with straightforward guidance for test practitioners, plus a selection of easy-to-use testing templates. Since then I have recommended *Testing IT* to numerous testers that I have met, as well as providing copies to the testers on projects I have managed, and have received positive feedback from them regarding the practical benefits that it provides.

With the publication of the second edition of *Testing IT*, John has built on the success of the first edition, revising and bringing it up to date to ensure it continues to be relevant for the next ten years and beyond. Having been a champion of the first edition, I was very pleased to have been invited to play a part in this process, having used my involvement in the Information Systems Examination Board (ISEB), International Software Testing Qualification Board (ISQTB), and the Test Maturity

Model Integrated (TMMi) initiatives to ensure the second edition continues to be relevant going forward.

So, back to my original question – what is this testing thing then? Well, although there is no single simple answer to this question, in my humble opinion, John's book goes a long way to helping practitioners involved in test process, test management, and testing make a really good stab at answering the question for themselves.

Foreword to the First Edition

Maurice Rosenburgh

Why is astronomy considered a science while astrology is considered only a pseudo-science? In other words, how can we prove that a theory faithfully describes reality, and that this theory can then be used to predict unknown facts? Karl Popper, the well-known philosopher, studied these problems and summarized his conclusions in one phrase: "The criterion of the scientific status of a theory is its falsability, or refutability, or testability."[*] For Popper, "confirming evidence should not count except when it is the result of a genuine test of the theory."

The testing process of a scientific theory is quite similar to the process of providing confirmation either to risky predictions or to attempts to falsify that theory. Testing is a complex activity. It has to simultaneously bear in mind the theory and the external reality; it has to provide objective answers to complex questions related to our own perceptions of a rational reality.

When developing software, we follow the same thought process, since one builds an abstract model between the external world and the user. In our software, we define strict processes that will guide our actions, and we build the data we want to manipulate in complex databases and templates.

Can we test our software with Popper's principles in mind? The answer is definitively yes, because software testing should not only be a confirmation that the application is working correctly but also that it will react correctly when unexpected conditions occur. This constant and complex relationship between the software one tests and external reality should guide testers in their daily work.

Although testing is usually perceived as a necessity in software development, it is rarely applied as a rigorous activity. Within many projects, testing is simply omitted; in others, it is executed with the distinct intent to prove that the application performs correctly under test conditions.

After reading John Watkins's *Testing IT* you will be convinced that testing is not as complex as it seems and that it can be managed like any other development activity.

[*] Karl Popper, *Conjectures and Refutations*. London: Routledge and Kegan Paul, 1963.

The first thing you notice in reading *Testing IT* is that John puts the accent on testing processes and real-world case studies, which are, in my opinion, the most important aspects of software testing, implicitly applying Popper's conclusions.

Testing IT is divided into three logical, distinct parts: Part 1 focuses on traditional testing processes. Although technology is evolving at lightening speed, processes remain. They become even more important because they are at the heart of any activity. You will find this part very useful since it presents the testing phases starting from unit testing up to regression testing in the order found on all projects. Each phase is presented in the same coherent plan, facilitating access to the information.

Part 2 gives practical case studies. Five projects are reported, each enhancing a different reality; we have again the confirmation that success is always related to a correct adaptation of processes to reality.

Part 3 presents ready-to-use templates and reference documents that you can adapt to your needs and that you will find very useful in your daily testing work.

Testing IT is not just another book on testing. It is, in addition, a guide for all testers who want to understand what testing is really about, and it proves once more that applying easy-to-understand processes is the key to success. In one word: indispensable.

I'm certain you will enjoy reading this book, as I did, and that you will keep it on your desk to profit in your daily work from John's rich experience.

Maurice Rozenberg, Paris
Author of *Test Logiciel* (1998, Eyrolles)

Acknowledgments

Second Edition Acknowledgments

I would like to express my gratitude to Dave Evans, Isabel Evans, Pete Kingston, and Jon Tilt for allowing me to cite their experiences in agile testing, and for their valuable insights into improving agile communications, revealing how to succeed with agile off-shore projects, and describing innovative solutions for visualizing project progress and defect detection (next time I see him, I must ask Dave Evans where he buys his lava lamps!). Thanks are also due to 2nd edition reviewers Anne Mills, Dave Burgin, and Nathalie Allen for their keen eyes and valuable observations and comments.

I am very grateful to Peter Quentin for his extensive knowledge of the ISEB and ISQTB syllabuses, and his advice and guidance on ensuring the content of the book was in line with current thinking.

Many thanks to independent testing guru Tom Gilb and Trond Johansen of Confirmit for allowing me to document their fascinating real-world agile software development and testing project in the form of a case study. Also, thanks to Gary Schwartz for his reviewing efforts on the Confirmit case study.

I would very much like to thank Geoff Thompson for his insightful, well-observed, and very flattering foreword to the 2nd edition (which is likely to cost me a fortune in beer), and for being such a fantastic ambassador and champion of the first edition of *Testing IT* (which I guess will more than cover the cost of the beers).

Special thanks to Simon Mills for kindly agreeing to join the *Testing IT* project, and for adding to and enhancing the quality of the 2nd edition by bringing his pragmatic and extensive experience and knowledge of testing and the testing process to the new edition.

Finally, many thanks to my editor Lauren Cowles and to David Jou for their support, encouragement, and encyclopedic knowledge of the publishing process.

First Edition Acknowledgments

I would very much like to thank the following people for their advice, assistance, and encouragement with the writing of the first edition of this book:

Martin Adcock, Steve Allott, Jo Armitage, Mike Ashton, James Bach, Chris Ball, Bob Bartlett, Clive Bates, Judith Bays, Lesley Beasant, Colin Bendall, Duncan Brigginshaw, Miriam Bromnick, Kevin Buchta, Dorothy Buck, Dave Burgin, Trevor J. Collins, Richard Coop, Victor Copeland, Chris Cupit, Jim Davies, Steve Dawson, Barbara Eastman, Will Eisner, Isabel Evans, Mark Fewster, Virpi Flyktman, Ian Francis, Ian George, Paul Gerrard, Peter Gillespy, Dot Graham, Sam Guckenheimer, Jon Hall, Marion Hampson, Richard Hands, Steve Harcombe, Kim Harding, David Hayman, Mark Hirst, Dave Hodgkinson, Alan and Alison Jones, John Kent, Shelagh Kidd, Sami Korppi, Shaun Legeyt, Carol Li, Neil Love, Nick Luft, Philip March, Andrew Martin, Peter McConnell, Alec McCutcheon, Aidus McVeigh, Simon Mills, Kevin Minier, Eric Nelson, Mike Newton, Tommi Oksanen, David Palfreeman, Richard Pollard, Andy Redwood, Susan and Andy Roach, Ranj Sekhon, Darran Shaw, David Shohet, Graham Shore, Michael Summerbell, Peter Terelak, Pete Thomas, Andrew Thompson, John Thompson, Richard Tinker, Julie Valentine, Paul Warne, Tony Wells, Martin Whitaker, and Helen White.

I would like to give particular thanks to Dorothy Graham for giving me the benefit of her extensive experience in the testing field; Graham Titterington for his comprehensive and informed review comments; Geoff Quentin for his testing insight, encyclopedic knowledge of testing standards, and extensive collection of testing references; and James Bach, Paul Gerrard, and Steve Hancock for their input and informed discussion regarding risk-based testing issues.

I would also like to thank the following people for their assistance in writing the case studies in Part 2 of this book, as well as for their general help and encouragement with the book and its contents: Morag Atkins, Ken Eves, Paul Goddard, Martin Kemble, David Marsh, Annette Philips, and James Toon.

I am also very grateful to Maurice Rozenberg for finding the time to both write the foreword to the book, and for giving me the benefit of his extensive testing expertise in reviewing the chapters, case studies, and appendices.

And last but certainly not least, I would like to express my appreciation for the insight and experience of my technical reviewer Kamesh Pemmaraju, and for the constant "encouragement" and guidance from my editor Lothlorien Homett.

1 Introduction

> "Hmm, The Wheel you say! Well, I don't wish to belittle your achievement, but I've travelled far and wide and I've seen a great many of these things invented by a great many people in a great many different caves!"
>
> **– Big Ugg, Neander Valley, 35,000 B.C.**

1.1 Purpose of the Book

This book provides comprehensive and rigorous guidance to workers in the field of software testing for researching or setting up a software testing process within organizations.

The book provides advice and guidance on all aspects of the testing process, including:

▶ The need to test software and the approach to testing
▶ Specific details of testing techniques, with examples
▶ The planning and management of testing projects
▶ Testing roles and responsibilities
▶ Comprehensive details of the testing phases
▶ Extensive testing document templates, proformas, and checklists
▶ Recommendations for testing process improvement and the role and use of metrics
▶ The testing challenges facing testers involved in quality assurance tasks on agile projects
▶ The testing challenges facing developers of object-oriented and component-based systems

The book covers the testing of software from a number of sources, including software developed or modified in-house, software that represents the modification or extension of existing legacy software systems, and software developed on behalf of an organization by a third party.

The book also covers acceptance testing of *commercial off-the-shelf* (COTS) software procured by an organization, or COTS software that has undergone bespoke development either internally or by a third party on behalf of an organization.

This book should be used in a pragmatic manner, in effect providing a testing framework that can be used by all members of staff involved in software development and testing within an organization to improve the quality of the software they deliver and to reduce time scales, effort, and cost of testing.

Alternatively, the testing process described in this book can be customized to match the specific testing requirements of any particular organization, and a series of real-world case studies are provided to illustrate how this can be achieved.

1.2 Readership

The target audience for this book includes the following people:

- ▶ **Technical directors/managers** who need to improve the software testing process within their organization (in terms of quality, productivity, cost, and/or repeatability of the process)
- ▶ **Quality assurance (QA) professionals** (such as company QA directors or managers) who need to put in place a formal organization-wide approach to software testing
- ▶ **Project managers/leaders** who need to save time, effort, and money, and improve quality by adopting a complete, standard, off-the-shelf solution to their testing requirements
- ▶ **Independent information technology (IT), QA,** or **management consultants** who provide advice and guidance to clients on software testing process, for whom the book will represent a key item in their "Consultants Tool Kit"
- ▶ **Testing/QA professionals** (such as test analysts, testers, or QA representatives) who wish to save time and effort by adopting predefined testing artifacts (such as standard templates for test scripts, test plan and test specification documents)
- ▶ **IT professionals** who need to understand the software testing process (such as developers involved in unit or integration testing)
- ▶ **Any staff members** who are keen to improve their career prospects by advocating a complete testing solution to their organizations' software testing needs, particularly where there is a need to improve quality or save time, effort, and cost
- ▶ **Training managers/trainers** who are in the process of writing or amending testing training materials and who need to obtain a pragmatic view of testing process and its application
- ▶ **Students** who need to obtain a pragmatic/real-world view of the application of testing theory and principles of organizational software testing requirements, or who have an interest in testing process improvement and the role and use of metrics

1.3 How to Read This Book

This book is divided into three parts, all closely linked, but each of which can be read and applied separately.

Part 1 (Chapters 2 to 14) documents the "traditional view" of the components comprising a software testing process. Part 1 provides detailed information that can be used as the basis of setting up a testing process framework tailored to the individual requirements of any organization involved in software testing.

Part 2 (Chapters 15 to 20) provides a series of case studies that show how a number of organizations have implemented their own testing process based on the "classic view" described in Part 1. These case studies can be read to provide real-world guidance on how an individual organization can implement a testing process framework to meet its own particular testing requirements.

Part 3 (the appendices) contains a set of standard testing document templates, proformas, and checklists, plus a number of appendices that expand on topics described in the main body of the book (such as worked examples of specific testing techniques). The standard testing document templates, proformas, and checklists are also available from the following link: http://www.cambridge.org/9780521148016, and can be used immediately without modification or customized to reflect the particular requirements of any organization (such as a corporate style, branding, or documentation standard).

Where terms appear in *italics*, these terms are more fully defined or expanded on in the glossary.

1.4 Structure and Content of This Book

Specifically, the chapters and appendices comprising this book are:

▶ Chapter 2, which discusses just how challenging it is to thoroughly test even the most simple software system, reviews a number of definitions of testing, provides a brief overview of the approach to software testing, and lists a number of definitive testing references for further reading
▶ Chapter 3, which describes the principal techniques used in designing effective and efficient tests for testing software systems and, where appropriate, provides references to illustrative worked examples in the appendices
▶ Chapter 4, which deals with the issues associated with the management and planning of the testing process, provides guidance on the organization of testing and testing projects and on the need for thorough planning, describing a number of techniques for supporting the planning process
▶ Chapters 5 to 11, which provide details on each of the testing phases (from unit testing to acceptance testing and on to regression testing[1]) and their interrelationships. Each chapter is presented in a standard format and covers:
  ▷ the overall testing approach for that phase
  ▷ test data requirements for that phase

---

[1] Although not strictly speaking a separate testing phase, regression testing is included in this list for the sake of completeness.

▷ the roles and responsibilities associated with that phase

▷ any particular planning and resourcing issues for that phase

▷ the inputs to and the outputs from that phase

▷ a review of the specific testing techniques appropriate to that phase

▶ Chapter 12, which discusses the need for process improvement within the testing process and reviews the role of metrics (proposing a pragmatic metrics set that can be used effectively within and across testing projects). It also provides references to further sources of information on test process improvement

▶ Chapter 13, which for organizations adopting the testing process described within this book or using it as the basis of setting up their own testing process framework, discusses the process of introducing the testing process into an organization, managing its successful adoption, and reviewing the need to maintain that testing process and proposing an approach to satisfy this requirement

▶ Chapter 14, which discusses the phenomenon of agile approaches to software development and testing, reviews a number of successful agile quality management practices being employed by testing practitioners on real-world projects, and concludes by making a series of recommendations about how to implement an effective and efficient agile testing approach

▶ Chapters 15 to 20, which provide a series of real-world case studies describing how a number of commercial organizations have implemented their own customized view of the testing process described in Chapters 2 to 12. Specifically, the organizations providing case studies are:

▷ The British Library

▷ Reuters Product Acceptance Group

▷ Crown Quality Assurance Group

▷ The Wine Society

▷ Automatic Data Processing (ADP) Limited

▷ Confirmit Agile Development and Testing

▶ Appendices A to J, which provide a set of testing document templates, proformas, and checklists:

▷ terms of reference for testing staff

▷ summary testing guides for each testing phase

▷ a test plan document template

▷ a test specification document template

▷ a test script template

▷ a test result record form template

▷ a test log template

▷ a test certificate template

▷ a reuse pack checklist

▷ a test summary report template

▶ Appendices K to N, which provide a series of worked examples of testing techniques described in Chapter 3

▶ Appendices O to S, each of which expand on topics described in passing in the main body of the book, and include:
  ▷ a scheme and set of criteria for evaluating the relative merits of commercially available automated software testing tools
  ▷ an overview of the process of usability testing and its application
  ▷ a scheme and set of criteria for performing an audit of a testing process
  ▷ a discussion of the issues involved in the testing of object-oriented and component-based applications
  ▷ an overview of a real-world example describing how it is possible to adopt a subset of the best practices described in this book in order to gain rapid-quality improvements.
▶ A list of the references cited in the book
▶ A glossary of terms used in this book

PART ONE

THE TRADITIONAL TESTING PROCESS

2 An Overview of Testing

"As we strive to implement the new features of our applications, there is one thing we can say with absolute certainty – that at the same time, we also introduce new defects."

2.1 Introduction

This chapter provides an overview of testing to provide an understanding of what testing is and why it is such a challenge. It also emphasizes that whenever we test software, the process must be made as efficient and effective as possible.

Readers familiar with the need for efficient and effective testing may not need to read this chapter.

2.2 The Challenge of Testing

So, just how difficult is testing? To help answer this question, consider the following example.

Imagine we have a requirement to test a simple function, which adds two, thirty-two bit numbers together and returns the result. If we assume we can execute 1,000 test cases per second, how long will it take to thoroughly test this function?

If you guessed seconds, you are way out. If you guessed minutes, you are still cold. If you guessed hours, or days, or even weeks you are not even slightly warm. The actual figure is – 585 million years.[1]

But surely this is a daft example. Nobody in his or her right mind would test such a function by trying out every single possible value! In practice, we would use some formal test design techniques such as *boundary value analysis* and *equivalence partitioning* to help us select specimen data for our test cases (see Chapter 3 for details of test design techniques). Using this test data, we would assume that if the function performed satisfactorily for these specimen values, it would perform satisfactorily for all similar values, reducing the time needed to test the function to an acceptable timescale.

---

[1] The calculation is quite straightforward (with a calculator) – $2^{(32+32)}/1000/60/60/24/365.25 = 584542046$ years.

However, as testers we should not start feeling too confident too soon – there are many other issues that can complicate the testing of our "simple" function. For example:

▶ What if the function needs to interoperate with other functions within the same application?
▶ What if the data for the calculation is obtained across a complex client/server system and/or the result is returned across the client/server system?
▶ What if the calculation is driven via a complex graphical user interface with the user able to type the addition values into fields and push the buttons to perform the calculation in any arbitrary order?
▶ What if this function has to be delivered on a number of different operating systems, each with slightly different features, and what if individual users are able to customize important operating system features?
▶ What if this function has to be delivered on a number of different hardware platforms, each of which could have different configurations?
▶ What if the application that this function belongs in has to interoperate with other applications, and what if the user could be running an arbitrary number of other applications simultaneously (such as email or diary software)?

These are all typical requirements for software systems that many testers face every day during their testing careers. They make software systems highly complex and make testing an immense challenge!

2.3 What Is Testing?

The process of testing is by no means new. The Oxford English Dictionary tells us that the term "test" is derived from the Latin expression – *testum*, an earthenware pot used by the Romans and their contemporaries in the process of evaluating the quality of materials such as precious metal ores.

Computer programs have undergone testing for almost as long as software has been developed. In the early days of software development there was little formal testing, and debugging was seen as essential to developing software.

As the software development process has matured, with the inception and use of formal methods (such as 6), the approach to testing has also matured, with formal testing methods and techniques (such as 8) being adopted by testing professionals.

Most workers in the field of modern software development have an intuitive view of testing and its purpose. The most common suggestions include:

▶ To ensure a program corresponds to its specification
▶ To uncover defects in the software
▶ To make sure the software doesn't do what it is not supposed to do
▶ To have confidence that the system performs adequately

▶ To understand how far we can push the system before it fails
▶ To understand the risk involved in releasing a system to its users.

Here are some more formal definitions of testing:

> Testing is any activity aimed at evaluating an attribute or capability of a program or system and determining that it meets its required results (1).

This definition addresses the traditional testing approach, that is, does the system conform to its stated requirements? This appears to be an intuitive view of testing; we have some statements about how the system should behave, and we confirm that these requirements are met. This approach is also known as *positive testing*.
   Here is another view of testing:

> Testing is the process of executing a program or system with the intent of finding defects (2).

This definition is less intuitive and does not, strictly speaking, consider the requirements of the system.[2] Instead, it introduces the notion of actively looking for defects outside the scope of the software requirements, which in practice could be any problem or defect in the system. This approach is also known as *negative testing*.
   In practice, testing will combine elements of positive and negative testing – checking that a system meets its requirements but also trying to find errors that may compromise the successful operation or usefulness of the system.[3]
   Most recently, the notion of defining testing in terms of risk has become increasingly popular. In this use, the term "risk" relates to the possibility that the *application under test (AUT)* will fail to be reliable or robust and may cause commercially damaging problems for the users. Here is a definition of testing in terms of risk:

> Testing is the process by which we explore and understand the status of the benefits and risk associated with the release of a software system (28).

Within this definition of testing, the role of the tester is to manage or mitigate the risk of failure of the system and the undesirable effects this may have on the user.
   Defining testing in terms of risk provides the tester with an additional strategy for approaching testing of the system. Using a risk-based approach, the tester is involved in the analysis of the software to identify areas of high risk that need to be tested to ensure the threat is not realized during operation of the system. Furthermore, the notion of risk in a project management context is well known and understood, and many tools and techniques exist that can be applied to the testing process (28, 29, 30).

---

[2] Although a "defect" could be considered a failure of the system to support a particular requirement.
[3] It is possible to argue that in a perfect world of complete requirements and accurate specifications, there would be no need for negative testing, because every aspect of the application under test (AUT) would be specified. Unfortunately, the reality is somewhat short of perfection, and so testing is always likely to include a degree of negative testing.

It may be difficult for the staff involved in planning and design of tests to identify specific risks for a particular AUT (especially where they may not be familiar with the domain of operation of the software). In assessing risk, it is essential that the following issues be considered:

▶ The business, safety, or security criticality of the AUT
▶ The commercial/public visibility of the AUT
▶ Experience of testing similar or related systems
▶ Experience of testing earlier versions of the same AUT
▶ The views of the users of the AUT
▶ The views of the analysts, designers, and implementers of the AUT.

The need to analyze risk in the testing process is addressed in Chapter 4 – the Management and Planning of Testing.

2.4   Verification and Validation

Two testing terms frequently used but often confused are *verification* and *validation*. Reference 40 provides a formal definition of these terms:

> Verification is the process by which it is confirmed by means of examination and provision of objective evidence that specific requirements have been fulfilled (during the development of the AUT)

> Validation is the process by which it is confirmed that the particular requirements for a specific intended use (of the AUT) are fulfilled

Reference 26 provides a succinct and more easily remembered definition of these terms:

> Verification: Are we building the product right?

> Validation: Are we building the right product?

Verification deals with demonstrating that good practice has been employed in the development of the AUT by, for example, following a formal development process (8).

Validation deals with demonstrating that the AUT meets its formal requirements, and in that respect conforms closely to the Hetzel (1) definition of testing discussed earlier in this chapter.

Both verification and validation (also termed *V&V*) are key to ensuring the quality of the AUT and must be practiced in conjunction with a rigorous approach to requirements management. Chapter 4 provides guidance on the role of requirements management and its role within V&V.

2.5 What Is the Cost of Not Testing?

Many examples exist, particularly those involving safety critical, business critical, or security critical applications, where the failure of the system has, either through litigation or loss of public confidence, resulted in the software provider going out of business.

Even where a system does not deal with a critical application, failure of high-profile systems, such as an organization's Web site, free shareware, or demonstration software, can still have serious commercial implications for the organization in terms of loss of public confidence and prestige.

Some defects are subtle and can be difficult to detect, but they may still have a significant effect on an organization's business. For example, if a system fails and is unavailable for a day before it can be recovered, then the organization may lose a day's effort per person affected. If an undetected defect simply causes the performance of a system to degrade, then users may not even notice that a problem exists. If, however, the defect causes a loss of productivity of just thirty minutes per day per user, then the organization could lose on the order of twenty days effort per person per year!

2.6 Testing – the Bottom Line

Phrases like "Zero Defect Software" or "Defect Free Systems" are hyperbole, and at best can only be viewed as desirable but unattainable goals.[4]

In practice, it is impossible to ensure that even relatively simple programs are free of defects because of the complexity of computer systems and the fallibility of the development process and of humans involved in this process.

In simple terms, it is impossible to perform sufficient testing to be completely certain a given system is defect free. When you combine this problem with the fact that testing resources are finite and (more typically) in short supply, then adequate testing becomes problematic. Testers must focus on making the testing process as efficient and effective as possible to find and correct as many defects as possible.

Ultimately, testing can only give a measure of confidence that a given software system is acceptable for its intended purpose. This level of confidence must be balanced against the role the system is intended for (such as safety critical, business critical, secure, confidential, or high-profile applications) and against the risk of the system failing in operation before the decision to release or accept software can be made.

The key to effective testing is making the process as efficient as possible: rigorous planning and project management must be employed; testers must use their

---

[4]   Even with mathematically rigorous methods (such as Z and VDM), it is still impossible to say that any but the simplest pieces of software will be defect free.

knowledge of testing techniques and experience to guide them in devising effective tests; reuse must be introduced and managed at all stages of the testing process; and organizations need to consider the benefits and role of automated software testing tools.

Each of these issues is considered in detail in the following chapters.

2.7 Additional Information

Both the Hetzel and Myers books (1, 2) are excellent general introductions to testing, as well as useful reference documents for more experienced testing practitioners. Bach's paper (28) provides a risk-based view of testing and offers guidance on performing testing from a risk-based perspective.

I also recommend the Fewster and Graham book (17), which although specifically dealing with software test automation, also provides a good general treatment of the subject.

Other testing books well worth reading include the Gilb and Graham book on software inspection (41), the Kit book (42), and the Beizer text on software testing techniques (43). I also recommend excellent testing books by Lee Copeland and Paul Jorgensen (73, 74) for further guidance on test design and on general testing best practices and principles. Last, I recommend Reference 54 as an excellent source of information on agile testing topics, as well as on the impact of new software development processes on testing and testers.

The CCTA IT Infrastructure Library series (5), published by the government center for information systems, provides thorough guidelines on setting up and administering a testing program within an organization.

The British Computer Society Specialist Group in Software Testing (BCS SIGiST) is very active in promoting the role of software testing and the use of best practice and process, and it is well worth a visit to the BCS Web site at www.bcs.org.uk (then search for SIGiST).

Other testing Web sites well worth a visit include:

▶ The Professional Tester: www.professionaltester.com
▶ Software Quality Engineering: www.sqe.com
▶ The Open University Faculty of Mathematics and Computing: www.open.ac. uk/courses
▶ The Software Testing Institute: www.softwaretestinginstitute.com
▶ The Information Systems Examinations Board (ISEB): www.bcs.org
▶ The International Software Testing Qualifications Board (ISTQB): www.istqb.org
▶ The Test Maturity Model Integrated (TMMi): www.tmmifoundation.org

Please also visit the Cambridge University Press Web site, where there are further references to testing books as well as links to other Web sites specializing in testing: www.cambridge.org

The following standards are worth obtaining for reference purposes:

▶ "IEEE Standard for Software Test Documentation," IEEE Std 829–2008, IEEE, 2008

▶ "International Software Testing Qualifications Board Glossary" – http://www. istqb.org/

3 Testing Techniques

> "I am for those means which will give the greatest good to the greatest number."

– Abraham Lincoln

3.1 Introduction

This chapter describes a number of testing techniques that the *test analyst* can employ in designing and developing effective *test cases*.

This chapter focuses on practical, pragmatic design techniques that test designers can employ in their everyday testing tasks, and does not try to provide an exhaustive list of every possible testing technique available (e.g., symbolic testing or other research-oriented testing methods).

The testing techniques are organized into three main groups:

▶ General testing techniques (i.e., high-level approaches to testing that can be applied to the specific testing techniques described in the second and third groups in the following), which include:
   ▷ Positive and negative testing
   ▷ White box and black box testing
   ▷ Experienced based testing or error guessing
   ▷ Automated software testing
▶ Functional testing techniques (i.e., testing techniques used to confirm that the *application under test (AUT)* meets its *functional requirements*), which include:
   ▷ Equivalence partitioning
   ▷ Boundary value analysis
   ▷ Intrusive testing
   ▷ Random testing
   ▷ State transition testing
   ▷ Static testing
   ▷ Thread testing
   ▷ Pairwise testing
▶ Nonfunctional testing techniques (i.e., testing techniques used to verify that the (AUT) meets its *nonfunctional requirements*), which include:
   ▷ Configuration/Installation testing
   ▷ Compatibility and interoperability testing

> ▷ Documentation and help testing
> ▷ Fault recovery testing
> ▷ Performance testing
> ▷ Reliability testing
> ▷ Security testing
> ▷ Stress testing
> ▷ Usability testing
> ▷ Volume testing

Where appropriate, examples illustrating the use of a particular test design technique are provided in the appendices.

3.2 General Testing Techniques

3.2.1 Positive and Negative Testing

Positive and negative testing are complementary testing techniques, and in practice both processes are likely to be used in the testing of a particular AUT (see Figure 3.1, for example).

The process of positive testing is intended to verify that a system conforms to its stated requirements. Typically, test cases will be designed by analysis of the *requirements specification document* for the AUT. The process of positive testing must be performed to determine if the AUT is "fit for purpose," and where the application will be delivered to a customer, the process is likely to be a compulsory aspect of contractual acceptance.

"A Compact Disk (CD) Player can be in one of three states: Standby, On or Playing.

When in Standby mode, the CD Player can be turned on by pressing the Standby button once (an indicator light turns from red to green to show the CD Player is On).

When the CD Player is On, it can return to Standby mode by pressing the Standby button once (an indicator light turns from green to red to show the CD Player is in Standby mode).

When the CD Player is On, pressing the Play button causes the currently loaded CD to play. Pressing the Stop button when the CD Player is playing a CD causes the CD Player to stop playing the disk."

Examples of positive tests could include:

- Verifying that with the CD Player in Standby mode, pressing the Standby button causes the CD Player to turn on and the indicator light changes from red to green
- Verifying that with the CD Player in the On state, pressing the Standby button causes the state of the CD Player to change to Standby and the indicator light changes from green to red."

Examples of negative tests could include:

- Investigating what happens if the CD Player is playing a CD and the Standby button is pressed
- Investigating what happens if the CD Player is On and the Play button is pressed without a CD in the CD Player.

3.1 Examples of Positive and Negative Testing

The process of negative testing is intended to demonstrate – "that a system does NOT do what it is not supposed to do." That is, test cases are designed to investigate the behavior of the AUT outside the strict scope of the requirements specification. Negative testing is often used to test aspects of the AUT that have not been documented or that have been poorly or incompletely documented in the specification.

Because the requirements for software systems are frequently poorly specified (or possibly missing, such as is the case with some legacy systems), it is likely that a certain amount of negative testing of the AUT will be required to provide confidence in the operation of the application. This must be balanced against the need to be as effective and efficient as possible in testing, because negative testing is an open-ended technique and is not bounded in terms of possible expended effort in the same manner as positive testing.

To illustrate the techniques of positive and negative testing consider the following extract (in Figure 3.1) from the specification for the operation of a compact disk player.

3.2.2 White Box and Black Box Testing

White box and black box testing are complementary approaches to testing the AUT that rely on the level of knowledge the test analyst has of the internal structure of the software.

White box tests are designed with the knowledge of how the system under test is constructed. For example, an analyst designing a test case for a particular function that validates the input of an integer within a specified range of values may be aware that the validation is performed using an "IF-THEN-ELSE" instruction, and so will structure the test to check that the appropriate logic has been implemented. It is anticipated that the test analyst will have access to the design documents for the system or other implementation documentation or will be familiar with the internal aspects of the system. Other sources of knowledge may include familiarity with similar or related systems to the AUT.

Black box tests are designed without the knowledge of how the system under test is constructed. This is not as unlikely an event as it may at first seem. For example, the test analyst may be called upon to design *regression tests* for extensions to legacy applications where the system documentation has been lost, or to design acceptance tests for *commercial-the-shelf* (*COTS*) products or systems implemented by third-party developers. In black box testing, the design of test cases must be based on the external behavior of the system. If requirements exist for the system, these must be tested against. Where there are no requirements, then user guides or documentation describing how the system should behave can be used as the basis of test design.

The terms *behavioral* and *structural testing* (45) are often used synonymously with the terms black box and white box testing. In fact, behavioral test design is slightly different to black box testing, as the knowledge of how the system under test is constructed is not strictly prohibited during test design, but is discouraged.

Because knowledge of how the software was constructed is necessary for white box testing, this technique is typically used during the early phases of the testing process where the programmer is responsible for designing and executing the tests (such as *unit testing* – see Chapter 5). Black box techniques are typically used during the later phases of the testing process (such as *system testing* – see Chapter 7), where the test analyst may not have access to information about how the software was constructed or where the software has been developed by a third party or brought in as COTS software. In practice, test analysts often use a mixture of black and white box techniques in the design of test cases, in effect following a "grey box" or "translucent box" approach.

3.2.3 Experienced Based Testing

Experienced based testing is not in itself a testing technique, but rather a skill that can be applied to all of the other testing techniques to produce more effective tests (i.e., tests that find defects).

Also termed error guessing, experienced based testing is the ability to find errors or defects in the AUT by what appears to be intuition. In fact, those testers who are effective at error guessing are actually using a range of techniques including:

▶ Knowledge about the AUT, such as the design method or implementation technology
▶ Knowledge of the results of any earlier testing phases (particularly important in regression testing)
▶ Experience of testing similar or related systems (and knowing where defects have arisen previously in those systems)
▶ Knowledge of typical implementation errors (such as division by zero errors)
▶ General testing rules of thumb or heuristics.

Experienced based testing is a skill that is well worth cultivating because it can make testing much more effective and efficient – two extremely important goals in the testing process. As suggested by its title, the skill of experienced based testing is obtained through experience, although there are some people who seem to have a natural flair for finding defects in software systems.

3.2.4 Automated Software Testing

Although strictly speaking not a testing technique, automated testing is included in this section for the sake of completeness.

The majority of test automation tools[1] allow reusable tests to be created by recording the expected behavior of the AUT under its typical operation, then subsequently replaying those tests (against a later build or release of the software) to compare the observed behavior against the expected behavior (i.e., the originally recorded

---

[1] Other examples of test automation tools include those where the test is created using a simple scripting language such as (47).

behavior). Where the observed behavior differs from the expected behavior, the tool logs this event and allows the tester to analyze how and why the differences have occurred.

Automated tools exist that support both the testing of functional and nonfunctional aspects of the AUT, such as testing against the functional requirements for the AUT and *performance*, *load*, *volume*, and *stress* testing (see [23], for example).

A significant benefit of such tools is their ability to operate unattended (e.g., to run overnight or over the weekend), providing significant gains in productivity for the testing task. Automated tools can also provide additional confidence in the AUT by allowing more tests to be executed in the same time as that taken for an equivalent manual test.

The principal use of such tools is in *regression testing* (see Chapter 11) or retesting of the AUT, where it becomes possible to rerun all of the previously generated tests against the application following modification or extension of the software, rather than the typical manual approach of attempting to assess the impact of the modifications on the AUT and selecting a "representative" subset of the tests to run. This is of particular benefit where an iterative approach to software development (8) has been adopted, because there is typically a demanding requirement to regression test the deliverables from earlier iterations.

Although these tools have many potential benefits, they will not be appropriate for all testing tasks, and a critical review and evaluation of the advantages and disadvantages must be undertaken before their introduction. Appendix O provides both a scheme and a set of criteria to support the process of evaluating automated software testing tools.

Examples of where automated testing tools may be particularly appropriate include:

▶ Testing of applications that have a rapid build and release cycle
▶ Testing of applications that have to be delivered across diverse platforms
▶ Testing of applications with complex GUI and/or client server architectures
▶ Testing of applications that require thorough, rigorous, repeatable testing (e.g., safety critical, business critical or security critical systems)
▶ Where there is a need to reduce testing timescales and effort
▶ Where there is a need to do more thorough testing in the same timescales.

Where automated testing tools are adopted, they must be integrated with the existing testing management process and not just "tacked on" to the current process with the expectation that they will provide instant benefits.

Finally, although it is possible to gain rapid benefits from the introduction of automated tools (see, e.g., [17]), typically the benefits such tools bring will not be realized during their initial use, because the tools will require integration into the existing testing process and there will be learning curve issues to overcome. However, it is important that organizations persevere with their use, otherwise such tools are likely to quickly become "Shelfware" and the initial investment in the tool and its use will be lost.

References (22) and (23) provide typical examples of such automated testing tools, whereas case studies in Chapters 17 and 19 provide examples of the successful use of such tools.

3.3 Functional Testing Techniques

3.3.1 Equivalence Partitioning

This technique relies on the fact that inputs and outputs from the AUT (which can include environment variables and logical operations) can be grouped or partitioned into coherent groups or classes, and that all instances of these classes will be treated in the same manner by the system. The principal assumption of this technique is that testing one instance of the class is equivalent to testing all of them.

The skill in using this technique lies in identifying the partition of values and selecting representative values from within this partition, and in deciding how many values to test.

There are a number of graphical methods that can be used to support this technique, which involve visualizing the partition and tabulating the test cases and their values (Appendix K provides a worked example that demonstrates the technique of equivalence partitioning).

3.3.2 Boundary Value Analysis

Boundary value analysis is a closely related technique to equivalence partitioning and relies on the same underlying principle – that inputs and outputs can be grouped into classes and that all instances of these classes will be treated similarly by the system.

Where equivalence partition deals with selecting representative values from within the class, boundary value analysis focuses on testing values from the boundary of the class. Specifically, the technique will design a test case for the boundary value itself, plus a test case for one significant value on either side of the boundary.

In practice, boundary value analysis and equivalence partitioning are used together to generate a complete set of test cases providing tests of the "edges" of the ranges of values as well as values from the "body" of the range of values.

As with equivalence partitioning, there are a number of graphical methods that can be used to support boundary value analysis, which involve visualizing the boundary (or boundaries) and tabulating the test cases and their values. (Appendix L contains a worked example that demonstrates the technique of boundary value analysis.)

In practice, when using boundary and/or equivalence techniques, the test analysts may face a combinatorial explosion in terms of the seemingly infinite number of possible combinations of values when considering the interaction between the different variables within the AUT. One possible solution the test analyst can use to control this complexity is the use of *pairwise testing* (Section 3.3.8).

3.3.3 Intrusive Testing

As the name suggests, intrusive testing involves the deliberate modification of the AUT or its behavior for the purposes of testing.

For example, where the result of a test would not be visible to the tester (such as the modification of the value of a variable that would not be displayed to the user during the execution of the AUT), the test analyst may introduce additional statements into the application to display the value of the variable. Other examples include directly setting the values of variables using symbolic debuggers or deliberately triggering error conditions within the AUT.

Clearly, any modifications made to the system for the purpose of testing must not be delivered to the customer/user of the system. Therefore rigorous change control and configuration management is essential.

Although this technique can be useful during testing, there is a fundamental objection to this form of testing, which is what you deliver after testing is not what you actually tested.

This technique should be used with extreme caution as there are many examples of systems that have been released containing changes introduced during intrusive testing that have manifested themselves during normal operation of the system.

3.3.4 Random Testing

Random testing is one of the few techniques for automatically generating test cases. Test tools are used to provide a harness for the AUT, and a generator produces random combinations of valid input values, which are input to the AUT. The results generated by each input are logged and the inputs and their respective results can be inspected following testing for defects.

Although it is relatively straightforward to automate the process of providing inputs and stimulating the AUT, it is difficult to automate the process of checking the outputs, which can make this a particularly labor-intensive process (as well as introducing the likelihood of human error). Depending on the approach employed, it may also be difficult to reproduce the results of a particular series of random tests. As a result, random testing is not a commonly used technique, but is one that is particularly appropriate to automated testing tool support.

Where it is used, this technique can be highly effective in identifying obscure defects; however, random testing should not be used as a substitute for other systematic testing techniques, but rather it should be considered an adjunct to the more rigorous techniques.

3.3.5 State Transition Analysis

This technique models the AUT in terms of the states the system can be in, the transitions between those states, the actions that cause the transitions, and the actions that may result from the transitions.

In designing test cases, state transition information can be derived from the requirements document, or may be documented in the design for those development methods that support state transition notations (such as the Unified Modeling Language or UML [6]).

Test cases are designed to exercise transitions between states and specify:

▶ The initial state
▶ The inputs to the system
▶ The expected outputs
▶ The expected final state.

As well as being useful in positive testing, this technique is particularly useful in negative testing, as the process of considering the system states and transitions will often suggest tests covering issues either overlooked or poorly specified in the specification document.

A number of graphical methods can be used to support this technique that involve visualizing the states and their transition. (Appendix M contains a worked example that demonstrates the technique of state transition analysis.)

3.3.6 Static Testing

As the name implies, static testing does not involve executing or running the AUT, but deals with inspecting the system in isolation.

There are a number of methods and tools typically used in static testing:

▶ Code review and inspection (by members of the development team)
▶ Code walk-through (using paper and pen evaluation)
▶ Static analysis tools (such as syntax and style checkers – see, e.g., [60])
▶ Complexity estimating tools (such as cyclic complexity analysis tools).

Static testing usually takes place early in the testing process, and is particularly appropriate as an adjunct to unit testing. See (24) for further information on static testing.

3.3.7 Thread Testing

This technique is used to test the business functionality or business logic of the AUT in an end-to-end manner, in much the same way a user or an operator might interact with the system during its normal use.

For example, if the AUT is a library system for managing the book lending process, one particular thread to test might be a request for a particular book. The process might involve the following steps:

▶ The operator logging onto the system
▶ Validation of the operator privileges
▶ Entry of the details of the book being requested
▶ Validation of the book details
▶ Access to the database to verify the availability of the book
▶ Modification of the database to show that the book has now been borrowed
▶ Printing of the appropriate paperwork to conclude the transaction.

This technique contrasts with earlier testing phases (such as unit and integration testing) where the tester is likely to have been more interested in the correct functioning of the object under test rather than on its business logic.

3.3.8 Pairwise Testing

As we discussed in Chapter 1, even with tool support it is a virtual impossibility to completely test all of the possible states that even moderately simple software can assume.

Where there are a number of different parameters that can be in a number of different states in a program, it appears that the two most effective approaches for finding defects are to change the state of a single parameter or to change the state of a pair of parameters (75). The tester sees diminishing returns in executing tests involving three or more parameters; with increasing test effort there are decreasing benefits in terms of finding defects.

The technique of pairwise testing (also termed all-pairs testing) looks to select a subset of all possible pairs of parameters and combinations of values to provide the most effective test coverage. Used in combination with the other test design techniques discussed within Section 3.3, pairwise testing provides good results in terms of identifying defects. (Appendix N contains a simple worked example that demonstrates the technique of pairwise testing).

In practice, for testing complex applications involving large numbers of parameters and possible states, the technique of pairwise testing may become unwieldy for manual test case design. Under such circumstances, there are numerous tools available that can be used to support the technique of pairwise testing (e.g., [76]).

3.4 Nonfunctional Testing Techniques

3.4.1 Configuration/Installation Testing

Configuration/Installation testing is used to ensure that hardware and software have been correctly installed, all necessary file and connections have been created, all appropriate data files have been loaded (such as database and/or historic information), system defaults have been correctly set, and interfaces to other systems or peripheral devices are all working.

3.4.2 Compatibility and Interoperability Testing

Compatibility testing verifies that when the AUT runs in the live environment, its operation does not impact adversely on other systems and vice versa. It is often required when a new system replaces an existing system, which had previously interacted with one or more other systems.

Interoperability testing verifies that when the AUT runs in the live environment it is able to communicate successfully with other specified systems (such as invoking, passing data to, or receiving data from another system).

3.4.3 Documentation and Help Testing

The testing of the documentation and help facilities of the AUT are frequently overlooked aspects of testing the complete system. The testing of these items is often omitted from the testing process (because of lack of time or resources), because it is thought to be outside the scope of the testing process or through simple carelessness. In fact, these aspects of the AUT may be vital to its successful operation and use, particularly for new or naive users of the system.

User documentation and help system information should be checked for conformance to the requirements specification document. Specific testing techniques involve review of the documentation, cross-referencing checks (e.g., against the document contents and index sections), and thread testing of typical user help scenarios.

3.4.4 Fault Recovery Testing

Fault recovery testing verifies that following an error or exception (such as a system crash caused by loss of power), the AUT can be restored to a "normal" state, such as the initial state of the application when it is first executed, and that the AUT can continue to perform successfully. Fault recovery testing may also be used to verify the successful rollback and recovery of the data used or manipulated by the AUT following an error or exception.

3.4.5 Performance Testing

Performance testing is traditionally a problem area because system performance is frequently poorly specified and can be measured using a variety of different criteria, including:

▶ User response times
▶ System response times
▶ External interface response times

▶ Central processor unit (CPU) utilization
▶ Memory utilization.

In conducting performance testing it is essential to have a "performance model" that specifies what aspect of system performance is being tested, what the performance requirements are, how they can vary under typical system usage, and how they will be tested. Once the performance model is established, the test analyst can design clearly defined test cases based on this information.

Another challenge in performance testing is the difficulty in accurately representing the test environment. For example, where there are likely to be large numbers of concurrent users and/or large amounts of data, it may be impractical or infeasible to set up and conduct realistic performance testing. Furthermore, recreating such a complex test environment to reproduce the test results or to rerun the tests against a new build or release of the AUT will be extremely difficult.

Because of these difficulties, performance (and volume and stress) testing is often conducted using automated testing tool support. Examples of such tools include "low-level" performance testing tools (such as [44]) that are able to identify sections of the AUT that are executed frequently and that may need to be optimized to improve application performance, or "high-level" tools that can simulate very large numbers of users and their typical tasks to realistically exercise the AUT (see [23]).

3.4.6 Reliability Testing

Reliability testing involves executing tests to ensure the robustness and reliability of the AUT under typical usage. Reliability testing typically includes integrity and structural tests.

Integrity tests focus on verifying the AUT's robustness (resistance to failure), compliance to language, syntax, and resource usage. For example, a particular unit could be executed repeatedly using a test harness to verify that there are no memory leak problems. Integrity tests can be designed, implemented, and executed during any testing phase.

Structure tests focus on verifying the AUT's adherence to its design and formation. For example, a structure test could be designed for Web-enabled applications to ensure that all links are connected, appropriate content is displayed, and there is no orphaned content.[2]

3.4.7 Security Testing

Depending on the intended role of the AUT, requirements may exist that specify the need to ensure the confidentiality, availability, and integrity of the data and software.

---

[2] Orphaned content are those files for which there is no "inbound" link in the current Web site, that is, there is no way to access or present the content.

Security testing is intended to test whether the features implemented within the AUT provide this required level of protection.

Security testing is mainly concerned with establishing the degree of traceability from the requirements through implementation, and in the validation of those requirements. Where particularly rigorous security testing is necessary, it is typically conducted by a dedicated team whose role is to evaluate the conformance of the AUT to the particular security requirements. Such teams may also verify that a standard approach or formal process has been followed in the development of the AUT.

Security tests can be designed, implemented, and executed within any testing phase but are typically conducted at system test and rerun during user acceptance testing.

3.4.8 Stress Testing

Stress testing (also termed load testing – [45]) examines the ability of the system to perform correctly under instantaneous peak loads with the aim of identifying defects that only appear under such adverse conditions. For example, if the specification for the AUT states that the system should accept thirty simultaneous users, what happens if a thirty-first user attempts to log on? Similarly, what happens if all thirty users attempt to log on simultaneously?

Simulation is a frequently used method in stress testing. In the previous example, it would be difficult from a planning and resource perspective to have thirty real-life users simultaneously logging on at thirty terminals; however, it may be more realistic to simulate thirty virtual users performing this activity.

It is also worth considering tool support for stress testing, and there are several software testing tools that automate the process, some of which also incorporate simulation techniques (e.g., [23]).

3.4.9 Usability Testing

The topic of software usability is increasingly important, particularly with the increase in popularity of visual programming environments and the use of development techniques such as user-centered design (9) and rapid prototyping (12).

Users themselves are also becoming increasingly sophisticated in their expectations of what a user interface should do for them and how it should support their business activities in a consistent and intuitive manner. Conversely, this must always be balanced by the inevitable occurrence of users unfamiliar with computer systems but who are still expected to be able to use a particular application with little or no guidance or training.

Specific techniques employed in usability testing include:

▶ Conformance checks – testing the application against agreed user interface (UI) standards (such as the Microsoft Windows standards – [10])

▶ User-based surveys – psychometric testing techniques to analyze user perceptions of the system (such as that documented in [11])

▶ Usability testing – where users are asked to perform a series of specified business tasks with the AUT under controlled conditions in order to test the usability goals or requirements of the AUT.

Appendix P describes usability testing in greater detail and provides an overview of one particular approach to usability testing. Also see (9) for a definitive treatment of usability.

3.4.10 Volume Testing

Volume testing (sometimes also termed "flood testing" – [45]) examines the system's ability to perform correctly using large volumes of data with the aim of identifying defects that only appear under such conditions.

Typically at the lower levels of testing (such as unit and integration testing) a representative sample or copy of the data the system will process is used. Only at the higher levels of testing (such as system and acceptance testing) is live data likely to be used. This may be an important issue where a system is expected to process particularly large quantities of data, because the ability of the system to function correctly under these circumstances will need to be tested.

Volume testing may involve rerunning appropriate tests from earlier testing phases (e.g., from the unit or integration reuse packs – see Appendix I), in addition to designing new test cases. One particular volume testing technique involves repeatedly running the same test while increasing the volume of data involved at each iteration to identify the point at which the system fails to cope with the volume of data.

The terms volume testing and stress testing are frequently confused with each other. Myers in (2) provides a useful typing analogy to help distinguish between these techniques: volume testing will confirm that a typist can cope with a very large document; stress testing will confirm that the typist can manage to enter forty words per minute.

3.5 Further Reading on Testing Techniques

The following references provide additional information on testing techniques and their role within the testing process.

The Beizer book (43) provides extensive information on testing techniques, as does the Kit text (42), although set in a process improvement context.

The testing unit of M301 (the third-level Open University Software Engineering course – [24]) provides a thorough treatment of testing techniques (and in particular on static analysis and review techniques) within the context of a formal engineering approach to software development, test, and deployment.

Reference (46) provides descriptions of the common testing techniques within the context of an end-to-end software development process.

Reference (45) provides an extensive and thorough coverage of software testing techniques, with particular emphasis on a quality assurance approach to validation and verification (*V&V*) of the AUT.

4 The Management and Planning of Testing

"Plans are worthless, the process of planning is invaluable"

– Eisenhower

4.1 Introduction

This chapter deals with the issues associated with the organization, management, and high-level planning of the testing process.

A generic approach to organizing the testing process is described, which can be applied to businesses involved in developing and/or testing software. The chapter discusses the implications for the testing process of the size of the business, its prevailing quality culture, and (where appropriate) the maturity of its software development process.

The case studies in Part 2 of this book provide specific examples of how a number of different businesses have customized this generic approach in response to their own particular organizational, management, and testing requirements.

This chapter also considers a number of key requirements that must be considered in implementing a rigorous, effective, and efficient testing process: the need for configuration management, defect tracking, and the need to ensure that each of the requirements of the *application under test* (*AUT*) has been verified. The issues associated with each of these requirements are discussed, and recommendations for supporting them are provided.

The chapter concludes with a discussion of the role of risk-based testing and its use in the management and planning of testing projects.

This chapter is structured as follows:

▶ Section 4.2 discusses the high-level organization of the testing process, the roles that are required and their interrelationships, and provides a diagram summarizing this information

▶ Section 4.3 provides specific details of the roles and responsibilities of the staff involved in a testing program

▶ Section 4.4 reviews the individual testing phases that comprise the complete testing cycle from *unit testing* through *acceptance testing*, and including *regression testing*

▶ Section 4.5 describes the *V Model*, its role in the management of testing, and its use in the process of planning the testing activities and in controlling risk

▶ Sections 4.6, 4.7, and 4.8 consider the need for requirements management, configuration management, and defect tracking in the testing process, and make recommendations for supporting these requirements

▶ Section 4.9 briefly reviews the role of risk-based testing in the management and planning of testing and provides a number of references that provide further information on this subject.

4.2 The Organization of Testing

One of the first steps in implementing a testing process is to consider the high-level organization of the staff involved in testing, their relationship to each other, and how the testing process will integrate with the existing management structure of the business.

The guiding principle in establishing the high-level organization is that there are a series of activities common to all testing tasks, which must be managed effectively and efficiently to ensure they are completed on time, to budget, and to an acceptable level of quality.

The challenge facing the majority of businesses involved in implementing a testing process is that this task cannot take place in isolation; there will be existing departments and groups within the company with which the testing process must integrate, and existing staff who will need to participate in the testing process. For example, many businesses incorporate the management of the testing process into the existing information technology (IT) group. Alternatively, for those businesses with a well-established quality culture, the testing process is often managed from within the quality assurance (QA) group.

Further issues to be considered include the size and complexity of the business, the geographic distribution of offices, and the balance of software developed/extended in-house, developed under contract by a third party, and bought-in as *commercial off-the-shelf* (*COTS*) products. All of these factors will affect the size and role of the testing process within a particular business.

Figure 4.1 provides a generic view of the organization of the testing process. Chapters 15 to 20 provide specific examples of how a number of different businesses have implemented the organization of their testing process based on their own particular organizational, management, and testing requirements. The testing roles shown in Figure 4.1 and their specific responsibilities are documented in the following section.

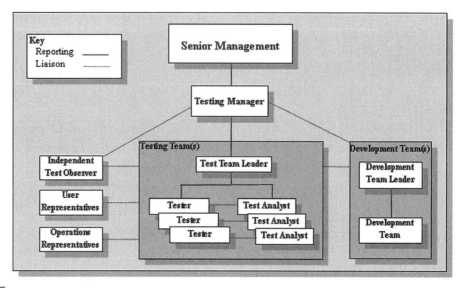

4.3 Roles and Responsibilities

4.3.1 Overview

This section describes the roles of the staff involved in the testing process, their individual responsibilities, and their requirements for reporting and liaison.

It is important to note when reading the following paragraphs that it is possible for a single person to assume more than one role within any given testing process. For example, in a small organization in which there are few testing staff, a single person could assume the roles of both *test analyst* and *tester* on a testing project. Similarly, the responsibilities of the *test manager* and *test team leader* could be assumed by one person if there was only one testing task or project to manage. The notable exception to this is the *independent test observer*, who must maintain complete independence from the testing project and its progress.

It is also possible for a single person to assume different roles on different projects. For example, a test analyst on one project could perform the role of test team leader on another. Again, this will depend on the size of the business and the number of staff involved in testing.

In addition to the traditional roles described in the following paragraphs, Section 4.3.7 describes a number of additional roles it may be beneficial to include in testing projects with particular characteristics or requirements – such as a project in which automated testing tools are employed (see [23] for example).

Concise terms of reference for the traditional testing roles described in this chapter can be found in Appendix A.

4.3.2 Testing Manager

The testing manager has the authority to administer the organizational aspects of the testing process on a day-to-day basis, and is responsible for ensuring that the individual testing projects produce the required products (i.e., the outputs from the testing phases, including the fully tested AUT), to the required standard of quality and within the specified constraints of time, resources, and cost.

The testing manager is also responsible for liaising with the development teams to ensure that they follow the *unit* and *integration testing* approach documented within the process. The testing manager will also liaise with the independent test observer(s) to receive reports on those testing projects that have failed to follow the testing process correctly.

The testing manager will report to a senior manager or director within the organization, such as the quality assurance (QA) manager, chief information officer (CIO), or information technology (IT) director. In larger organizations, and particularly those following a formal project management process (such as that described in [3]), the testing manager may report to a *testing program board*, which is responsible for the overall direction of the project management of the *testing program*.[1] (Appendix A contains details of a typical testing program board.)

The testing manager may also be called upon to formally represent his or her parent organization during acceptance testing of bespoke software developed by a third-party company, or COTS products acquired from a vendor. In this capacity, the testing manager will be expected to represent the interests of his or her organization as well as cosigning any *acceptance test certificate* documentation (see Appendix H).

The position of testing manager may be implemented as a part-time role, which is given as an additional responsibility to an existing senior manager or director (such as the QA manager, CIO, or IT director). This will be particularly likely for smaller organizations, where the total number of staff involved in testing is relatively low.

4.3.3 Test Team Leader

The test team leader is given the authority to run a testing project. Her or his responsibilities include tasking one or more test analysts and testers, monitoring their progress against agreed plans, setting up and maintaining the testing project filing system, and ensuring the generation of the testing project artifacts, including:

▶ The *test plan document*, which will be used as the basis of project management control throughout the testing process. (Appendix C contains a specimen test

---

[1] The term testing program is used by organizations such as the British Library to denote the complete organizational specification of their testing process, which is run under the PRINCE project management method (see Chapter 15 for the British Library case study).

plan document template.) This document will be produced by the test team
leader and will be approved by the testing manager

▶ The *test specification document*, which will detail the approach to testing the
AUT, the resources needed, the testing environment, the evaluation criteria and
acceptable defect frequencies, halting criteria, etc. (Appendix D contains a specimen test specification document template.) Although the test team leader is
responsible for ensuring that this document is produced, responsibility for its
completion may be delegated to a test analyst.

The test team leader reports to the test manager, and is reported to by one or
more test analysts and testers. The test team leader will liaise with the independent
test observer (e.g., to discuss their availability to attend a particular test), and (where
appropriate) the development team leader (in order to undertake early planning of
the testing project and preliminary test design, and to determine the availability of
the AUT for testing). During acceptance testing, the test team leader will also be
responsible for liaising with the *user representative* and *operations representative*
to obtain one or more users to perform user and/or operations acceptance testing.

4.3.4 Test Analyst

The test analyst is responsible for the design and implementation of one or more *test
scripts* (and their associated *test cases*), which will be used to accomplish the testing
of the AUT. (Appendix E contains a specimen test script template, whereas Chapter 3
provides guidance on test case design.)

The test analyst may also be called upon to assist the test team leader in the
generation of the test specification document.

During the design of the test cases, the test analyst will need to analyze the
requirements specification for the AUT to identify specific requirements that must
be verified. During this process the test analyst will need to prioritize the test cases
to reflect the importance of the feature being verified and the risk (see Section 4.9)
of the feature failing during normal use of the AUT. The approach adopted can be
as simple as assigning a high, medium, or low value to each test case. This is an
important exercise to undertake, because such an approach will assist the test team
leader in focusing testing effort should time and resources become critical during
testing.

At the completion of the testing project, the test analyst is responsible for the
back-up and archival of all testing documentation and materials, as well as the
creation of a testing *reuse[2] pack* (Appendix I). These materials will be delivered to

---

[2] Reuse is a key technique in ensuring that the testing process is as effective and efficient as possible.
This book promotes the philosophy of reuse within the testing process by providing a set of specimen
templates, proformas, and checklists that staff involved in the testing process can use as the basis of
developing their own project artifacts.

the test team leader for filing. The test analyst is also responsible for completing a test summary report briefly describing the key points of the testing project.

The test analyst reports to the test team leader and liaises with one or more testers to brief them on their tasks before testing of the AUT commences.

4.3.5 Tester

The tester is primarily responsible for the execution of the test scripts created by the test analyst, and the interpretation and documentation of the results of the test cases.

Prior to the execution of the test scripts, the tester will set up and initialize the test environment, including the test data and test hardware, plus any additional software required to support the test (such as *simulators* and *test harnesses*).

During test execution, the tester is responsible for filling in the *test result record forms* (TRRFs – see Appendix F) to document the observed result of executing each test script, and for cosigning the bottom of each TRRF with the independent test observer to confirm that the test script was followed correctly and the observed result recorded accurately. In interpreting the results of executing a test script, the tester will make use of the description of the expected result recorded on the test script, the *test result categories* specified in the test specification document, and his or her own personal experience. The tester is also responsible for the recovery of the test environment in the event of failure of the system.

Following test execution, the tester is responsible for the back-up and archival of the test data, any simulator or test harness software, and the specification of the hardware used during testing. These materials will be delivered to the test team leader for filing. (In practice, much of this material will be provided to the test team leader in electronic format, on digital optical disk, or copied to a shared area on a computer server.) The tester will also deliver the completed TRRFs to the test team leader.

The tester reports to the test team leader and liaises with the test analyst and the independent test observer.

4.3.6 Independent Test Observer

In general terms, the independent test observer is responsible for providing independent *verification* that correct procedures (i.e., those specified in the testing process for the organization) are followed during the testing of the AUT.

Specifically during testing, the independent test observer is responsible for ensuring that the tester executes the tests according to the instructions provided in the test scripts, that he or she interprets the observed result correctly according to the description of the expected result, and where the observed and expected results differ, that the tester records the correct test result categories score for the defect (as specified in the test specification document).

In organizations where there is a formal quality assurance group, independent test observers may be drawn from the ranks of the *quality assurance representatives* (*QARs*). In smaller organizations or where there is not such a strong quality culture, the independent test observer may be a member of staff drawn from another group or project within the organization. The key criteria in selecting an independent test observer is that she or he must be impartial and objective, that is, he or she must not have any other responsibilities within the project, be affected by the progress of the project, and be able to accurately report any failure to follow the testing process to the testing manager.

The independent test observer liaises with the testing manager to report any deviations from the testing process, liaises with the test team leader to schedule attendance at the test execution, and liaises with the tester to confirm the result of executing an individual test script and to cosign the test result record form. The independent test observer may also be invited to review some of the testing project artifacts produced during the testing project, such as the test specification document or test script(s) as part of the quality assurance process for the testing project.

4.3.7 Supplementary Testing Roles

Depending on the specific testing requirements of a particular testing project, it may be appropriate to include a number of additional testing roles.

In practice, the responsibilities given to each of these supplementary testing roles may be assigned to existing testing roles within the project. This will depend on the size of the testing project, the number of testing staff available, the amount of testing that is required, and the duration of the testing project. A review of the case studies presented in Part 2 of this book will provide additional insights into how organizations and testing teams of varying sizes and with a wide variety of testing requirements have organized their roles and responsibilities to support effective and efficient testing.

The supplementary testing roles covered in this section include: *test automation architect*, *automation analyst*, and *exploratory tester*.

Test Automation Architect
The test automation architect has the following responsibilities:

▶ Definition of the test automation architecture
▶ Specification of all hardware and software configurations needed
▶ Assisting the test team leader to plan any programming and set-up tasks needed to install a new automation environment, including deploying the testing tools and environment-specific support code.

The test automation architect reports to the test team leader and liaises with the test analyst (test automation analyst – see next section) and testers.

Test Automation Analyst

The test automation analyst has the following responsibilities:

▶ Implementation of automated tests as specified in the test specification document and any supplementary design documents
▶ Implementation of test support code required for efficiently executing automated tests
▶ Setting up and executing automated tests against the AUT
▶ Reviewing the automated test log following testing to identify and report on defects found within the AUT during testing.

The test automation analyst reports to the test team leader and liaises with the test automation architect.

Exploratory Tester

The exploratory tester has the following responsibilities:

▶ Autonomous testing of a product without following a specified set of test cases
▶ Focusing on finding the highest severity defects in the most important features of the system using a risk-based testing approach.

This role requires a high degree of testing expertise, as well as knowledge about the AUT (such as the design method or implementation technology), knowledge of the results of any earlier testing phases (particularly important in regression testing), experience of testing similar or related systems (and knowing where defects have arisen previously in those systems), knowledge of typical implementation errors (such as division by zero errors), and general testing rules of thumb or heuristics. Although there are no detailed test cases to follow, an exploratory tester may follow a specified general strategy based on a combination of previously mentioned skills and experience.

The exploratory tester role is especially useful in testing projects with particularly demanding timescales (such as e-business development projects) and testing projects where it is essential to find show-stopping defects before release to the client.

4.4 The Testing Phases

4.4.1 Overview

This section describes the management issues associated with each of the phases of testing that the AUT undergoes during its development lifecycle. For each testing phase, the following items are covered:

▶ A brief overview of the testing phase
▶ A discussion of who is responsible for conducting the testing within that phase

▶ A discussion of who is responsible for managing the testing within that phase
▶ A discussion of the requirements for independent observation of the results of testing.

Chapters 5 to 11 describe in detail all aspects of each of the testing phases covered in the following sections (including their common synonyms), and Appendix B contains a set of one-page testing guides, which can be used to provide summary advice and support to staff involved in the various phases of software testing.

This section concludes with a discussion of an important aspect of the management of testing and of each testing phase, that is, when to stop the testing process. The traditional halting criteria are reviewed and a number of practical examples are also discussed.

4.4.2 Unit Testing

Unit testing (also termed "software component testing") represents the lowest level of testing that the AUT can undergo, and it is conducted to ensure that reliable program units[3] (or software components) are produced that meet their requirements.

Unit testing is typically conducted by the development team and specifically by the programmer who coded the unit, who is responsible for designing and running a series of tests to verify that the unit meets its requirements.

The development team leader has responsibility for ensuring the unit testing is completed, and will be responsible for incorporating the testing task into the overall development plan and monitoring progress against that plan. Because of this, it is unlikely that the development team leader will need to produce detailed test plan and test specification documents for unit testing (particularly as the testing resources are likely to be provided from within the existing development team).

The results of unit testing should be formally documented using a test result record form, which will be filed by the development team leader. The development team leader may also produce a reuse pack (Appendix I) to allow selected unit tests to be rerun during the later phases of testing or during regression testing of the AUT.

"Independent" observation of the testing process is likely to be performed by the development team leader or by another member of the team, who will be expected to countersign the appropriate test result record form to confirm that the correct procedures (i.e., those specified in the testing process) were followed during the testing of the AUT. If the organization has a particularly well-established quality culture, observation of the testing may be performed by a quality assurance representative assigned to assure the quality of the development project.

Chapter 5 provides comprehensive details of all aspects of unit testing.

---

[3] Chapter 5 provides a number of possible interpretations of the term "unit."

4.4.3 Integration Testing

The objective of integration testing is to demonstrate that the modules that comprise the AUT interface and interact together in a correct, stable, and coherent manner.

The development team typically conducts integration testing, with responsibility for managing the testing falling to the development team leader. Occasionally in large organizations with well-established quality and/or mature software development and testing processes, integration testing will be conducted by a dedicated *testing team*, who will be responsible for all aspects of the testing.

Where the development team is responsible for integration testing, the development team leader has responsibility for ensuring the integration testing is completed, and will be responsible for incorporating the testing task into the overall development plan and monitoring progress against that plan. Because of this, it is unlikely that the development team leader will need to produce detailed test plan and test specification documents (particularly as the testing resources are likely to be provided from within the existing development team).

The results of integration testing should be formally documented using a test result record form, which will be filled by the development team leader. The development team leader should also produce a reuse pack (Appendix I) to allow selected integration tests to be rerun during the later phases of testing or during regression testing of the AUT.

During integration testing and the later testing phases, it is increasingly important that truly independent observation of the testing process is performed. An independent test observer may be drawn from another development project or, if the organization has a particularly well-established quality culture, independent observation may be performed by a quality assurance representative assigned to assure the quality of the development project. Even where a dedicated testing team performs the testing, independent observation is essential.

Another key issue to consider is the need to manage the user[4] expectations regarding the look and feel, and operation and performance of the AUT. Many applications have successfully reached acceptance testing only to encounter difficulties because the user is dissatisfied with some aspect of the AUT (even though the software has already demonstrably satisfied its requirements during the earlier testing phases). Similarly, it is also possible for the requirements to have been misinterpreted and for the specification to be incorrect. The development team leader must consider inviting the user representative to the integration test (and even unit testing) in an informal capacity to observe the testing process. In this way, the user representative will be exposed to the AUT prior to formal acceptance testing, and any show-stopping issues can be discussed and resolved in a timely manner.

Chapter 6 provides comprehensive details of all aspects of integration testing.

---

[4] Where the user could be the customer representative for a bespoke development or customization of an existing system with responsibility for formally accepting the AUT, or could be an "internal" user with responsibility for accepting software developed by the IT department of the same organization.

4.4.4 System Testing

The fundamental objective of *system testing* is to establish confidence that the AUT will be accepted by the users (and/or operators), that is, that it will pass its acceptance test.

System testing is typically conducted as an independent testing project by a dedicated testing team, with responsibility for managing the testing falling to the test team leader.

For those small organizations where there are few IT staff, it is possible that the development team will conduct system testing. (Where this is the case, it is essential that the development team leader take on all of the responsibilities of the test team leader [as described in Section 4.3], and that they nominate appropriately experienced staff from within the development team to fulfill the roles of test analyst and tester.)

During system testing it is essential that truly independent observation of the testing process be performed. The independent test observer may be drawn from another development project or, if the organization has a particularly well-established quality culture, independent observation may be performed by a quality assurance representative assigned to assure the quality of the testing project.

As with integration testing, the test team leader should consider inviting the user representative to the system test in an informal capacity to observe the testing process in order to manage their expectations of the AUT prior to formal acceptance testing.

Chapter 7 provides comprehensive details of all aspects of system testing.

4.4.5 Systems Integration Testing

The objective of *systems integration testing* is to provide confidence that the AUT is able to successfully interoperate with other specified systems and does not have an adverse effect on other systems that may also be present in the live operating environment or vice versa.

Systems integration testing will only be introduced into the testing process if there is a significant requirement for the AUT to interoperate with a number of other software systems (such as the requirement for the British Library IT systems to communicate for the purposes of exchanging data – see Chapter 15).

For many software systems with less rigorous requirements for interoperability, it is more likely that any aspects of systems integration testing will be performed during the system test.

Where systems integration testing does appear as a distinct testing phase, it is typically conducted as an independent testing project with responsibility for managing the testing falling to the test team leader.

During systems integration testing it is essential that independent observation of the testing process be performed. The independent test observer may be drawn from another development project or, if the organization has a particularly well-established quality culture, independent observation may be performed by a quality assurance representative assigned to assure the quality of the testing project.

Chapter 8 provides comprehensive details of all aspects of systems integration testing.

4.4.6 Acceptance Testing

The purpose of acceptance testing is to confirm that the system meets its business requirements and to provide confidence that the system works correctly and is usable before it is formally "handed over" to the users. Acceptance testing is often divided into *user acceptance testing* (involving the business or end users of the AUT) and *operations acceptance testing* (involving the operations or administrative users of the AUT).

Acceptance testing is performed by nominated user representatives under the guidance and supervision of the testing team. The test team leader will obtain these staff by liaising with the appropriate user and/or operations representative.

During acceptance testing it is important that independent observation of the testing process be performed, particularly where the user representatives are IT-naive business staff. The independent test observer may be drawn from another development project or, if the organization has a particularly well-established quality culture, independent observation may be performed by a quality assurance representative assigned to assure the quality of the testing project.

Chapters 9 and 10 provide comprehensive details of all aspects of user acceptance testing and operations acceptance testing.

4.4.7 Regression Testing

The purpose of regression testing is to provide confidence that the AUT still functions correctly following modification or extension of the system (such as user enhancements or upgrades or following new builds or releases of the software).

Regression testing is not strictly speaking a testing phase, but it is a testing technique that can be applied to any of the other testing phases (e.g., following enhancements to the AUT, it will be necessary to perform a system regression test to ensure the existing functionality of the application is unaffected by the changes). Typically regression testing is applied to the higher levels of testing and to system and acceptance testing in particular.

Because of the need for effective and efficient testing, regression testing relies heavily on the reuse of existing test scripts and test cases created for previous testing phases such as system and acceptance testing. Similarly, it is unlikely that all of the test scripts from previous testing phases will be executed. Instead, the test analyst will consider the scope of changes to the AUT, the structure of the AUT, and the manner in which it was developed, and experience of testing the AUT (or related software) and select a subset of test scripts to reuse. Clearly, where higher confidence in the quality of the AUT is required (e.g., for safety critical or business critical systems), more elaborate and complete testing will be necessary.

The responsibility for conducting and managing a particular regression test will be determined by the specific testing phase the testing is associated with. Similarly, the need for independent observation will also depend on the observation requirements for the associated testing phase.

Chapter 11 provides comprehensive details of all aspects of regression testing.

4.4.8 When to Stop Testing

One of the most difficult decisions the manager responsible for any testing phase has to make is when to stop testing.

Often, the reason for halting the testing process is completely arbitrary and can include running out of the time allotted for testing, exhausting the allocated testing resources, or hitting a fixed milestone such as a contractual delivery date. From a testing perspective, such halting criteria are far from ideal and take no account of the quality of the AUT at the instant testing has to stop.

Where the testing manager is able to influence the planning aspects of the software development and testing process, there are a number of additional criteria that can be employed to provide greater confidence in the decision to halt the testing process and that provide a much clearer indication of the risk involved in stopping testing. These criteria include:

▶ Test requirement coverage – has it been demonstrated that all the requirements for the AUT have been verified? If it has not been possible to test all the requirements, have those with the highest risk associated with them been tested? (Section 4.9 discusses the need to review the requirements for the AUT and prioritize them according to their impact and likelihood of failure.)
▶ Test code coverage – has it been demonstrated that all "parts" of the software have been exercised during testing (including exception handling and error handling routines)?
▶ Test case metric – how many test cases have been planned, designed, implemented, executed, and passed or failed? This is a useful metric to collect to measure the progress of the testing activity
▶ Defect detection metric – has the rate of defect detection been plotted, and has the rate of defect detection leveled off? This provides a reasonable indication that the majority of defects have been detected (however, caution must be exercised using this approach because tester fatigue could also produce similar results).

There are other, more esoteric methods of estimating the numbers of defects in the AUT, such as seeding the software with "known" defects and comparing the ratio of known to unknown defects observed during testing. Mathematically, this ratio can provide an estimate of the total number of defects in the AUT, and hence provide an

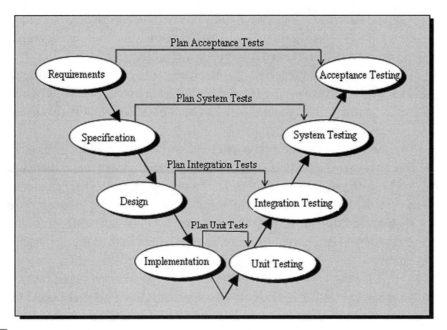

Plan Acceptance Tests

Requirements

Acceptance Testing

Plan System Tests

Specification

System Testing

Plan Integration Tests

Design

Integration Testing

Plan Unit Tests

Implementation

Unit Testing

4.2 The V Model

effective halting criterion. In practice, such methods are difficult to manage, provide imperfect results, and may be hazardous (e.g., it is essential that the AUT is delivered without any seeded defects still in place).

4.5 Role of the V Model in Planning

Typically, between 25% and 50% of the total costs of developing a software system are spent on test activities (1). This figure is likely to be significantly larger for high reliability, business critical, and safety critical systems. Project plans must reflect this issue in their allocation of time, effort, and resources to testing.

The V Model (see Figure 4.2) is a software development and testing model, which helps to highlight the need to plan and prepare for testing early in the development process. The left-hand descending arm of the "V" represents the traditional Waterfall development phases (18), while the ascending right-hand arm of the "V" shows the corresponding testing phase.

In the V Model, each development phase is linked to a corresponding testing phase. As work proceeds on a particular development phase, planning and some preliminary design work are performed for the corresponding testing phase. The benefits of the V Model include:

▶ The testing phases are given the same level of management attention and commitment as the corresponding development phases in terms of planning and resourcing, allowing any risks to be addressed early in the development cycle (e.g., if a highly specialized piece of hardware is necessary to perform acceptance testing, which has a long order and delivery time, identifying this requirement early allows the hardware to be ordered in a timely manner – mitigating the risk of late delivery of the tested system)

▶ The outputs from the development phases (such as specification and design documents) can be reviewed by the testing team to ensure their testability (e.g., ensuring that a given requirement has been documented in such a manner that it is easily verifiable)

▶ The early planning and preliminary design of tests provides additional review comments on the outputs from the development phase (e.g., if there are errors in the initial requirements, they have a greater chance of being detected if the acceptance test specification is produced before development proceeds to detailed analysis and design. During this process, it is possible to identify duplicated and/or contradictory requirements and feed these back to the analyst for clarification.)

Although the testing manager is responsible for the timely set-up and initiation of testing for a particular software development project, the main responsibility for exploiting the power of the V Model will fall to the test team leader, who will need to liaise with the development team leader to ensure early planning and preliminary design tasks are completed.

Although the V Model is described in terms of the traditional Waterfall view of software development, the principles of forward planning and design equally apply to the more modern iterative approaches to development (such as those described in [8] and [12]). In an iterative approach, each iteration can be viewed as a "mini-waterfall" with stages analogous to those seen in the Waterfall view of development.

In practice, the V Model provides a powerful tool for managing and controlling risk within the testing component of a software development project. The process of bringing testing planning and design into the development process as early as possible enables risks to be identified and strategies for removing or mitigating them to be put in place in a timely manner.

4.6 The Management of Test Requirements

In performing effective and efficient testing, it is essential that the test analyst know precisely what the requirements of the AUT are. This information is the basis of the formal *validation* that the AUT meets its requirements. Without access to this information, the test analyst has virtually no formal basis for performing the design of the test scripts and test cases.

Incomplete or poorly maintained requirements may result in the test analyst not designing a test for an important requirement, or may cause the test analyst to duplicate testing effort by generating several tests that verify the same requirement.

The acquisition, maintenance, management, and communication of requirements is a traditional source of quality problems in software development and testing projects. Because of the complexity of the task combined with the number of requirements generated for any but the most trivial of development projects, the majority of software development projects use requirements management tools.

However, even where tools are used, the problem is often exacerbated by poor communication between the various roles involved in the development and testing process, with analysts, developers, and testers all using different tools to represent requirements, design information, and testing data.

If tool support for requirements management is to be employed on a project, it is essential that analysts, developers, and testers all have access to the same tool, and that it is easy to communicate the requirements information between the project roles. In this way, the test analyst can examine the most up-to-date copy of the requirements, ensuring complete testing coverage of the features of the AUT and avoiding duplication or omission of tests. (Reference [19] provides a typical example of a requirements management tool that satisfies the above requirements.)

4.7 The Role and Use of Configuration Management

A major requirement of the management of the testing process is that the results of testing be reproducible, allowing testers to recreate the conditions of a previous test and be able to exactly repeat the testing and accurately reproduce the results (e.g., it may be necessary to repeat a particular test in response to an observation raised against the tested AUT by the users on the live system).

To support this requirement, it is essential that testing be conducted under strict and effective configuration management (CM). The minimum testing artifacts that must be placed under CM control are:

▶ The AUT
▶ The test plan and test specification
▶ The test data
▶ Any supporting software (such as test harnesses, simulators, or stimulators)
▶ The specification of the test hardware or test rig (if this is not already included in the test specification document)
▶ The test scripts and component test cases.

The CM of testing projects is a complex and difficult task, and tool support should be considered (a number of CM tools are commercially available, such as [20]).

4.8 The Role and Use of Defect Tracking

Effective testing is nothing without an accurate means of reporting defects, monitoring their progress, and managing their resolution. A formal approach to defect tracking must be employed to make sure the effort expended on testing is well spent by ensuring defects detected during testing are corrected.

In setting up a defect tracking system, the following facilities must be provided:

▶ The ability to register a defect and its characteristics and associate the defect with a unique identifier
▶ The ability to associate a severity value with that defect (see *test result category* in the Glossary)
▶ The ability to associate a priority of resolution with that defect
▶ A defined workflow in which the details of the defect are provided to the appropriate staff within the organization, and its status (such as new, open, closed) is altered as it progresses through the system
▶ Defined rights and privileges for the staff involved in the defect tracking process (e.g., in a particular organization, a tester may be able to report a defect, but only the testing manager may close a defect following successful retesting)
▶ The ability to customize the above attributes of the defect tracking system to more closely match the particular requirements of the host organization.

As with CM, rigorous and effective defect tracking is a complex and difficult task, particularly where there are multiple development and testing projects operating simultaneously. The majority of organizations involved in testing employ one of the many defect tracking tools that are available (such as [21]) or develop one of their own in-house. The latter approach suffers from a number of problems including reliability, maintenance costs, lack of professional support, and possible loss of tool expertise due to career change.

4.9 The Role of Risk in Test Planning and Management

The term "risk" has appeared in several places in this chapter, including the planning and design of tests. The management of risk and mitigation of risk are popular terms in project management, and particularly in IT project management.

Chapter 2 showed how testing can be defined in the context of risk, and this leads us to consider the management and planning of testing in a risk-based manner as well. In this context, effective management and planning of the testing process provide opportunities for identifying risk within the AUT[5] in a timely manner and allow such risks to be investigated (by means of testing), removed, or mitigated as quickly as possible.

The V Model provides the testing manager and test team leader with an effective means of identifying risk as early as possible in the software development lifecycle, and allowing the removal or mitigation of the risk. This process can involve all the stakeholders in the development process, including the managers (e.g., in terms of the need to modify plans), developers (e.g., in terms of the need to rework some

---

[5] Such as the risk of failure of some key feature during its normal operation following delivery of the software, or the failure of the AUT to meet a specific requirement specified by the user.

aspect of the AUT), and even the users (e.g., allowing respecification of missing, duplicate, or contradictory requirements).

Within the testing process, the test analyst must take account of risk during the design of the test cases, ensuring that the test cases are prioritized in such a way as to test high-risk aspects of the AUT before less risky aspects of the software.

Reference (28) provides a high-level view of risk-based testing process:

▶ generate a prioritized list of risks
▶ perform testing to explore each risk
▶ as risks are removed (and new ones are identified), adjust the testing effort to focus on the remaining list of risks.

There are a number of strategies for achieving this high-level approach to risk-based testing, which are described in Reference 28, while References 29 and 30 provide further reading on methods and tools that can be used for risk management within testing projects.

5 Unit Testing

> "(The Programmer) personally defines the functional and performance specifications, designs the program, codes it, tests it, and writes its documentation... They need great talent, ten years experience and considerable systems and applications knowledge, whether in applied mathematics, business data handling, or whatever!"
>
> **– Fred P. Brooks**

5.1 Overview

The objective of *unit testing* is to ensure that reliable program units are produced that meet their requirements. The process is primarily intended to identify errors in program logic. Unit testing is conducted by the development team under the supervision of the *development team leader*. Typically, the software engineer or programmer who coded the unit will design and run a series of tests to verify that the unit meets its requirements. Unit testing may also be termed *component testing*.

Each unit should be tested individually and in isolation (although it may be necessary to employ a *test harness*) by exercising its inputs and observing its outputs. It may also be possible for the unit to be tested using the facilities available in the development environment (such as stepping through the statements of code using a debugger). Once confidence has been established in the unit, it should then be tested in collaboration with other interoperating units.

Unit testing is typically a *white box* testing activity, based primarily on the functional and data requirements expressed in the *requirements specification* for the *application under test* (*AUT*), as well as any supplementary material (such as design documentation, user guides, or prototype code). Examples of areas typically covered in unit testing include:

▶ Correctness of calculations/manipulations performed by the unit (as per the requirements specification document for the AUT)
▶ Low-level performance issues (such as performance bottlenecks observed under repeated invocation of the unit and its functionality)
▶ Low-level reliability issues (such as memory leaks observed under repeated and extended invocation of the unit and its functionality)

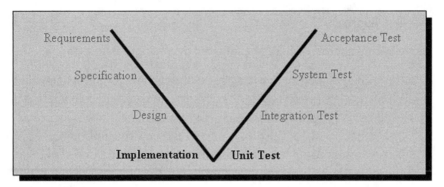

5.1 Unit Testing and the V Model

▶ Screen/window contents and navigation (for graphical user interface [GUI] units) including consistency of the "look and feel" of the window, use of "hot keys," function keys, and keyboard short cuts
▶ Report contents, layouts, and calculations
▶ File/record creation, update, and deletion
▶ Communication between interoperating units.

The precise definition of a "unit" will depend on the approach to design of the AUT and the implementation technology employed in its development. For example:

▶ A unit in an application developed using a procedural programming language could be represented by a function or procedure, or a closely related group of functions or procedures
▶ A unit in an application developed using an object-oriented programming language could be represented by a class or an instance of a class, or the functionality implemented by a method
▶ A unit in a visual programming environment or a GUI context could be a window or a collection of related elements of a window such as a group box
▶ A unit in a component-based development environment could be a predefined reusable component. In such circumstances, the developer testing the component will need to consider the components origin, maturity, and previous testing history and determine how much testing needs to be performed.

In terms of the *V Model*, unit testing corresponds to the implementation phase of the software development lifecycle (see Figure 5.1).

Testing issues associated with unit testing (such as test planning and resourcing, and the review of testing requirements and high-level test design), should be considered during the implementation phase of the AUT. The V Model and its role in testing is described in Chapter 4.

A flow chart providing a high-level overview of the unit testing process can be found at the end of this chapter (see Figure 5.2).

5.2 Unit Test Approach

The following approach should be followed in conducting unit testing:

▶ Determine how a given unit may be invoked and what its response will be under each invocation (by reviewing the appropriate design documentation produced during the development of the AUT, for example)

▶ Determine what states the unit can be in and how the unit moves between these states (consider using the state transition techniques described in Chapter 3)

▶ Determine the expected results for each state the unit may be in (or combination of states) and what will be necessary to confirm these results (it may be useful to generate a table of inputs and outputs to record this information)

▶ Review the requirements specification document for the AUT and the unit under test to confirm that the previous steps have identified all possible test conditions and add further conditions as necessary (consider data initialization, boundary values, error conditions, and division by zero, for example)

▶ Determine any prerequisites for testing the unit (such as output from other units, the need for a test harness, or specific handcrafted test data)

▶ Use the previous information to generate a set of *test cases* to test the unit and incorporate them into a *test script*, describing in detail the steps to be followed during testing. Formal test case design techniques should be employed to ensure boundary values and error conditions are correctly exercised.

Where they are available, consider reusing test cases from earlier unit tests. These can be obtained from the appropriate unit test *reuse packs* (see Appendix I).

5.3 Unit Test Data Requirements

The data used during unit testing is unlikely to be *live data* because:

▶ Of the risk of corrupting commercially important or business critical information

▶ Live data may contain sensitive information (such as commercial or personal details)

▶ The data may contain information of a secure nature (such as user passwords).

Where the function of the unit under test does not involve the manipulation or use of large volumes of data, it is likely that the *test analyst* will use a small representative set of handcrafted test data. In creating the test data, the test analyst must employ formal design techniques such as the *boundary value analysis* or *equivalence partition* methods described in Chapter 3, to ensure the data adequately tests the boundary conditions for the unit as well as to provide truly representative values.

Where the unit under test is responsible for manipulating large volumes of data, and where this will be a requirement for a number of units, it may be worth considering taking a copy of the live data (which may need to be "sanitized"[1] if it contains sensitive information), or a smaller representative sample of the live data, for purposes of testing. The test analyst may still need to consider the introduction of some handcrafted data into the sampled data for the purpose of testing a specific feature of the unit, such as the response to error conditions.

Where a unit will receive data from a remote source when it is incorporated into the complete AUT (e.g., from a client/server system), it may be necessary to *simulate* access to such data during the unit test using test harness software. In considering such an option, the test analyst must bear in mind the effort involved in developing the test harness software and the need to test the test harness itself before it can be used. Time and effort may be saved if such software is already available for reuse, perhaps having been developed for earlier testing of the AUT.

Similarly, in identifying the data requirements for unit testing, it is important for the test analyst to consider the role of reuse as a means of obtaining data for current testing (from previous tests). If it has been necessary to handcraft some data for the purposes of conducting a unit test, the test analyst must make sure that a copy of this data is included in the reuse pack (see Appendix I) for possible use in later testing phases or for *regression testing*.

5.4 Roles and Responsibilities

Unit testing is typically conducted by the development team under the supervision of the *development team leader*, who is responsible for ensuring that adequate testing is performed using appropriate testing techniques and under suitable quality control and supervision (as defined in the unit test plan and *test specification documents*).

Typically, the same member of the development team who coded the unit will design the required test case(s), test the unit, and correct any defects (effectively performing the roles of test analyst and *tester*). Testing includes the design and execution of the test scripts and test cases, and the completion of the *test result record form* and *unit test log*.

At unit testing, it is desirable that the testing process is monitored by an *independent test observer* who will formally witness the results of individual test cases. The need for a genuinely independent test observer is not as stringent at unit test as it is during subsequent testing phases, hence the observer could be drawn from the development team (such as the development team leader or another member of the development team). A quality assurance representative (QAR) could also fill the independent test observer role, if such a staff exists within the organization.

---

[1] Where live data contains confidential data or information relating to security issues, it may be inappropriate to conduct system testing using the original data. One solution is to use a copy of live data that has been altered to remove or change those items of a confidential or secure nature.

The development team leader will liaise with the *test team leader* (assuming a *testing team* for the AUT has been constituted at this stage of the development project) to report on the progress of the development of the AUT and likely dates for delivery of the AUT for subsequent testing purposes, and should invite the test team leader to observe one or more unit tests (although in practice it is likely that the test team leader will simply review copies of the deliverables produced during the unit test process to assure themselves that testing was conducted adequately).

The development team leader may consider inviting a *user representative* to informally observe unit testing, particularly where the testing involves aspects of the AUT that deal with the business logic of the system or the operation of the user interface. Unit testing provides a valuable opportunity to expose the user representative to aspects of the operation and appearance of the AUT, allowing (informal) feedback to be obtained and helping to manage the expectations of the user representative prior to formal *acceptance testing* (see Chapter 4 for a fuller explanation of the need to involve users in the testing process).

The development team leader will provide the test team leader with copies of a number of outputs produced as a result of the unit testing process (and listed in Section 5.8), including the completed test result record forms, unit test log, and a brief unit test summary report when unit testing is complete. In the event that the testing team is constituted after unit testing has been completed, the development team leader should provide the test team leader with copies of appropriate outputs as soon as possible.

5.5 Planning and Resources

The planning of unit testing is the responsibility of the development team leader and should be developed with reference to the overall development and testing plan for the AUT.

Human resources required for unit testing will be drawn from the development team (with the exception of the independent test observer, who may be drawn from another project or the quality assurance group, should one exist within the organization). At unit test, the independent test observer role could be performed by the development team leader or another nominated member of the development team.

It is assumed that unit testing will not take place in the *live environment*, but will take place in the *development environment* or a separate *testing environment*. The time and duration for unit testing must be integrated into the development plan for the AUT to minimize the impact on the development process caused by unit testing and to ensure that no contention for resources will occur.

It is essential that the unit test plan take account of the time and effort required for any correction of defects and retesting.

5.6 Inputs

The following items are required as inputs to unit testing and should be complete and available to the development team leader before test execution can begin:

▶ The requirements specification document (for the AUT)
▶ The design documents for the AUT
▶ Any supplementary material, such as user guides or prototype software
▶ The unit testing plan (see Appendix C)
▶ The unit test specification document (see Appendix D)
▶ The unit testing guide (see Appendix B)
▶ Any unit test scripts and unit test cases (see Appendix E)
▶ Blank test result record forms (see Appendix F)
▶ Any appropriate reuse packs, such as any from previous unit tests (see Appendix I).

5.7 Testing Techniques for Unit Testing

The following testing techniques are appropriate for unit testing:

▶ *Functional testing* against the requirements for the unit under test
▶ *Static testing* (such as code review and code walkthrough)
▶ White box testing (because the structure of the unit will be known to the developer)
▶ *State transition testing* (particularly where it is possible for the unit to be in a number of different states, and to assist in negative testing of the unit)
▶ *Nonfunctional testing* (e.g., where appropriate, for *performance*, *stress*, or *reliability testing* of the unit).

See Chapter 3 for details of these testing techniques.

5.8 Outputs

The following items are generated as outputs from unit testing:

▶ The fully tested units
▶ The completed unit test certificate (see Appendix H)
▶ Any revised test script and test cases (where appropriate)
▶ The archived test data
▶ The completed test result record forms (see Appendix F)
▶ The unit test log (see Appendix G)
▶ The unit test reuse pack (see Appendix I)
▶ A brief unit test summary report (see Appendix J).

Unit testing will be considered complete when all of the previously mentioned deliverables (under strict configuration management, as described in Chapter 4) are complete and have been provided to the development team leader.

Appropriate deliverables (i.e., all of the previously mentioned except the fully tested units) should be stored in the project file. The fully tested units (plus any associated test harness or simulation code and test data) should be backed up and archived.

Copies of the filed deliverables (under strict configuration management) should be provided to the test team leader.

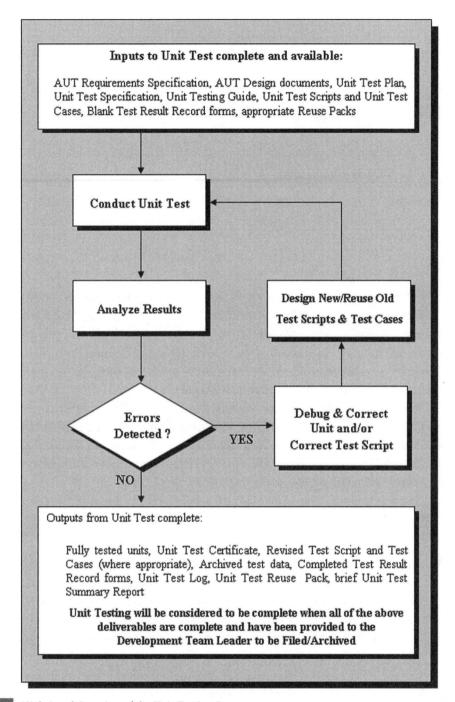

Inputs to Unit Test complete and available:

AUT Requirements Specification, AUT Design documents, Unit Test Plan, Unit Test Specification, Unit Testing Guide, Unit Test Scripts and Unit Test Cases, Blank Test Result Record forms, appropriate Reuse Packs

Conduct Unit Test

Analyze Results

Design New/Reuse Old Test Scripts & Test Cases

Errors Detected ?

YES

NO

Debug & Correct Unit and/or Correct Test Script

Outputs from Unit Test complete:

Fully tested units, Unit Test Certificate, Revised Test Script and Test Cases (where appropriate), Archived test data, Completed Test Result Record forms, Unit Test Log, Unit Test Reuse Pack, brief Unit Test Summary Report

Unit Testing will be considered to be complete when all of the above deliverables are complete and have been provided to the Development Team Leader to be Filed/Archived

5.2 High-Level Overview of the Unit Testing Process

6 Integration Testing

> "Computers are like Old Testament gods; lots of rules and no mercy."
>
> **– Joseph Campbell**

6.1 Overview

The objective of *integration testing* is to demonstrate that modules comprising the *application under test* (*AUT*) interface and interact together in a correct, stable, and coherent manner prior to *system testing*. Integration testing is typically conducted by the development team and involves independent observation of the testing process. Integration testing may also be termed *link* or *module testing*, but it should not be confused with *systems integration testing* (see Chapter 8).

Testing should be performed against the *functional requirements* of the AUT using *black box* testing techniques. *Test case* design should demonstrate correct interfacing and interaction between modules but should avoid duplication of *unit testing* effort (however, where appropriate, reuse of unit tests should be considered to reduce testing timescales and effort).

The precise definition of a "module" depends on the approach to design of the AUT and the implementation technology. For example:

▶ A module in an application developed using a procedural programming language could be represented by a closely related group of functions or procedures that perform a well-defined service within the AUT and that communicate with other component modules via strictly defined interfaces

▶ A module in an application developed using an object-oriented programming language could be represented by a collection of objects that perform a well-defined service within the AUT and that communicate with other component modules via strictly defined interfaces

▶ A module in a visual programming environment could be a window or a collection of subwindows that perform a well-defined service within the AUT and that communicate with other component modules via strictly defined interfaces

▶ A module in a component-based development environment could be a reusable component that performs a well-defined service within the AUT and that communicates with other modules via a strictly defined (and documented) interface.

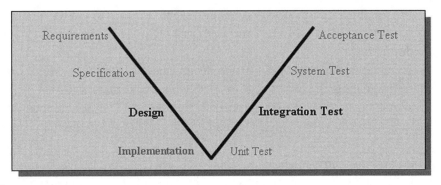

Integration Testing and the V Model

Under such circumstances, the developer testing the component will need to consider the components origin, maturity, and previous testing history to determine how much additional testing is required.

In terms of the V Model, integration testing corresponds to the design phase of the software development lifecycle (see Figure 6.1).

Testing issues associated with integration testing (such as test planning and resourcing, and the review of testing requirements and high-level test design), should be considered during the design phase of the AUT. The V Model and its role in testing is described in Chapter 4.

A flow chart providing a high-level overview of the integration testing process can be found at the end of this chapter (see Figure 6.2).

6.2 Integration Test Approach

Integration testing is typically a black box testing activity, based primarily on the design of the AUT plus functional and data requirements expressed in the specification document(s). Examples of areas typically covered in integration testing include:

▶ Invocation of one module from another interoperating module
▶ Correct transmission of data between interoperating modules
▶ Compatibility (i.e., checking that the introduction of one module does not have an undesirable impact on the functioning or performance of another module)
▶ Nonfunctional issues (such as the reliability of interfaces between modules).

The following approach should be followed in conducting integration testing:

▶ Identify the relationships between the modules that comprise the complete system (e.g., by reference to the design documentation for the AUT)
▶ Review the requirement for interaction and communication between modules and identify the interfaces between the modules (e.g., by reference to the requirements specification document for the AUT)

▶ Use the above information to generate a set of *test cases* to test the module(s) and incorporate them into a *test script*, describing in detail the steps to be followed during testing

▶ Incremental testing should be employed where successive modules are added to the (enlarging) system and the new combination tested (use of reuse packs should be considered). This process is repeated in a logical/functional sequence until all modules have been successfully integrated to form the complete system.

Configuration management is an important aspect of integration testing; are the proper versions of the components going into the integration build? Have the components themselves passed their earlier tests? Do the components compile together without any problems?

Where they are available, consider reusing test cases from earlier unit tests to verify the quality of the components. These can be obtained from the unit test reuse pack compiled during unit testing.

6.3 Integration Test Data Requirements

Because the principal purpose of integration testing is to demonstrate that the modules comprising the AUT interface and interact together correctly, the data requirement (both in terms of volume and content) is typically not very demanding.

Live data is unlikely to be used during integration testing because of the risk of corrupting commercially important or business critical information, because the live data may contain sensitive information (such as commercial or personal details), or because the data may contain information of a secure nature (such as user passwords).

Under these circumstances, it is likely that the *test analyst* will use a small representative set of handcrafted test data. In creating the test data, the test analyst must employ formal design techniques, such as the *boundary value analysis* or *equivalence partition* methods described in Chapter 3, to ensure the data adequately tests the boundary conditions for the module as well as provide truly representative values.

Where a module receives data from a remote source when it is incorporated into the complete AUT (e.g., from a client/server system), it may be necessary to *simulate* access to such data during the integration test using *test harness* software. In considering such an option, the test analyst must bear in mind the effort involved in developing the test harness software and the need to test the test harness before it can be used. Time and effort may be saved if such software is already available for reuse, perhaps having been developed during unit testing of the AUT.

Similarly, if it has been necessary to generate test data during unit testing, it may be appropriate to reuse this data during integration testing. This data should be available from the unit test reuse pack.

6.4 Roles and Responsibilities

Integration testing is typically conducted by the development team under the supervision of the development team leader, who is responsible for ensuring that adequate integration testing is performed using appropriate testing techniques and under suitable quality-control and supervision (as defined in the integration test plan and test specification documents).

At integration testing, it is important that the testing process is monitored by an *independent test observer*, who will formally witness the results of individual test cases. The independent test observer could be drawn from the QA group in an organization where such a group exists, or from another development team or project.

The development team leader will liaise with the *test team* leader to report on the progress of the development of the AUT, and likely dates for delivery of the AUT for system testing purposes, and will invite the test team leader to informally observe the integration test, or to nominate a suitably qualified member of the *testing team* to attend in his or her place.

The development team leader should consider inviting a *user representative* to informally observe integration testing, particularly where testing involves aspects of the AUT that deal with the business logic of the system or the operation of the user interface. Integration testing provides a valuable opportunity to expose the user representative to aspects of the operation and appearance of the AUT, allowing (informal) feedback to be obtained and helping to manage the expectations of the user representative prior to formal *acceptance testing* (see Chapter 4 for a fuller explanation of the need to involve users in the testing process).

The development team leader will provide the test team leader with copies of a number of outputs produced as a result of the integration testing process (and listed in Section 6.8), including the completed test result record forms, integration test log, and an integration test summary report when integration testing is complete.

6.5 Planning and Resources

Planning of integration testing is the responsibility of the development team leader and should be conducted with reference to the overall development plan for the AUT.

The human resources required for integration testing will be drawn from the development team (with the exception of the independent test observer who may be drawn from another project or the quality assurance group, should one exist within the organization).

It is assumed that integration testing will not take place in the *live environment*, but will take place in the *development environment* or a separate *test environment*. The time and duration for the integration testing must be integrated into the development plan for the AUT to minimize the impact on the development process caused by integration testing and to ensure that no contention for resources will occur.

In the event that integration testing takes place on the live environment, the development team leader must liaise with the IT systems administrator to plan installation of the AUT prior to testing and to ensure that the manager is aware of the date, time, and duration of the integration test.

It is essential that the integration test plan take account of the time and effort required for any correction of defects and retesting.

6.6 Inputs

The following items are required as inputs to integration testing and should be complete and available to the development team leader before testing can begin:

▶ The requirements specification document (for the AUT)
▶ The design documents for the AUT
▶ Any supplementary material, such as user guides or prototype software
▶ The integration testing plan (see Appendix C)
▶ The integration test specification document (see Appendix D)
▶ The integration testing guide (see Appendix B)
▶ Any integration test scripts and test cases (from the test analyst)
▶ Blank test result record forms (see Appendix F)
▶ Any appropriate *reuse packs*, such as the unit test reuse pack (see Appendix I).

6.7 Testing Techniques for Integration Testing

The following testing techniques are appropriate for integration testing:

▶ *Functional testing* using black box testing techniques against the interfacing requirements for the module under test
▶ Nonfunctional testing (where appropriate, e.g., for *performance* or *reliability testing* of the module interfaces)
▶ Where appropriate, some functional testing against relevant intermodule functionality (again using black box testing techniques).

See Chapter 3 for details of these testing techniques.

6.8 Outputs

The following items are generated as outputs from integration testing:

▶ The fully tested and integrated modules
▶ The completed integration test certificate (see Appendix H), where formal proof of testing is required
▶ Any revised *test scripts* and test cases (where appropriate)

▶ The archived test data
▶ The completed test result record forms (see Appendix F)
▶ The integration test log (see Appendix G)
▶ The integration test reuse pack (see Appendix I)
▶ A brief integration test summary report (see Appendix J).

Integration testing will be considered complete when all of the above deliverables (under strict configuration management, as described in Chapter 4) are complete and have been provided to the development team leader.

Appropriate deliverables (i.e., all of the previous except for the fully tested modules) should be stored in the project file. The fully tested modules (plus any associated test harness or simulation code and test data) should be backed up and archived.

Copies of the filed deliverables should be provided to the test team leader prior to the commencement of system testing.

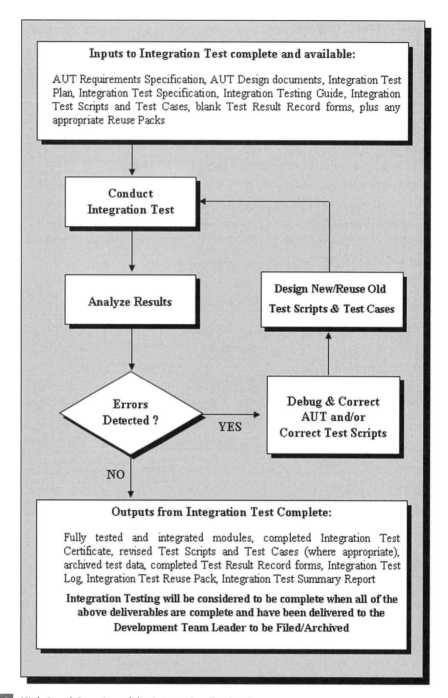

Inputs to Integration Test complete and available:

AUT Requirements Specification, AUT Design documents, Integration Test Plan, Integration Test Specification, Integration Testing Guide, Integration Test Scripts and Test Cases, blank Test Result Record forms, plus any appropriate Reuse Packs

Conduct
Integration Test

Analyze Results

Design New/Reuse Old
Test Scripts & Test Cases

Errors
Detected ?

YES

Debug & Correct
AUT and/or
Correct Test Scripts

NO

Outputs from Integration Test Complete:

Fully tested and integrated modules, completed Integration Test Certificate, revised Test Scripts and Test Cases (where appropriate), archived test data, completed Test Result Record forms, Integration Test Log, Integration Test Reuse Pack, Integration Test Summary Report

Integration Testing will be considered to be complete when all of the above deliverables are complete and have been delivered to the Development Team Leader to be Filed/Archived

6.2 High-Level Overview of the Integration Testing Process

7 System Testing

> "The process of system testing is like removing the needles from the haystack without disturbing the straws"

7.1 Overview

The objective of *system testing* is to establish confidence that the *application under test (AUT)* will be accepted by its users (and/or operators), that is, that it will pass its *acceptance tests*. During system testing, the functional and structural stability of the system will be demonstrated, as well as *nonfunctional* requirements such as performance and reliability. System testing is conducted by the *testing team* under the supervision of the *test team leader*.

Where the AUT has a moderate requirement to interoperate with one or more collaborating software systems, this may be tested during systems testing. Where the AUT has a significant requirement to interoperate with several collaborating software systems and/or the nature of the interoperation is complex, this will typically be tested during a separate testing phase – termed *systems integration testing* (see Chapter 8 for further details).

System testing should employ *black box* testing techniques and will test high-level requirements of the system without considering the implementation details of component modules (e.g., performing *thread testing* and/or testing complete transactions).

In terms of the *V Model*, system testing corresponds to the specification phase of the software development lifecycle (see Figure 7.1).

Testing issues associated with system testing (such as test planning and resourcing and the review of testing requirements and high-level test design), should be considered during the specification phase of system development. The V Model and its role in testing is described in Chapter 4.

A flow chart providing a high-level overview of the system testing process can be found at the end of this chapter (see Figure 7.2).

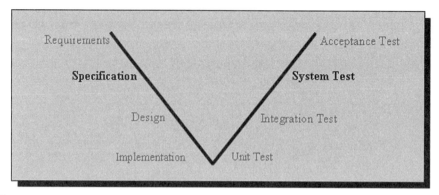

System Testing and the V Model

7.2 System Test Approach

The following approach should be followed in conducting system testing:

▶ Review the requirements for the system (e.g., by reference to the *requirements specification* document for the AUT) and identify:
  ▷ the high-level business requirements
  ▷ the requirement for data handling and transaction rates for the live system
  ▷ the requirements for system performance
  ▷ back-up and recovery requirements
  ▷ any security requirements
▶ Identify any requirements for the AUT to communicate with other systems and the means of communication (where this is not addressed by systems integration testing – see Chapter 8)
▶ Review the computing environment in which the live system will run to identify interoperability or compatibility issues with other systems (where this is not addressed by systems integration testing – see Chapter 8)
▶ Examine the requirement for testing system procedures (such as the installation procedure), system documentation (such as user manuals), and help facilities (both paper-based and interactive), as well as recovery, back-up, and archive
▶ Use the previous information to generate a set of *test cases* to test the system and incorporate them into a *test script*, describing in detail the steps to be followed during testing.

Where they are available, consider reusing test cases from earlier *unit* and *integration testing*. These can be obtained from the appropriate unit and integration test reuse packs.

7.3 System Test Data Requirements

Because one of the major goals of system testing is to establish confidence that the AUT will pass its acceptance test, the data used for testing must be as accurate and as representative of the *live data* as possible. Similarly, because *performance testing* will take place at system testing, the quantity of data available for testing must also be of equivalent size and complexity.

One approach to achieving the previous requirement for test data is to use live data. A significant benefit of this approach is that the system test will use the same data as the acceptance test, which will be one less issue to consider in maintaining uniformity between the system and acceptance tests and increasing confidence in test results.

In those circumstances where it is not possible to use live data either because of risk to the live system (and other applications that rely on live data) or because of security reasons, a copy of the live data should be used. The quality, accuracy, and volume of the copied data must be as representative of live data as possible, and where confidentiality or security considerations result in "sanitization"[1] of the data, great care must be taken to ensure the altered data adequately supports system testing data requirements.

Where live data or a copy of the live data is used, it may still be necessary to introduce some handcrafted data (e.g., to exercise boundary or error conditions). In creating the handcrafted test data the *test analyst* must employ formal design techniques, such as the *boundary value analysis* or *equivalence partition* methods described in Chapter 3, to ensure the data adequately test the boundary conditions for the AUT as well as provide truly representative values.

7.4 Roles and Responsibilities

System testing is typically conducted by the testing team under the supervision of the test team leader, who is responsible for ensuring that adequate system testing is performed using appropriate testing techniques and under quality control and supervision (as defined in the system test plan and test specification documents).

Within the *testing team*, the test analyst is responsible for designing and implementing (and/or reusing) the test script and component test cases used in testing the AUT.

The *tester* is responsible for executing the test cases documented within the test script. In a large test team, it is possible for several test analysts and testers to report to the test team leader, whereas in small test teams, the test analyst and tester roles may be filled by single members of staff or even by a single person with joint responsibility for design and execution of tests.

At system testing, it is essential that the testing process is monitored by an *independent test observer* who formally witnesses the results of individual test cases. The independent test observer could be drawn from the QA group in an organization where such a group exists, or from another testing team or project.

---

[1] Where live data contains confidential data or information relating to security issues, it may be inappropriate to conduct system testing using original data. One solution is to use a copy of the live data that has been altered to remove or change those items of a confidential or secure nature.

The test team leader will liaise with the development team leader to determine the progress of the development of the AUT and likely dates for delivery of the AUT for system testing purposes. The test team leader will invite the development team leader to informally observe the system test or to nominate a suitably qualified member of the development team to attend in his or her place.

The test team leader should consider inviting a *user representative* to informally observe system testing. System testing provides a valuable opportunity to expose the user representative to aspects of the operation and appearance of the AUT, allowing (informal) feedback to be obtained and helping manage expectations of the user representative prior to formal *acceptance testing* (also see Chapter 4 for an explanation of the need to involve users in the testing process).

The test team leader must liaise with the *IT systems administrator* (i.e., the member of staff with responsibility for administering the corporate IT facilities) to install the AUT prior to testing. This will be particularly important if the system test is scheduled to take place on the live environment. Similarly, the IT systems administrator should be kept fully appraised of the date, time, and duration of the system test to ensure there is no contention for system resources, there are no scheduled IT tasks (such as preventive maintenance), and to allow the IT manager the opportunity to perform contingency operations (such as backing up the system) prior to testing.

The test team leader will file copies of a number of outputs produced as a result of the system testing process (and listed in Section 7.8), including the completed *test result record forms*, system test log, and a comprehensive system test summary report on completion of system testing.

7.5 Planning and Resources

System testing planning is the responsibility of the test team leader and should be developed with reference to the overall development and testing plan for the AUT to minimize the impact on the development process caused by system testing and to ensure that no contention for resources will occur.

The human resources required for system testing will be drawn from the testing team (with the exception of the independent test observer, who may be drawn from another project or the quality assurance group, should one exist within the organization).

It is assumed that system testing will take place either in a dedicated *test environment* or in the *live environment*. The choice will depend on a number of issues including:

▶ The availability of a suitably specified test environment (i.e., one that is representative of the live environment)
▶ An assessment of the commercial or safety critical nature of the live environment and the likelihood of the system test adversely affecting it

▶ The occurrence of commercially or confidentially sensitive data, or security critical information within the live environment.

In the event that system testing takes place on the live environment, the test team leader must liaise with the IT systems administrator to plan installation of the AUT prior to testing and to ensure that the manager is aware of the date, time, and duration of the system test.

It is essential that the system test plan take account of the time and effort required for any correction of defects and retesting.

7.6 Inputs

The following items are required as inputs to system testing:

▶ The requirements specification document (for the AUT)
▶ Design documents for the AUT
▶ Any supplementary material, such as user guides or prototype software
▶ System test plan (see Appendix C)
▶ The system test specification document (see Appendix D)
▶ The system testing guide (see Appendix B)
▶ The system test scripts and test cases (from the test analyst)
▶ Blank test result record forms (see Appendix F)
▶ Any appropriate reuse packs, such as the unit and integration test reuse packs (see Appendix I).

7.7 Testing Techniques for System Testing

The following testing techniques are appropriate for system testing:

▶ Black box testing against high-level system requirements
▶ *Thread testing* against high-level business requirements for the AUT
▶ Nonfunctional testing (such as volume, stress, and performance testing)
▶ *Static testing* (review of system documentation, e.g., user manuals)
▶ The role and use of automated testing tools.

See Chapter 3 for details of these testing techniques.

7.8 Outputs

The following items are generated as outputs from system testing:

▶ The fully tested system
▶ The completed system test certificate (see Appendix H)
▶ Any revised test scripts and test cases (where appropriate)
▶ Archived test data

▶ The completed test result record forms (see Appendix F)
▶ The system test log (see Appendix G)
▶ The system test reuse pack (see Appendix I)
▶ A system test summary report (see Appendix J).

System testing will be considered complete when all previously mentioned deliverables are complete and copies (under strict configuration management, as described in Chapter 4) have been provided to the test team leader.

Appropriate deliverables (i.e., all of the previous except the tested system) should be stored in the project file. The fully tested system (plus any associated test harness or simulation code and test data) should be backed up and archived.

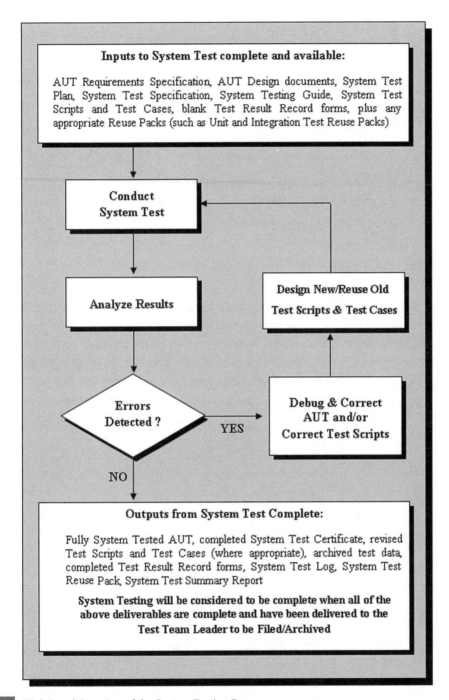

Inputs to System Test complete and available:

AUT Requirements Specification, AUT Design documents, System Test Plan, System Test Specification, System Testing Guide, System Test Scripts and Test Cases, blank Test Result Record forms, plus any appropriate Reuse Packs (such as Unit and Integration Test Reuse Packs)

Conduct System Test

Analyze Results

Design New/Reuse Old Test Scripts & Test Cases

Errors Detected ?

YES

Debug & Correct AUT and/or Correct Test Scripts

NO

Outputs from System Test Complete:

Fully System Tested AUT, completed System Test Certificate, revised Test Scripts and Test Cases (where appropriate), archived test data, completed Test Result Record forms, System Test Log, System Test Reuse Pack, System Test Summary Report

System Testing will be considered to be complete when all of the above deliverables are complete and have been delivered to the Test Team Leader to be Filed/Archived

7.2 High-Level Overview of the System Testing Process

8 Systems Integration Testing

> "There has never been an unexpectedly short debugging period in the history of computing"
>
> **– Steven Levy, "Hackers"**

8.1 Overview

The objective of *systems integration testing* is to provide confidence that the *application under test* (*AUT*) is able to successfully interoperate with other specified software systems[1] and does not have an adverse affect on other systems that may also be present in the *live environment* or vice versa. Systems integration testing is conducted by the *testing team* under the supervision of the *test team leader*. Systems integration testing may also be termed *compatibility testing* or simply integration testing[2] (as termed in the British Library testing process for example – see Chapter 15).

It is possible that the testing tasks performed during systems integration testing may be combined with *system testing*, particularly if the AUT has little or no requirement to interoperate with other systems.

Systems integration testing should employ *black box* techniques and will test high-level interoperability requirements of the AUT without considering the internal construction of the AUT (e.g., testing business processes and complete transactions that require intersystem communication or interaction). The use of *negative testing* and *error guessing* techniques (see Chapter 3) are particularly appropriate during compatibility testing for uncovering unanticipated problems.

In terms of the *V Model*, systems integration testing corresponds to the specification phase of the software development lifecycle (see Figure 8.1).

Testing issues associated with systems integration testing (such as test planning and resourcing and the review of testing requirements and high-level test design) should be considered during the specification phase of system development. The V Model and its role in testing is described in Chapter 4.

---

[1] Software systems refers both to applications that may be coresident in memory as well as external systems with which the AUT may need to communicate.

[2] Where systems integration testing is termed integration testing, the traditional integration testing phase will need to have a different title, such as link testing.

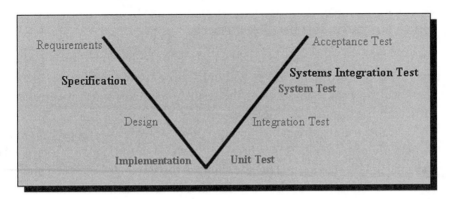

Systems Integration Testing and the V Model

A flow chart providing a high-level overview of the systems integration testing process can be found at the end of this chapter (see Figure 8.2).

8.2 Systems Integration Test Approach

The following approach should be followed in conducting systems integration testing:

▶ Review the interoperability requirements for the system (e.g., by reference to the *requirements specification* document for the AUT) and identify:
  ▷ any requirements for the AUT to communicate with other systems and the means of communication
  ▷ the high-level business requirements that involve communication with other systems
  ▷ the requirement for data handling and transaction rates for the live environment
  ▷ the requirements for system performance
  ▷ back-up and recovery requirements (where these involve other systems)
  ▷ any security requirements (where these involve interoperability issues)
▶ Review the computing environment in which the live system will run to identify interoperability or compatibility issues with other systems
▶ Use the previous information to generate a set of *test scripts* and *test cases* to test the system.

Where appropriate, reusing test cases from *unit*, *integration*, and system testing should be considered. These can be obtained from the unit, integration, and system test *reuse packs* (see Appendix I).

Where the AUT interoperates with external systems over which the *test team* has no control, the use of a *test harness* should be considered to provide reproducible testing results.

8.3 System Integration Test Data Requirements

Systems integration testing should take place in the live environment, and consequently, it will utilize *live data*. Without testing on the live environment, it will be difficult to have confidence in the results of systems integration tests (and in particular, the compatibility testing).

Typically, the requirements for data within systems integration testing are not particularly demanding. This is because the focus of testing is on interoperability and compatibility testing and not the ability of the system to access and process large volumes of data, a test requirement that should have been dealt with during system testing.

The guiding principle in identifying data requirements for systems integration testing is to consider what data will be required in support of the *thread testing* that will be needed to verify interoperability – such as passing, requesting, or receiving data from other systems. In most cases it will be possible to reuse or modify system tests and their associated data during systems integration testing.

8.4 Roles and Responsibilities

Systems integration testing is typically conducted by the *testing team* under the supervision of the test team leader, who is responsible for ensuring that adequate testing is performed using appropriate testing techniques and under quality control and supervision (as defined in the systems integration test plan and test specification documents).

Within the testing team, the *test analyst* is responsible for designing and implementing (and/or reusing) the test script and component test cases used in testing the AUT.

The *tester* is responsible for executing the test cases documented within the test script. In a large test team, it is possible for several test analysts and testers to report to the test team leader, whereas in small test teams, the test analyst and tester roles may be filled by single members of staff or by a single person with joint responsibility for design and execution of tests.

At systems integration testing, it is essential that the testing process is monitored by an *independent test observer* who will formally witness the results of individual test cases. The independent test observer could be drawn from the *quality assurance (QA) group* in an organization where such a group exists, or from another testing team or project.

The test team leader will liaise with the *development team leader* to determine the progress of the development of the AUT and likely dates for delivery of the AUT for systems integration testing purposes. In the event that systems integration testing takes place as part of system testing or immediately after, then the AUT should already be available for testing. The test team leader will invite the development team leader to informally observe the systems integration test or to nominate a suitably qualified member of the development team to attend in his or her place.

The test team leader should consider inviting a *user representative* to informally observe systems integration testing. Systems integration testing provides another valuable opportunity to expose the user representative to aspects of the operation and appearance of the AUT, allowing (informal) feedback to be obtained and helping to manage the expectations of the user representative prior to formal *acceptance testing* (see Chapter 4 for a fuller explanation of the need to involve users in the testing process).

The test team leader must liaise with the *IT systems administrator* (i.e., the member of staff with responsibility for administering corporate IT facilities) for the purpose of installing the AUT prior to testing (this will be particularly important if the systems integration test is scheduled to take place on the live environment, and if it is planned to make use of networked/intra/Internet access to other systems or data). Similarly, the IT systems administrator should be kept fully appraised of the date, time, and duration of the systems integration test to ensure that there is no contention for system resources, there are no scheduled IT tasks (such as preventive maintenance), and the IT manager has the opportunity to perform contingency operations (such as backing up the system) prior to testing.

The test team leader will file copies of a number of outputs produced as a result of systems integration testing process (and listed in Section 8.8), including the completed *test result record forms*, systems integration *test log*, and a comprehensive systems integration *test summary report* on completion of systems integration testing.

8.5 Planning and Resources

The planning of systems integration testing is the responsibility of the test team leader and should be developed with reference to the overall development and testing plan for the AUT in order to minimize the impact on the development process caused by systems integration testing and to ensure that no contention for resources will occur.

The human resources required for systems integration testing will be drawn from the testing team (with the exception of the independent test observer who may be drawn from another project or the quality assurance group, should one exist within the organization).

It is assumed that systems integration testing will take place in the live environment. The use of a dedicated *test environment* should only be considered after considering the following issues:

▶ The availability of a suitably specified test environment (i.e., one that is representative of the live environment)

▶ An assessment of the commercial or safety critical nature of the live environment and the likely hood of the system test adversely affecting it
▶ The occurrence of commercially or confidentially sensitive data, or security critical information within the live environment
▶ The ability to simulate representative interactions with the external system.

In the event that systems integration testing takes place on the live environment, the test team leader must liaise with the IT systems administrator to plan installation of the AUT prior to testing and to ensure that the manager is aware of the date, time, and duration of the systems integration test.

It is essential that the system test plan take account of the time and effort required for any correction of defects and retesting.

8.6 Inputs

The following items are required as inputs to systems integration testing:

▶ The requirements specification document (for the AUT)
▶ The design documents for the AUT
▶ Any supplementary material, such as user guides or prototype software
▶ The systems integration test plan (see Appendix C)
▶ The systems integration test specification document (see Annex D)
▶ The systems integration testing guide (see Annex B)
▶ Any systems integration test scripts and test cases (from the test analyst)
▶ Blank test result record forms (see Annex F)
▶ Any appropriate reuse packs such as the unit, integration, and system test reuse packs (see Appendix I).

8.7 Testing Techniques for Systems Integration Testing

The following testing techniques are appropriate for systems integration testing:

▶ Black box testing against high-level system requirements (and specifically, those requirements addressing interoperability issues)
▶ Thread testing against the high-level business requirements for the AUT (again, focusing on interoperability requirements)
▶ Negative testing and error guessing to uncover any unanticipated problems (such as contention for system resources)
▶ Consider the role and use of automated testing tools.

See Chapter 3 for full details of these testing techniques.

8.8 Outputs

The following items are generated as outputs from systems integration testing:

▶ The systems integration tested system
▶ The completed systems integration *test certificate* (see Annex H)
▶ Any revised test scripts and test cases (where appropriate)
▶ The archived test data
▶ The completed test result record forms (see Appendix F)
▶ Systems integration test log (see Annex G)
▶ Systems integration test reuse pack (see Annex I)
▶ A systems integration test summary report (see Appendix J).

Systems integration testing will be considered to be complete when all of the previous deliverables are complete and copies (under strict configuration management, as described in Chapter 4) have been provided to the test team leader.

Appropriate deliverables (i.e., all of the previous except the tested system) should be stored in the project file. The fully tested system (plus any associated test harness or simulation code and test data) should be backed up and archived.

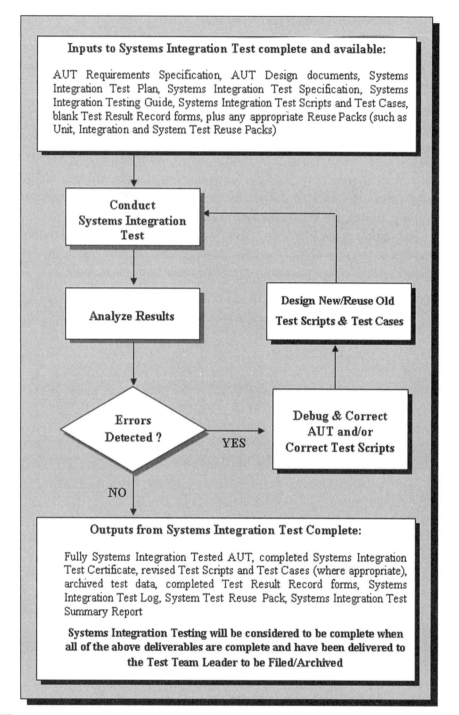

Inputs to Systems Integration Test complete and available:

AUT Requirements Specification, AUT Design documents, Systems Integration Test Plan, Systems Integration Test Specification, Systems Integration Testing Guide, Systems Integration Test Scripts and Test Cases, blank Test Result Record forms, plus any appropriate Reuse Packs (such as Unit, Integration and System Test Reuse Packs)

Conduct Systems Integration Test

Analyze Results

Design New/Reuse Old Test Scripts & Test Cases

Errors Detected ?

YES

NO

Debug & Correct AUT and/or Correct Test Scripts

Outputs from Systems Integration Test Complete:

Fully Systems Integration Tested AUT, completed Systems Integration Test Certificate, revised Test Scripts and Test Cases (where appropriate), archived test data, completed Test Result Record forms, Systems Integration Test Log, System Test Reuse Pack, Systems Integration Test Summary Report

Systems Integration Testing will be considered to be complete when all of the above deliverables are complete and have been delivered to the Test Team Leader to be Filed/Archived

8.2 High-Level Overview of the System Integration Testing Process

9 User Acceptance Testing

> "If love is like an extended software Q.A. suite, then true love is like a final Acceptance Test – one often has to be willing to endure compromise, bug fixes and work-arounds; otherwise, the software is never done."
>
> **– The Usenet Oracle**

9.1 Overview

The objective of *user acceptance testing* is to confirm that the *application under test* (*AUT*) meets its business requirements and to provide confidence that the system works correctly and is usable before it is formally "delivered" to the *end user(s)*. User acceptance testing is conducted by one or more *user representatives* with the assistance of the *test team*.

User acceptance testing is considered distinct from *operations acceptance testing*, which is used to verify the operations and administrative aspects of the AUT (e.g., the installation of updates to the AUT, back-up, archive, and restoring the AUT and its data, and the registration of new users and assigning of their privileges).[1] In practice, where the AUT supports simple administrative facilities, user and operations acceptance testing are often combined into a single testing exercise. Also see Chapter 10 – Operations Acceptance Testing.

User acceptance testing should employ a *black box* approach to testing and should make use of *thread testing* techniques to verify the high-level business requirements of the system. In practice, the user representative(s) will test the AUT by performing typical tasks they would perform during normal usage of the system.

User acceptance testing should also address testing of system documentation (such as user guides) by the user representative(s).

In terms of the *V Model*, user acceptance testing corresponds to the requirements phase of the software development lifecycle (see Figure 9.1).

User acceptance testing issues (such as test planning, review of testing requirements, and identification of user representative[s]) must be considered during the requirements phase of the AUT. The V Model and its role in testing are described in Chapter 4.

---

[1] Typically, the operations users will be experienced IT staff and will require less guidance and assistance in the testing process than the business users of the application under test.

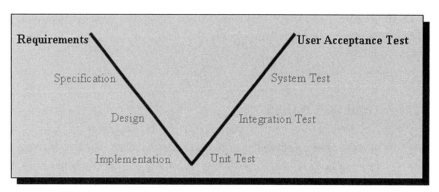

9.2 User Acceptance Test Approach

Typically, user acceptance testing involves the *test analyst* selecting a representative subset of the system test scripts and asking the user representative to execute them. The selection of these *test cases* can be based upon:

▶ Discussion with the user representative
▶ Reviewing the requirements for the AUT to identify any particularly important areas or functions that should be verified.

It is also likely that the test analyst will implement a number of additional test scripts to verify specific user-oriented aspects of the AUT, such as:

▶ Usability aspects of the AUT
▶ System documentation (such as the user manual)
▶ User help facilities (both document based and on-line).

Additional scripts should be produced using formal design techniques as described in Chapter 3.

If the system test for the AUT did not take place in the *live environment* and/or without the *live data*, the following steps must be considered:

▶ Rerun those system tests that address requirements for the AUT to communicate/exchange data with other systems (e.g., to validate user privileges)
▶ Rerun system tests addressing the *interoperability/compatibility* requirements for the AUT.

It is important for the success of the acceptance test that the user representatives' expectations have been carefully managed throughout the development and testing process. For example, the *test team leader* should have invited the user representative to attend the earlier testing phases in an informal capacity so that they will be used to the look and feel of the AUT. In this way, the risk of the user representative rejecting the AUT at acceptance testing because it does not conform to the appearance they anticipated will be minimized. Chapter 4 discusses the need to involve the user representative(s) as early as possible in the development and testing process.

9.3 User Acceptance Test Data Requirements

Wherever possible, live data should be used during user acceptance testing.

Where the live data contains confidential or secure information, and this data is observable during part or all of the acceptance test, steps must be taken to ensure that:

▶ The user representative is cleared to work with such data
▶ The test team leader is cleared to work with such data, or the testing is organized to avoid the need for the test team leader to see the data
▶ The *independent test observer* is cleared to work with such data, or is able to confirm and document the success or failure of the test cases without having to see the data.

In the event that it is not possible to use live data, acceptance testing should be conducted against a realistic and representative copy of the live data. Where secure or confidential information needs to be altered or removed from the test data, care should be taken to ensure that "sanitizing" the data will not have undesirable effects on the accuracy of the user acceptance test.

Where it is necessary to introduce handcrafted data for the purposes of exercising boundary behavior or error conditions, this data should be produced using formal design techniques (see Chapter 3).

9.4 Roles and Responsibilities

User acceptance testing is typically conducted by the user representative(s) with the assistance of the testing team. User acceptance testing is supervised by the test team leader, who is responsible for ensuring that adequate testing is performed using appropriate testing techniques and under quality control and supervision (as defined in the user acceptance test plan and test specification documents).

The user acceptance test typically employs a subset of the tests run during the system test for the AUT. The test analyst is responsible for liaising with the user representative to determine which test scripts and test cases will be rerun during the acceptance test, as well as to determine the need to design and implement any additional test scripts to exercise specific aspects of the AUT that the user representative may request. Any such additional effort must be discussed and agreed with the test team leader.

The *tester* shall assist the user representative in executing the test scripts comprising the user acceptance test, and shall also assist in the interpretation of the results of test cases in collaboration with the independent test observer. The tester shall also be responsible for the set-up and initialization of the *test bed* prior to testing. In a large test team, it is possible for several test analysts and testers to report to the test team leader, whereas in small test teams, the test analyst and tester roles may be filled by single members of staff or even by a single person with joint responsibility for test design and execution.

It is particularly important in user acceptance testing that the testing process is monitored by an independent test observer involved in formally witnessing the result of executing the individual test cases. The independent test observer can act as a safeguard against overenthusiastic testers attempting to coerce or persuade the user representative (who, although being very knowledgeable about his or her domain of expertise, may be IT naive) into accepting the results of a test with which they may have a genuine concern. The independent test observer could be drawn from the QA group in an organization where such a group exists, or from another testing team or project.

The test team leader will liaise with the development team leader to determine progress of the development of the AUT and likely dates for delivery of AUT for user acceptance testing purposes. This will be particularly important if the AUT required rework as a result of the system or systems integration testing.

The test team leader must liaise with the *IT systems administrator* (i.e., the member of staff with responsibility for administering corporate IT facilities) for the purpose of installing the AUT on the live environment. Similarly, the IT systems administrator should be kept fully appraised of the date, time, and duration of the user acceptance test to ensure there is no contention for system resources, there are no scheduled IT tasks (such as preventive maintenance), and to allow the IT manager to perform contingency operations (such as backing up the system) prior to testing.

The test team leader will file copies of a number of outputs produced as a result of the user acceptance test (and listed in Section 9.8), including the completed *test result record forms*, acceptance *test log*, and a comprehensive acceptance *test summary report* on completion of user acceptance testing.

9.5   Planning and Resources

The planning of user acceptance testing is the responsibility of the test team leader and should be developed with reference to the overall development and testing plan for the AUT to minimize the impact on the development process caused by acceptance testing and to ensure that no contention for resources will occur.

The human resources required for user acceptance testing will be drawn from the testing team (with the exception of the independent test observer who may be drawn from another project or the *quality assurance [QA] group*, should one exist within the organization) and the user representative(s).

The test manager will liaise with the customer[2] to identify one or more user representatives selected from the user community for the AUT. It is important that the user representatives are genuine users of the system, and not, as often happens, line managers. For effective acceptance testing it is key that the user representatives have a thorough understanding of both the business aspects of the system as well as typical scenarios employed to achieve business goals.

It is assumed that user acceptance testing will take place on the live environment. However, under certain circumstances acceptance testing may have to be performed using a dedicated *test environment*. The choice will depend on a number of issues including:

▶ An assessment of the commercial or safety critical nature of the live environment and the likelihood of the user acceptance test adversely affecting it
▶ The occurrence of commercially or confidentially sensitive data, or security critical information within the live environment
▶ The availability of a suitably specified test environment (i.e., one that is fully representative of the live environment)
▶ The success of the system test, the possible detection of a significant number of defects, and large-scale rework of the AUT.

Assuming that the user acceptance test takes place on the live environment, the test team leader must liaise with the IT systems administrator to plan installation of the AUT prior to testing and to ensure that the administrator is aware of the date, time, and duration of the system test.

It is essential that the user acceptance test plan take account of the time and effort required for correction of defects and retesting.

9.6 Inputs

The following items are required as inputs to user acceptance testing:

▶ The requirements specification document for the AUT
▶ The design documents for the AUT
▶ Supplementary material, such as user guides or prototype software
▶ The user acceptance test plan (see Appendix C)
▶ The user acceptance test specification document (see Appendix D)
▶ The user acceptance testing guide (see Appendix B)
▶ The user acceptance test scripts and test cases (from the test analyst)
▶ Blank test result record forms (see Appendix F)
▶ Any appropriate reuse packs, such as the system test reuse pack (see Appendix I).

---

[2] The "customer" could be an external client for whom the development of the AUT is conducted under contract, or could be another member of staff within the same organization.

9.7 Testing Techniques for User Acceptance Testing

The following testing techniques are appropriate for user acceptance testing:

▶ Black box testing against high-level system requirements
▶ Thread testing against high-level business (i.e., user) requirements for the AUT
▶ *Usability testing* to ensure the GUI for the AUT is intuitive, consistent, and easy to use, and to ensure the on-line help facilities are satisfactory
▶ Static testing of system documentation (such as user manuals) and their use with the AUT.

See Chapter 3 for details of these testing techniques.

9.8 Outputs

The following items are generated as outputs from user acceptance testing:

▶ The user accepted system
▶ The completed user acceptance test certificate (see Appendix H)
▶ Any revised test scripts and test cases (where appropriate)
▶ The archived test data
▶ The completed test result record forms (see Appendix F)
▶ The user acceptance test log (see Appendix G)
▶ The user acceptance test reuse pack (see Appendix I)
▶ A user acceptance test summary report (see Appendix J).

User acceptance testing will be considered complete when all of the previous deliverables are complete and copies (under strict configuration management, as described in Chapter 4) have been provided to the test team leader.

Appropriate deliverables (i.e., all of the previous except the tested system) should be stored in the project file. The fully tested system (plus any associated test harness or simulation code and test data) should be backed up and archived.

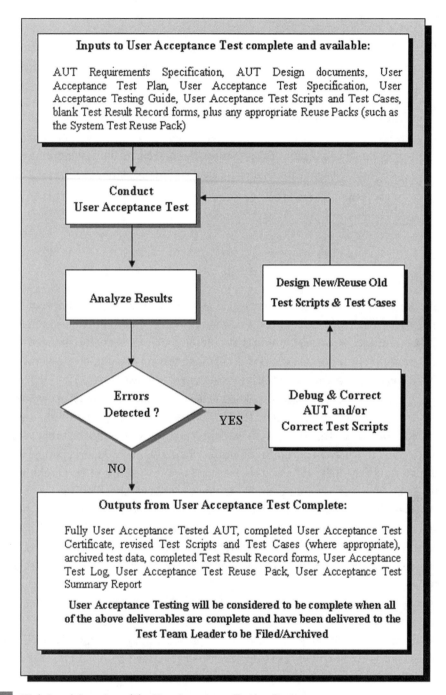

Inputs to User Acceptance Test complete and available:

AUT Requirements Specification, AUT Design documents, User Acceptance Test Plan, User Acceptance Test Specification, User Acceptance Testing Guide, User Acceptance Test Scripts and Test Cases, blank Test Result Record forms, plus any appropriate Reuse Packs (such as the System Test Reuse Pack)

Conduct
User Acceptance Test

Analyze Results

Design New/Reuse Old
Test Scripts & Test Cases

Errors
Detected ?

YES

NO

Debug & Correct
AUT and/or
Correct Test Scripts

Outputs from User Acceptance Test Complete:

Fully User Acceptance Tested AUT, completed User Acceptance Test Certificate, revised Test Scripts and Test Cases (where appropriate), archived test data, completed Test Result Record forms, User Acceptance Test Log, User Acceptance Test Reuse Pack, User Acceptance Test Summary Report

User Acceptance Testing will be considered to be complete when all of the above deliverables are complete and have been delivered to the Test Team Leader to be Filed/Archived

9.2   High-Level Overview of the User Acceptance Testing Process

10 Operations Acceptance Testing

> "If a man will begin with certainties, he shall end in doubts; but if he will be content to begin with doubts, he shall end in certainties"
>
> **– Francis Bacon**

10.1 Overview

The objective of *operations acceptance testing* is to confirm that the *application under test (AUT)* meets its operations requirements, and to provide confidence that the system works correctly and is usable before it is formally "handed over" to the *operations user(s)*. Operations acceptance testing is conducted by one or more *operations representatives* with the assistance of the *test team*.

Operations acceptance testing is considered distinct from *user acceptance testing*, which is used to verify that the AUT meets its business requirements, and to provide confidence that the system works correctly and is usable before it is formally "delivered" to the *end user(s)*. In practice, where the AUT supports simple administrative facilities, operations and user acceptance testing are often combined into a single testing exercise. Also see Chapter 9 – User Acceptance Testing.

Operations acceptance testing should employ a *black box* approach to testing and should make use of *thread testing* techniques to verify high-level operations requirements of the system. In practice, the operations representative(s) will test the AUT by performing typical tasks they would perform during normal usage of the system.

Operations acceptance testing should also address testing of system documentation (such as operations guides) by the operations representative(s).

In terms of the *V Model*, operations acceptance testing corresponds to the requirements phase of the software development lifecycle (see Figure 10.1).

A flow chart providing a high-level overview of the operations acceptance testing process can be found at the end of this chapter (see Figure 10.2).

Operations acceptance testing issues (such as test planning, review of testing requirements, and identification of the operations representative[s]), must be considered during the requirements phase of the development of the AUT. The V Model and its role in testing are documented in Chapter 4.

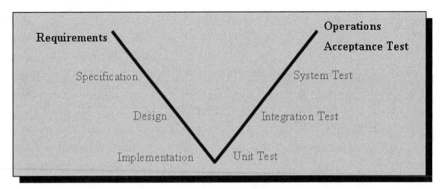

Operations Acceptance and the V Model

10.2 Operations Acceptance Test Approach

For applications that support significant operations facilities, the operations aspects of the AUT are typically key to the successful running of the system. Under such circumstances, a high degree of confidence in the operations aspects of the system (and hence, greater testing coverage) is required, and the additional time, effort, and resources required for operations acceptance testing must be reflected in the test plan.

Typically, operations acceptance testing involves the *test analyst* selecting a representative subset of the system test scripts and asking the operations representative to execute them. The selection of these *test cases* can be based upon:

▶ Discussion with the operations representative to identify key aspects of the operations functionality
▶ Review of the requirements for the system to identify particularly important areas or functions.

It is also likely that the test analyst will implement a number of additional test scripts to verify specific operations-oriented aspects of the AUT, such as:

▶ The usability of operations aspects of the AUT
▶ System procedures (such as the installation procedure)
▶ System documentation (such as the operations manual)
▶ Operations help facilities (both document-based and on-line).

These additional scripts should be produced using the formal design techniques described in Chapter 3.

If the system test for the AUT did not take place in the *live environment* and/or without the *live data*, the following steps must be considered:

▶ Rerun the system tests addressing requirements for the AUT to communicate/exchange data with other systems (e.g., to validate administrator privileges)
▶ Rerun the system tests addressing the *interoperability/compatibility* requirements for the AUT.

The *test team leader* should consider the benefits of involving the operations representative(s) in the early testing phases in an informal capacity to manage their expectations of the software they will ultimately be expected to accept. This approach is likely to be less critical to the success of operations acceptance compared with user acceptance because operations representatives are typically more *information technology* (*IT*) oriented than *user representatives* and hence are likely to have more realistic expectations regarding capabilities of the AUT and are more likely to accept compromises in terms of the facilities provided. Chapter 4 discusses the need to involve the user and operations representative(s) as early as possible in the development and testing process.

10.3 Operations Acceptance Test Data Requirements

Although it is preferable to use live data during operations acceptance testing, it is not as critical as it is for user acceptance testing. In practice, it is possible to use a copy of the live data or even a handcrafted data set for operations acceptance as long as:

▶ The available test data is realistic and representative of the live data
▶ The test data set provides a sufficient quantity and complexity of data to support those operations acceptance testing tasks involving manipulation of large volumes of data (e.g., the back-up and recovery of system data, or installation of the system database)
▶ The operations acceptance test does not involve significant data access or manipulation.

Where the live data contains confidential or secure information, and this data is observable during part or all of the acceptance test, steps must be taken to ensure that:

▶ The operations representative is cleared to work with such data (this will be likely if, for example, the operations representative is the system administrator, who is likely to have sufficient clearance)
▶ The test team leader is cleared to work with such data, or the testing is organized to avoid the need for the test team leader to see the data
▶ The independent test observer is cleared to work with such data or is able to confirm and document the success or failure of the test cases without having to see the data.

Where it is necessary to introduce handcrafted data for the purposes of exercising boundary behavior or error conditions, this data should be produced using formal design techniques (see Chapter 3).

10.4 Roles and Responsibilities

Operations acceptance testing is typically conducted by the operations representative(s) with the assistance of the testing team. Operations acceptance testing is supervised by the test team leader, who is responsible for ensuring that adequate testing is performed using appropriate testing techniques and under quality control and supervision (as defined in the operations acceptance test plan and test specification documents).

The operations acceptance test typically employs a subset of the tests run during the system test for the AUT (however, if the operations aspects of the AUT are considered vital to successful functioning of the software, it may be decided to execute all of the system tests that deal with operations facilities). The test analyst is responsible for liaising with the operations representative to determine which test scripts and test cases will be rerun during the operations acceptance test.

The *tester* assists the operations representative in executing the test scripts comprising the operations acceptance test and shall also help in the interpretation of the results of test cases in collaboration with the independent test observer. The tester shall also be responsible for the set-up and initialization of the *test bed* prior to testing.

Although it is important that the testing process is monitored by an independent test observer who is involved in formally witnessing the individual test cases, this requirement is not as strenuous as it is for user acceptance testing. This is because the operations representative(s) are typically more IT aware then the user representatives, and will require less support against overly enthusiastic testers attempting to coerce or persuade the operations representative into accepting the results of a test with which they may have expressed a genuine concern. The independent test observer could be drawn from the *quality assurance (QA) group* in an organization where such a group exists, or from another testing team or project.

The test team leader will liaise with the development team leader to determine the progress of the development of the AUT and likely dates for delivery of AUT for operations acceptance testing purposes. This will be particularly important if the AUT required rework as a result of the system or systems integration testing.

The test team leader must liaise with the *IT systems administrator* (i.e., the member of staff with responsibility for administering the corporate IT facilities to install the AUT on the live environment. Similarly, the IT systems administrator should be kept fully appraised of the date, time, and duration of the operations acceptance test to ensure there is no contention for system resources, there are no scheduled IT tasks (such as preventive maintenance), and to allow the IT manager the opportunity to perform contingency operations (such as backing up the system) prior to testing.

The test team leader will file copies of a number of outputs produced as a result of the operations acceptance test (and listed in Section 10.8), including the completed *test result record forms*, acceptance *test log*, and a comprehensive acceptance *test summary report* on completion of operations acceptance testing.

10.5   Planning and Resources

The planning of operations acceptance testing is the responsibility of the test team leader and should be developed with reference to the overall development and testing plan for the AUT to minimize the impact on the development process caused by operations acceptance testing and to ensure that no contention for resources will occur.

The human resources required for operations acceptance testing will be drawn from the testing team (with the exception of the independent test observer who may be drawn from another project or the quality assurance group, should one exist within the organization) and the operations representative(s).

The test manager will liaise with the customer[1] to identify one or more operations representatives who will be selected from the operations user community (typically the IT systems group) for the AUT.

Because operations acceptance testing does not deal with the execution of typical business scenarios dealing with the normal use of the AUT by the user representatives, the requirement for using live data may be relaxed. However, typically, the volume and complexity of the test data should be representative of the live data to accurately exercise the administrative scenarios typically followed by the operators (such as back-up and recovery of the system and archival of the data). In making such a decision regarding the use of live data the following criteria should be considered:

▶ The need for realistic volumes of data to accurately exercise the administrative operations of the AUT
▶ An assessment of the commercial or safety critical risk involved in using the live environment and the likelihood of the operations acceptance test adversely affecting it
▶ The occurrence of commercially or confidentially sensitive data, or security critical information within the live environment. (This is not normally an issue because the operations staff are likely to be cleared to work with such material.)
▶ The availability of a suitably specified test environment (i.e., one that is sufficiently representative of the live environment).

If the operations acceptance test takes place on the live environment, the test team leader must liaise with the IT systems administrator to plan installation of the AUT prior to testing and to ensure that the administrator is aware of the date, time, and duration of the system test.

It is essential that the operations acceptance test plan take account of the time and effort required for any correction of defects and retesting.

10.6 Inputs

The following items are required as inputs to operations acceptance testing:

▶ The requirements specification document

---

[1] The "customer" could be an external client for whom the development of the AUT is being conducted under contract, or could be another member of staff within the same organization.

▶ The design documents for the AUT, and specifically those dealing with the operations aspects of the software
▶ Any supplementary material, such as user guides or prototype software
▶ The operations acceptance testing plan (see Appendix C)
▶ The operations acceptance test specification document (see Appendix D)
▶ The operations acceptance testing guide (see Appendix B)
▶ The operations acceptance test scripts and test cases (from the test analyst)
▶ Blank test result record forms (see Appendix F)
▶ Any appropriate *reuse packs*, such as the system test reuse pack (see Appendix I).

10.7 Testing Techniques for Operations Acceptance Testing

The following testing techniques are appropriate for operations acceptance testing:

▶ Black box testing against high-level system requirements
▶ Thread testing against the operations requirements for the AUT
▶ *Usability testing* to ensure the GUI for the AUT is intuitive, consistent, and easy to use, and to ensure on-line help facilities are satisfactory
▶ Static testing of system documentation (such as operations manuals), and their use with the AUT.

See Chapter 3 for details of these testing techniques.

10.8 Outputs

The following items are generated as outputs from operations acceptance testing:

▶ The operations accepted system
▶ The completed operations acceptance test certificate (see Appendix H)
▶ Any revised test scripts and test cases (where appropriate)
▶ The archived test data
▶ The completed test result record forms
▶ The operations acceptance test log (see Appendix G)
▶ The operations acceptance test reuse pack (see Appendix I)
▶ An operations acceptance test summary report (see Appendix J).

Operations acceptance testing will be considered complete when all of the previous deliverables are complete and copies (under strict configuration management, as described in Chapter 4) have been provided to the test team leader.

Appropriate deliverables (i.e., all of the previous except the tested system) should be stored in the project file. The fully tested system (plus any associated test harness or simulation code and test data) should be backed up and archived.

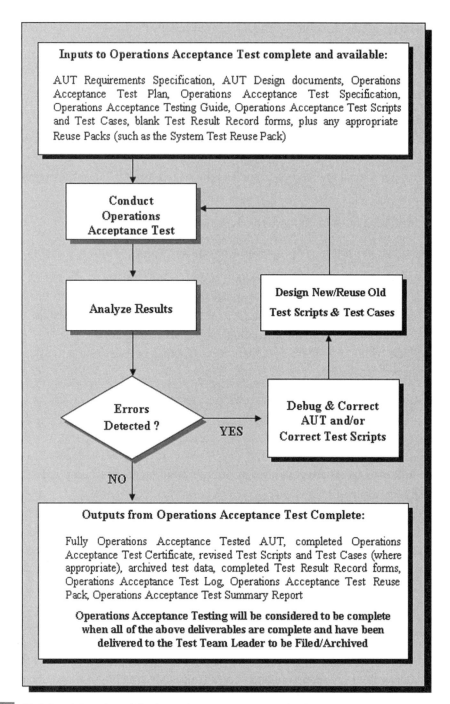

Inputs to Operations Acceptance Test complete and available:

AUT Requirements Specification, AUT Design documents, Operations Acceptance Test Plan, Operations Acceptance Test Specification, Operations Acceptance Testing Guide, Operations Acceptance Test Scripts and Test Cases, blank Test Result Record forms, plus any appropriate Reuse Packs (such as the System Test Reuse Pack)

Conduct Operations Acceptance Test

Analyze Results

Design New/Reuse Old Test Scripts & Test Cases

Errors Detected ?

YES

Debug & Correct AUT and/or Correct Test Scripts

NO

Outputs from Operations Acceptance Test Complete:

Fully Operations Acceptance Tested AUT, completed Operations Acceptance Test Certificate, revised Test Scripts and Test Cases (where appropriate), archived test data, completed Test Result Record forms, Operations Acceptance Test Log, Operations Acceptance Test Reuse Pack, Operations Acceptance Test Summary Report

Operations Acceptance Testing will be considered to be complete when all of the above deliverables are complete and have been delivered to the Test Team Leader to be Filed/Archived

10.2 High-Level Overview of the Operations Acceptance Testing Process

11 Regression Testing

"Quality comes for free as long as you pay for it"

11.1 Overview

The purpose of *regression testing* is to ensure that the *application under test* (*AUT*) still functions correctly following modification or extension of the system (e.g., user enhancements or upgrades).[1] Typically, the new modifications or extensions will be tested to verify that they meet their requirements, after which a series of tests will be run to verify that the existing functionality still meets its requirements.

Regression testing is not strictly speaking a testing phase, but it is a testing technique that can be used with any of the testing phases described in the previous chapters. For example, if a test team were conducting a *system test* of a new release of the AUT, the *test analyst* would need to design a number of tests to verify the correctness of the new or modified functionality. In addition to the new tests, the test analyst would select (perhaps from the appropriate reuse pack – see Appendix I) a number of the tests from the previous system test(s) of the AUT in order to determine if any defects had been introduced into the AUT during the implementation of the new functionality.

Regression testing can also be employed following changes to the environment in which an AUT runs, such as the installation of a new version of the operating system, changes to the hardware platform (e.g., addition of memory), or a particular event external to the AUT. For example, *millennium testing* can be considered to have been a special case of *regression testing*. During a typical millennium test, the AUT would not have been altered, but it would still be necessary to ensure the AUT performed correctly following a particular event (e.g., the year 2000 date change).

Typically regression testing is employed in the context of system and *acceptance testing* (and where the AUT has a significant requirement to interoperate with other

---

[1] The literal meaning of regression testing, is testing to ensure the AUT has not regressed or lost functionality or reliability following the addition of new functionality or changes to existing functionality.

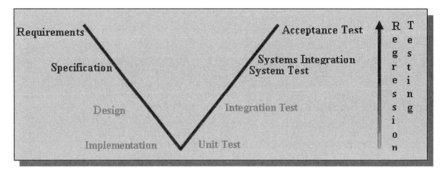

Regression Testing and the V Model

applications, at *systems integration testing*), ensuring that the complete AUT still functions correctly following a new build or release, or ensuring that the existing business functionality of the AUT is still intact.

Regression testing should employ *black box* techniques to test the high-level requirements of the AUT without considering the implementation details of the system (e.g., testing business processes and complete transactions). In addition, some *nonfunctional tests* may be required to check whether the enhancements or extensions have affected the performance characteristics of the system. The role of *error guessing* is an important one in *regression testing*, with the test analysts using their testing experience to determine the scope and extent of the testing required to provide confidence in the modified system (see Chapter 3).

Regression testing is a particularly appropriate candidate for support by means of an *automated testing tool* (e.g., see [22]), especially if frequent new builds and releases of the AUT are anticipated. The advantages of using a tool include:

▶ The ability to run the regression test unattended, that is, overnight or over the weekend, without the need for testing staff to be present
▶ The ability to rerun all of the *automated test scripts* or a selected subset of scripts against the new build or release as required to provide maximum confidence in the software
▶ Establishing a high degree of confidence that the modifications or extensions to the system have not impacted unduly on its functionality.

A number of the case studies presented in Part 2 of this book describe organizations that have successfully incorporated the use of automated testing tools in their testing process for use in regression testing (e.g., see Chapters 16 and 18).

As mentioned earlier in this chapter, although regression testing can be employed at all testing phases, it is particularly appropriate during the higher testing phases. Figure 11.1 shows the relationship between *regression testing* and the *V Model*.

11.2 Regression Test Approach

The following approach should be followed in conducting regression testing:

▶ Complete the functional testing of the new enhancements or extensions to the AUT to verify that they meet their requirements as appropriate to the particular testing phase (e.g., system, systems integration, or acceptance testing)
▶ Obtain the testing reuse pack(s) (see Appendix I) for the relevant testing phase(s)
▶ Update the reuse pack as necessary by reviewing the requirements for the enhancements or extensions to the AUT and the *test scripts* contained within the reuse packs, to identify any existing test cases that may be redundant or need to be updated (e.g., a change to the requirements for the AUT may have led to the modification of an existing feature of the AUT, rendering the corresponding test obsolete or incorrect)
▶ Review the computing environment in which the *live system* will run in order to identify any *interoperability* or *compatibility* issues with other systems that may occur with respect to the enhancements or extensions to the system, and the need to design and implement appropriate tests
▶ Compile a set of regression test cases by reusing appropriate tests from the reuse packs, and execute these against the new version of the AUT. These tests should be selected on the basis of verifying that key aspects of the AUT still perform correctly, and by using experience and judgment, deciding which other aspects of the AUT may have been affected by the new extensions or enhancements.

For organizations employing an automated testing tool approach to regression testing, the need to determine which tests to reuse is not an issue, because all of the tests can be rerun. This is possible because of the ability of such tools to operate unattended, allowing more thorough testing of the AUT by allowing tests to be run overnight or over the weekend.

Those organizations employing automated tools most efficiently, use them to record the execution of the manual test script(s) for a particular testing phase (e.g., system testing). The resulting automated test script can then be replayed against a later build or release of the AUT to ensure the behavior of the AUT has not regressed. In addition, the new manual tests used to verify the new extensions or enhancements to the AUT are recorded, allowing these tests to be added into the existing library of automated test scripts (the case studies presented in Chapters 17 and 19 provide details of how this approach has been applied successfully within the context of a commercial software testing process).

11.3 Regression Test Data Requirements

Whereas the purpose of conducting regression testing is to determine whether the existing reliability and functionality of the AUT are unaffected because of the modification or extension of the software, it is important to keep other factors that may influence the outcome of the testing as similar as possible to those under which the tests were originally run on the unmodified software. Test data is one such factor.

For example, if live data is to be used within the regression test, it may be difficult to ensure that any defects observed are not due to changes in data rather than changes to the AUT. Where live data is to be used, the ideal approach to regression testing the AUT will involve first running the regression test against the test data set that was archived following the previous testing of the AUT, in order to isolate any observed defects from concerns about the data. If these tests are satisfactory, the regression test (or selected elements of it) can be rerun against the live data to provide further confidence in the software.

Where it has been necessary to introduce handcrafted data into the regression test (to exercise boundary or error conditions for the extended or enhanced functionality for example), the test analyst must employ formal design techniques, such as the *boundary value analysis* or *equivalence partition* methods described in Chapter 3.

11.4 Roles and Responsibilities

For regression testing associated with system, systems integration or acceptance testing, the *test team leader* will supervise the testing process and will be responsible for ensuring that adequate regression testing is performed using appropriate testing techniques and quality-control procedures (as defined in the *regression test plan* and *test specification* documents).

Within the testing team, the test analyst is responsible for obtaining and reviewing the reuse packs from previous testing phases for the purposes of selecting an appropriate set of test scripts and test cases to rerun against the new version of the software, and for designing and implementing any new test scripts and test cases required to verify the new extensions or enhancements to the AUT. The test analyst will also be responsible for updating the reuse pack where existing tests are found to be incorrect or obsolete. Additionally, the test analyst may be required to create or modify existing test data for the purposes of exercising the new functionality or for verifying boundary or error conditions using the formal design techniques described in Chapter 3.

The *tester* is responsible for executing the *test scripts* created by the *test analyst*, and for observing and recording the results of testing with reference to the *test result categories* recorded in the regression test specification document (see Appendix D).

At regression testing, it is important that the testing process is monitored by an *independent test observer* who will formally witness the results of individual test cases. The independent test observer could be drawn from the *quality assurance (QA) group* in an organization where such a group exists, or from another testing team or project.

The test team leader must liaise with the *information technology (IT) systems administrator* (e.g., the member of staff with responsibility for administering the corporate IT facilities) for the purpose of installing the AUT prior to testing (this will be particularly important if the regression test is scheduled to take place on the live environment). Similarly, the IT systems administrator should be kept fully appraised of the date, time, and duration of the regression test to ensure that there is no contention for system resources, there are no scheduled IT tasks (such as preventative maintenance), and to allow the IT manager the opportunity to perform contingency operations (such as backing up the system) prior to testing.

The test team leader is responsible for filing and archiving copies of a number of the outputs generated as a result of regression testing (and listed in Section 11.8), including the completed *test result record forms* and *regression test log*, and a brief *regression test summary report* on completion of *regression testing*.

There is unlikely to be any significant benefit to inviting any *user or operations representatives* to informally attend *regression testing* associated with *system* or *systems integration testing* because the need to manage their respective expectations of the AUT should already have been considered in the previous testing phases. Clearly, the appropriate users should be invited to assist in any *regression testing* associated with *acceptance testing* of the AUT.

Where automated testing tools are being used to support the regression testing process, the test analyst will have responsibility for designing the automated test scripts and the *verification points* (analogous to *test cases*). The tester will be responsible for setting up and executing the automated test scripts, and for reviewing and interpreting the automated test log at the completion of testing.

11.5 Planning and Resources

The planning of regression testing is the responsibility of whoever is managing the associated testing phase. Thus for regression testing conducted in conjunction with system, systems integration or acceptance testing, the test team leader will plan the testing process with reference to the overall development and testing plan to ensure no contention for resources will occur.

The human resources required for regression testing will be drawn from the testing team (with the exception of the independent test observer who may be drawn from another project or from the quality assurance group, should one exist within the organization).

It is assumed that regression testing will take place either in a dedicated test environment or in the live environment. The choice will depend on a number of issues including:

▶ The availability of a suitably specified test environment (that is, one that is representative of the live environment)
▶ An assessment of the commercial or safety critical nature of the live environment and the likely hood of the regression test adversely affecting it

▶ The occurrence of commercially or confidentially sensitive data, or security critical information within the live environment.

In the event that regression testing does take place on the live environment, the test team leader must liaise with the IT systems administrator to plan installation of the AUT prior to testing and to ensure that the manager is aware of the date, time, and duration of the regression test.

It is essential that the regression test plan take account of the time and effort required for correction of defects and retesting.

11.6   Inputs

The following items are required as inputs to regression testing:

▶ Any appropriate reuse packs from previous testing phases (see Appendix I)
▶ The *requirements specification* document and any supplementary design documents for the AUT (to assist the test analyst in determining the scope and extent of regression testing)
▶ Any supplementary material, such as user guides or prototype software
▶ The regression test specification document (see Appendix D)
▶ The regression testing plan (see Appendix C)
▶ The regression testing guide (see Appendix B)
▶ Any additional regression test scripts and test cases (created where needed by the test analyst)
▶ Blank *test result record forms* (see Appendix F).

11.7   Testing Techniques for Regression Testing

The following testing techniques are appropriate for regression testing:

▶ Black box testing against high-level system requirements to verify that key aspects of the AUT still perform correctly
▶ Black box testing against other aspects of the AUT which may have been compromised by the new extensions or enhancements
▶ Thread testing against the high-level business requirements for the AUT
▶ Nonfunctional testing (e.g., volume, stress and performance testing), where appropriate.

See Chapter 3 for details of these testing techniques.

11.8   Outputs

The following items are generated as outputs from regression testing:

▶ The fully regression tested system

▶ The completed regression test certificate (see Appendix H)
▶ Any revised test scripts and test cases (where appropriate)
▶ The archived test data (where appropriate)
▶ The completed test result record forms (see Appendix F)
▶ The regression test log (see Appendix G)
▶ The regression test reuse pack (see Appendix I).

Regression testing will be considered complete when all of the previous deliverables are complete and copies (under strict configuration management, as described in Chapter 4) have been provided to the test team leader.

Appropriate deliverables (that is, all of the previous except the tested system) should be stored in the project file. The fully tested system (plus any associated test harness or simulation code and test data) should be backed up and archived.

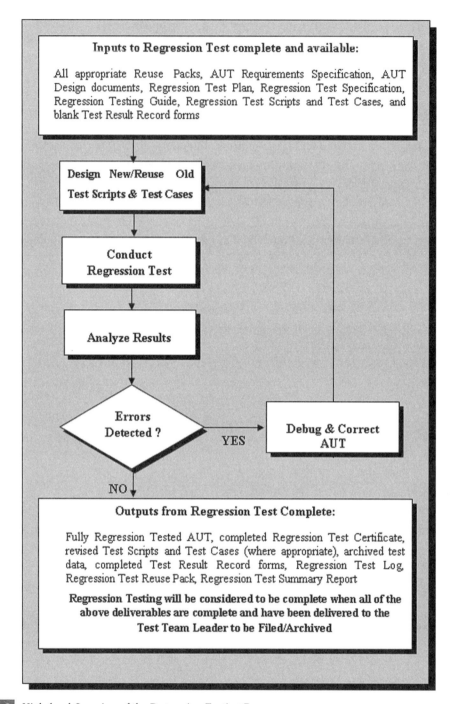

Inputs to Regression Test complete and available:

All appropriate Reuse Packs, AUT Requirements Specification, AUT Design documents, Regression Test Plan, Regression Test Specification, Regression Testing Guide, Regression Test Scripts and Test Cases, and blank Test Result Record forms

Design New/Reuse Old Test Scripts & Test Cases

Conduct Regression Test

Analyze Results

Errors Detected ?

YES

Debug & Correct AUT

NO

Outputs from Regression Test Complete:

Fully Regression Tested AUT, completed Regression Test Certificate, revised Test Scripts and Test Cases (where appropriate), archived test data, completed Test Result Record forms, Regression Test Log, Regression Test Reuse Pack, Regression Test Summary Report

Regression Testing will be considered to be complete when all of the above deliverables are complete and have been delivered to the Test Team Leader to be Filed/Archived

11.2 High-level Overview of the Regression Testing Process

12 Improving the Testing Process

"Those who forget the Lessons of History, are Doomed to Repeat its Mistakes."

– George Santayana

12.1 Introduction

The idea that we should try to learn by our experiences is both natural and intuitive, but one we frequently seem to ignore in the software development and test context.

One particular approach to learning by experience in a project environment is to collect and use metrics observed during the course of the project, such as how much effort was expended in completing the project, how many defects were found during testing, or how many defects were found by the client[1] following delivery of the tested system. This information subsequently can be used to determine whether the testing process is improving over time, for example, by comparing the current effectiveness in finding defects against previously observed results.

Metrics can also be used to investigate the benefits of adopting a specific approach to testing – such as the introduction of automated testing – by comparing the efficiency of the testing process before introduction with that observed following rollout of the tool. The Crown Management Systems case study (Chapter 17) provides just such an example of the role and use of metrics in a testing project environment.

If no formal, quantitative measurements are made, it is only possible to make qualitative statements about the effectiveness of the testing process. This may assure senior management in the short term, but in the long term will not help to improve the testing process. Typical examples of where metrics can be used in the testing process include:

▶ For objective assessment of testing quality against agreed standards
▶ For estimating the testing effort required to complete a given testing project/task
▶ For highlighting complex elements of the system under test, which may be error prone and require additional testing effort
▶ To measure and track the cost of testing

---

[1] The term client could refer to an external customer for whom the AUT was developed under contract or could represent an internal customer within the same organization.

▶ To measure the return on investment (ROI) of a particular approach or tool, such as an automated software testing tool (e.g., see [25])

▶ To assess and track the progress of the testing task

▶ To predict when it is appropriate to stop testing a particular *application under test (AUT)*.

Formally, metrics are objective numerical measures obtained by inspection and analysis of the products and processes of a software project. Although metrics can be collected at all stages of the software development lifecycle, this chapter will focus on those of relevance to the testing process.

This chapter discusses the role and use of metrics in process improvement, reviews the metrics typically employed in such programs, discusses the issues involved in setting up and adopting a metrics program, and makes a number of proposals for a simple and effective metrics set, which can be used to improve the testing process.

12.2 Overview of the Role and Use of Metrics

Although the statistical techniques clause of ISO 9001 provides guidance on the adoption of a metrics-based approach, there is presently no single universal standard for software metrics in the information technology (IT) or software development arena. However, a great deal of work has been done in the IT industry on software metrics, and many metrics and metrics sets have been proposed and adopted by different authors and organizations.

The following statement provides a useful working definition of a metric:

A Software Metric is a standard means of measuring some attribute of the software development (and testing) process (11).

A further useful distinction can be made between primitive and computed metrics:

▶ A primitive metric is one that can be measured directly. Examples include:
  ▷ the number of defects (e.g., the total number of reported defects)
  ▷ the complexity of the AUT (e.g., based on function points within the AUT)
  ▷ the cost of testing (e.g., the combined total cost of testing the AUT).
▶ A computed metric is one that must be calculated from other data or metrics. Examples include:
  ▷ the number of noncomment lines of code written per day
  ▷ the defect density (e.g., number of defects per line of noncomment code)
  ▷ the number of defects detected/reported per unit time or per development phase.

Primitive metrics typically form the raw data for a metrics program and will represent the observed data collected during the project. Often, plotting the progress of primitive metrics over time is a powerful means of observing trends within the testing project (or projects). For example, plotting the numbers of defects detected during a testing project against time can provide the test team leader with one means of determining when to stop testing by observing when the rate of detection of defects declines.[2]

Computed metrics typically form the basis of forming conclusions regarding the progress of a process improvement program. For example, observing the defect detection effectiveness percentage achieved by a testing team across a number of testing projects (which is based on the relative effectiveness of the testing team at detecting defects as compared with those reported by the user(s) following delivery of the AUT – see Section 12.3), provides a valuable indication of the changing efficiency of the testing process over time.

12.3 Metrics Typically Used Within the Testing Process

This section reviews the commonly collected and calculated metrics that can be used in improving the testing process. Where the metric discussed is computed, the means of calculating the metric is described with reference to the appropriate primitive metrics.

Size (How big is the AUT?)

This metric is typically measured as NCSS (Noncomment Source Statements or lines of code). In an object-oriented or GUI-based development, information about the number of objects (and their methods), or windows could be collected. This metric must be collected pragmatically – it does not make good sense to manually count every line of code of a huge application (however, an automated approach using a line-counting tool might be appropriate).

In using the information on the size of different applications, it is important to compare like with like (e.g., comparing lines of code in a traditional application with numbers of objects is unlikely to provide meaningful conclusions). However, if enough information is collected within organizations using a number of different implementation technologies, it may be possible over time – and with sufficient observation – to determine some form of conversion factor between such technologies, which will allow for useful comparisons.

Size metrics on their own may prove insufficient to enable any significant conclusions to be made. The complexity of the software should also be considered within any metrics program.

Complexity (How complicated is the AUT?)

This metric attempts to take account of the complexity of the AUT in terms of iteration, recursion, conditional branching points, function points. Caution must be exercised in the use of this metric, because it will be difficult to produce generally

---

[2] Great care must be taken when using such information within the planning process for the testing project, because decline in numbers of observed defects could be based on other factors, such as tester fatigue.

applicable conclusions for those organizations involved in a number of software development and testing projects, each of which utilizes different implementation technologies.

This is a difficult metric to collect; however, complexity-estimating tools are commercially available, which will simplify the collection and use of complexity information (e.g., [33]).

As with size of the AUT, this metric works best where like is compared with like.

Cost/Effort (How much does it cost? How much effort is expended to test a given piece of software and associated documentation?)

This metric is typically measured as payroll month, and includes time taken by staff doing testing, as well as time spent by managers engaged on testing tasks.

It may also be beneficial to measure the cost/effort involved in administering and collecting the metrics, because comparison of this value with the total effort expended in the testing process will provide information about the efficiency of the metrics program.

Total Defects Found in Testing (How many defects were detected during testing?)

In this context, a defect can be defined as anything in the output of the software process that would not exist if the software were fit for purpose. It may be beneficial to consider recording the severity of observed defects to help in comparing their relative impact. A simple three point scale of critical, serious, and minor is often sufficient for this purpose.[3]

Total Defects Found by Client (How many defects were reported by the client after the software's release?)

This value should be recorded consistently after a standard interval following release of the AUT (such as after three months and/or six months – clearly the time period adopted will depend on the usage and expected lifetime of the system, as well as its planned release schedule).

If a severity scale has been adopted to record the total defects found in testing metric, the same scale should be employed with this metric as well.

Test Development Progress (How many tests have been planned, designed, run, and passed/failed?)

This category also includes test coverage (How much of the AUT has been tested?). These metrics are particularly appropriate for generation by testing tools (such as the reporting facilities provided by a test management tool – e.g., see [25]).

This metric also could consider the numbers of defects reported but not rectified, and the progress of correcting defects over time and/or by developer.

Difficulty (How difficult is the software to develop and test?)

---

[3] Although high, medium, and low, or even 1, 2 and 3, are commonly used.

Although the difficulty of a software project may seem to be a subjective issue, it is possible to introduce a qualitative approach by breaking the project down into subitems and considering each in turn. Examples of categories could include:

▶ The stability of the requirements for the AUT (Are the requirements for the AUT fixed or do they change frequently in response to client requests?)
▶ The level of experience of the testing staff (e.g., Are the testers experienced practitioners or are they new IT graduates who have been assigned to a testing project as their first task after joining an organization?)
▶ The level of familiarity of the testing staff with the technology being tested (Have the testers worked with applications developed using similar technologies, other applications in the same product family, or previous releases of the AUT?)
▶ The ease of access to facilities used in the testing process (Do the testers have full and free access to the AUT for testing? Are there issues with confidentiality or security, which means real data cannot be used in testing? Are productivity tools – such as automated testing tools – available to support the testers?)

For the majority of organizations using traditional tried and tested implementation technologies and methods, the use of this metric is unlikely to provide much benefit. It may be beneficial for projects using leading-edge methods or technologies.

Communications (How much effort is spent in communicating with other entities?)

This metric is typically measured as the number of interfaces that a given project team has, with the purpose of characterizing the constraints on the project team due to dependencies with entities politically and physically distant, such as users, managers, and/or the supplier.

This metric is most useful for large and/or complex organizations where development and testing takes place across geographically distinct sites. In particular, the metric can be used to identify possible improvements to the organization of complex testing projects and provide a means for assessing the effectiveness of such improvements. For small testing projects, involving few staff located in the same office or site, there is unlikely to be a great deal of benefit from the use of this metric.

Defect Detection Effectiveness Percentage or DDE

This computed metric will provide an indication of how effective the testing process is over time (the DDE should increase with an increase in the effectiveness of testing). DDE is calculated as follows:

DDE = (TDFT / (TDFC + TDFT)) × 100, where

TDFT = Total Defects Found by Testing (i.e., by the testing team)

TDFC = Total Defects Found by Client (measured up to some standard point after release – after six months for example)

Defect Removal Effectiveness Percentage or DRE

This computed metric will provide an indication of how effective the testing task is at removal of defects. DRE is calculated as follows:

DRE = (TDCT / TDFT) × 100, where

TDCT = Total Defects Closed During Testing

TDFT = Total Defects Found During Testing

Test Case Design Efficiency Percentage or TDE

This computed metric will provide information about the effectiveness of the test case design process. TDE is calculated as follows:

TDE = (TDFC / NTC) × 100, where

TDFT = Total Defects Found by Testing

NTC = Number of Test Cases Run

12.4 Setting Up and Administering a Metrics Program

Prior to setting up an effective metrics program, there are a number of high-level issues that must be considered.

It is important that measurable or objective targets should be set. Similarly, the temptation to set targets too low in order to obtain good results, or the editing/ optimistic interpretation of information to produce the desired result, must be avoided.

Care must be taken to ensure that, when setting up the administrative aspect of the approach to metrics collection, excessive control through measurement is avoided. An overly intrusive and stringent regime may result in the stagnation of initiative in the staff involved and limit experimentation and imagination.

Similarly, care must be taken to ensure that the process of collecting a metric does not affect the item being measured (e.g., the manner in which you phrase a question can directly influence the way someone answers the question. This is known as the Hawthorne Effect – (9) and (32). It is important that the collection of metrics be as unobtrusive as possible.

In adopting such an approach, it is important to remember that the metrics program is itself an additional overhead to the software development and testing process, and will involve additional effort as part of the initial learning curve. It is important to employ the KIS principle (Keep It Simple), at least in the beginning, expanding and extending the scope of the program with increasing familiarity and success. Project control can be achieved using metrics quite quickly, project improvement will take longer – so be prepared to persevere.

Do not underestimate the importance of the involvement and motivation of the staff involved in the metrics program. Without staff buy-in, the process will be much more difficult. Often, staff perceive metrics to be career threatening, and under such circumstances may (deliberately or accidentally) provide incorrect or overly optimistic information. It must be made clear that the metrics program is not being set up to apportion blame, but rather to improve the software development and testing process.

The following requirements need to be considered in setting up a typical metrics program and should be reviewed to determine those appropriate within the context of the scheme planned as part of any specific testing process:

▶ The need to define organizational objectives for the process improvement program to establish:
  ▷ the methods to be used
  ▷ the costs that will be deemed acceptable in running the program
  ▷ the urgency of the program
  ▷ the required support from management for the program (which should be formally recorded if possible).
▶ The need to establish the following roles and responsibilities:
  ▷ what part of the organization will have responsibility for the program
  ▷ who will manage, implement, and administer the program
  ▷ who will submit/collect the metrics
▶ The need to research which metrics to record and what analysis is required. During this process the following issues must be considered:
  ▷ Whatever metrics are selected initially will almost certainly change. They will be modified by experience during the metrics program itself.
  ▷ Ensure that results of analysis are immediately useful to project management. If you continue to collect metrics with no visible benefit, management will become discouraged with the process.
  ▷ Be aware of what is realistic (i.e., although of potential interest, the number of keystrokes made by an engineer is not a realistic metric to record).
  ▷ Err on the side of generosity when selecting metrics to collect. It may be difficult to go back and obtain metrics for a parameter that was not initially thought to be needed, but which subsequently turns out to be useful. You can always drop a metric later if it turns out to be of no use.
  ▷ Be aware that the more metrics you decide to record, the greater the effort to collect, the greater resistance to the process, the larger requirements for storage and processing of the metrics.
▶ The need to set up the infrastructure for recording the metrics. The following steps are likely to be implemented:
  ▷ Set up a system for holding the metrics (such as a database or spreadsheet)
  ▷ Generate simple procedures for defining what metrics are to be collected and how this is to be achieved and formally document them in a form that can be distributed and easily understood

▷ Set up the means for staff to retrieve metrics information (such as database access)

▶ The need to "sell" the initial set of metrics. The success of the metrics program will depend upon the accuracy and coverage of the data collected, and this will depend upon the commitment of your staff in taking the time to collect and submit it. They will need to be convinced of the benefits. In particular, try to identify staff who may hamper the process and try to involve them to gain their acceptance. Where such staff can be involved, they often become powerful advocates for the process.

▶ The need to obtain tools for data collection and analysis. Tools will help simplify collection of metrics, reduce time expenditure of staff, promote accuracy and consistency, and help reduce staff resistance to performing the collection. A tool could be as simple as a customized spreadsheet, which staff can complete each week and email to the administrator, or could be as elaborate as a commercial metrics package.

▶ The need to review the process. It is important to ensure that the software metrics program is not static. It will be necessary to review the metrics being recorded and question their benefit at regular intervals. This will allow those not proved useful to be discontinued and allow for the introduction of new metrics. However, it will be important to be aware of the impact of constant changes on the staff involved in recording and using the metrics, and as a major goal of the program, you should aim to standardize a metrics set as quickly as possible.

12.5 A Proposal for a Simple and Effective Metrics Set

This section makes a number of recommendations for a basic set of metrics that can be used over time to improve the effectiveness of the testing process. The following metrics are straightforward to collect (and calculate in the case of computed metrics), and should not impose a significant overhead on the overall testing effort.

▶ Testing Effort – the total effort expended in testing (and retesting) calculated as person/hours

▶ Metrics Effort – an estimate of the effort expended in the reporting, collection, storage, and analysis of the metrics information. This information will be invaluable in determining how much influence the metrics program itself is having on the overall testing project results

▶ Metrics Efficiency Percentage – a computed metric that shows the relative influence of the metrics program on the overall effort expended during the testing project. Clearly, the goal should be for this value to be as small as possible. If the value becomes a significant fraction of the overall testing project effort, and if the benefits of running the metrics program are not clear (i.e., it has not been possible to demonstrate any significant improvements in the testing process over time), then the continued role of the metrics program should be reviewed.

Metrics Efficiency Percentage = (Metric Effort / Testing Effort) $* 100$

▶ Test Planning, Design and Execution Coverage – information should be collected to show how many tests have been planned, designed, run, and passed/failed. If a test management tool is being used, such products typically provide built-in reports to analyze and display this information. This information is a key input to the management aspects of the testing process in terms of the ability to measure and report progress

▶ Number of *Test Cases* (*NTC*) – the total number of test cases run against the AUT for a particular testing phase. In addition, this will be useful for estimating how many test cases can be created for a given amount of effort, and how many test cases were run to find a given number of defects

▶ Size – an estimate of the size of the AUT based on the implementation technology (used in combination with NTC, this provides a useful planning metric for estimating the effort required to test other AUTs of a similar implementation technology)

▶ Total Defects Found by Testing (TDFT) – the severity value associated with each reported defect should be recorded when using this metric (perhaps based on the *test result category* assigned to the defect during testing). For example, a simple three value system of critical, serious, and minor could be adopted to categorize observed defects, to allow more meaningful comparisons of defects to be made

▶ Total Defects Found by Client (TDFC) – the same severity values adopted for recording the TDFT metric should be used to allow meaningful comparison between TDFT and TDFC to be made. It is recommended that this metric is measured consistently at two standard points after delivery to the user(s), such as three and six months (but this will clearly depend on the release schedule for the AUT. For example, a six-month sampling period will not be appropriate for software with a four-month release schedule)

▶ Defect Detection Effectiveness Percentage – to determine how the effectiveness of the testing process improves over time, based on the numbers of defects detected during testing and those observed during normal operation of the AUT by the user(s)

▶ Defect Removal Effectiveness Percentage – principally used to determine the progress of the testing process during testing

▶ Test Case Design Efficiency Percentage – to determine how the efficiency of test case design changes over time (such as between testing different releases of the same AUT)

▶ Rate of Defect Detection – the rate of defect detection by the testing team during testing (and optionally, in live use by the client). It is recommended that defects are categorized as either serious or minor bugs to simplify analysis. Analysis of this information is useful in determining when to stop testing,[4] as well as for showing defect trends across the duration of the testing project

---

[4] If the rate defect detection is plotted against time, inspection of the resulting graph can be used to predict the most effective point to stop testing, such as when the graph trace has leveled off.

▶ Rate of Defect Correction – the rate at which the developers correct defects, deliver them for retesting, and are verified as being rectified. It is also recommended that where several developers are responsible for correcting defects, their individual rates of defect correction are collected. This is very useful information for both the planning and management of testing, because it can be used to estimate timescales for correction of defects, and also to predict which developers are most effective at clearing defects.

12.6 Further Reading

Reference 1 provides good advice regarding the role and use of metrics within the context of testing projects. Reference 17 contains useful information regarding the use of metrics in association with automated software testing tools. Reference 31 is an excellent general text on the role and use of metrics in the context of the software development process.

13 Introduction, Adoption, and Maintenance of the Testing Process

"Learn to Test, Test to Learn," motto of the Empire Test Pilot School.

13.1 Introduction

Even the very best software testing process is nothing without the acceptance and consistent use by a community of testers within an organization. Technical issues aside, the introduction and adoption of a testing process is likely to be the most difficult step in providing a formal, rigorous, and reusable process within an organization.

This chapter examines the issues involved in introducing a testing process into an organization, and the management of its successful adoption and use. This chapter also addresses the issues associated with the subsequent maintenance and update of the testing process, and its ongoing evolution and enhancement.

The chapter concludes by providing process adoption guidance for those test practitioners who may be under pressure to deliver immediate quality improvements, but who may not have the luxury of sufficient time, resources, or budget.

13.2 Introduction and Adoption of a Testing Process

13.2.1 Overview

This section discusses the need to first establish that there is a requirement for a formal testing process within an organization, and where this is the case, goes on to discuss the need to develop a strategy for the introduction and adoption of the process.

Establishing the Requirement

The first step in introducing a testing process within an organization is to establish there is a requirement for such a process. In determining whether a particular organization has a requirement for a formal testing process, the following issues should be considered:

▶ How much software testing does the organization conduct and how frequently does testing take place? Clearly, if an organization performs very little testing and/or this task takes place infrequently, there will be a weak requirement for introducing a large testing process and the associated infrastructure. However, there may still be significant benefit to be gained from documenting a standard approach to testing with some associated testing templates, to ensure that when testing does occur, it is as consistent and economical as possible

▶ How many departments/divisions of the organization are involved in software testing, with how many distinct testing projects? For each project, how many staff are involved in testing tasks? If there are many staff engaged on a number of different testing projects in separate departments across the organization, then there may be a significant benefit from standardizing the testing process, and setting up a testing process infrastructure to provide guidance on testing, and to provide access to standard reusable templates, checklists, and proformas

▶ How diverse is the testing requirement? Is the organization engaged in testing of software developed in-house, under contract by third-party developers, or bought in as *commercial-off-the-shelf* (*COTS*) software, and does the organization have a requirement for all phases of testing from *unit* through to *acceptance testing* and on to *regression testing*? Under such circumstances, an organization is highly likely to benefit from the introduction of a standard, reusable testing process, with well-defined roles and responsibilities, and testing phases, each with well-defined relationships with well-defined inputs and outputs.

One of the main reasons for adopting and using a testing process is to save the organization time, effort, and money. If the cost of introducing and using a testing process is greater than the cost of continuing with the current approach to software development and testing, then the benefits of introducing a process must be carefully considered.

Although an important issue for a great many organizations, saving time, effort, and money are not the only reasons for adopting a formal development and testing process. Other reasons for introducing and following a process could include: the need to address a serious flaw in the existing development and testing process – such as widespread quality problems; the need to formalize the software development and testing process as a prelude to gaining some form of quality certification (14); or as part of a software process improvement initiative (27).

Strategy for Introduction and Adoption

Once the requirement for a formal testing process has been established, it will be necessary to determine a strategy for the introduction and adoption of the process. The process of formulating such a strategy will include the following key tasks:

▶ Gain management commitment and involvement
▶ Identify a testing-process champion
▶ Baseline current software testing practices
▶ Identify related organizational processes
▶ Consider scope and scale of the testing process

▶ Ensure training and mentoring are available
▶ Monitor progress and improve the process
▶ Advertise results.

Each of these tasks is described in the following sections.

The first key task is to ensure that the introduction of the testing process is fully supported by the appropriate management within the organization. It is important that they are made aware of the importance of a formal testing process as well as the potential cost of not following good testing practice, perhaps by means of a brief proposal. A good indication of management commitment will be the promise of resources to the project, and a major goal of any strategy should be to obtain a guarantee of appropriate staff and facilities.

An important part of the process of gaining both management commitment as well as adoption by the other staff in the organization is to identify a testing-process champion to help promote the introduction and adoption of the testing process. The champion will need to be a relatively senior and/or well respected member of staff who can communicate at all levels within the organization from junior members of staff all the way through to senior management. He or she will need to have the appropriate technical skills to understand the testing process as well as an appreciation of the need to introduce a formal approach to testing. Clearly, good communication skills combined with enthusiasm will be key attributes of such a person. The responsibilities of the champion can include lobbying individuals, making presentations to management, holding speaking events (such as lunchtime seminars), advertising events and successes, and identifying points of resistance and working to overcome them.

To understand how to introduce a testing process, it will be important to identify the baseline for introduction of the process by taking stock of just where the organization is in terms of its current practices for software testing. Appendix Q provides a Testing Process Health Check (i.e., a set of criteria and a scoring scheme which can be used to conduct a testing audit), which can be used to help identify exactly where an organization is in terms of its testing practices, identifying the positive aspects of the process, as well as those that are capable of improvement. This activity should be documented in a brief report summarizing the findings of the health check, which can be used as supporting information in the proposal to management for implementing a testing process.

Next it will be necessary to identify what other existing processes within the organization may impact on the testing process, such as development standards and management practices, because the testing process cannot exist in a vacuum. It must interface and interact with other processes. For example, a particular software development process may already mandate an approach to unit testing, which will have to be reflected in the overall testing process. Similarly, the existing management infrastructure may have implications for which part of the organization will administer the testing process (such as the quality assurance [QA] or *information technology* [*IT*] groups). The output from this activity will be a brief report, which will document the current organizational processes and how they will interface to the proposed testing process, as well as a diagram showing the present organizational infrastructure, and how and where the testing process infrastructure will fit.

For a number of reasons, it is very unlikely that an organization (and particularly a medium- to large-sized enterprise) will attempt to rollout an organization-wide testing process.[1] A more likely strategy will be to conduct a small-scale rollout of the process, which will have the benefit of being a much more attractive alternative to risk-conscious management. The use of a pilot study or project may represent a useful option to enable the testing process to be rolled out on a small scale to one or two testing projects within the organization, which will allow the benefits of the testing process to be demonstrated prior to attempting a large-scale rollout. A pilot study will also allow the lessons learned during the use of the testing process to be addressed prior to large-scale adoption. If the launch of the pilot study and its subsequent achievements are effectively advertised to the rest of the organization (perhaps by the champion), this can provide an effective means of promoting the benefits of the testing process.

In ensuring the success of the introduction and adoption of the testing process, it will be essential to provide suitable training for those staff expected to use the process, and appropriate mentoring to ensure the continued successful use of the process. One of the goals of the pilot study should be to ensure that the staff involved will acquire the appropriate skills to be able to provide subsequent training and mentoring to other staff. The champion also should be considered a resource to provide training and mentoring to other staff in need of guidance. The testing health check provided in Appendix Q can be used to assess the progress of individual projects. This check can identify aspects of the process that may need improvement.

From the outset of the introduction of a formal testing process, it is vital that progress be monitored so that the benefits of introducing the process can be quantified, and that the process can be improved. Management for example, will certainly demand progress reports, which are likely to include figures on the return on investment of introducing a formal testing process. Tangible metrics will be needed to promote the success of the testing process to the rest of the organization. Chapter 12 provides good advice on what metrics to measure, and how they can be used to both show the progress of the introduction and adoption of the testing process. Chapter 12 also has information to help improve the overall effectiveness of testing.

The need to advertise the results of the introduction and use of the testing process has been discussed a number of times in the preceding paragraphs. However, the importance of letting the rest of the organization know about the benefits a formal

---

[1] Reasons include cost and organizational difficulties of large scale roll out of any novel process, the risk of failure of the process in practice, and the cost of reverting to the original state, organizational inertia, and (particularly in very large distributed organizations) traditional staff resistance to change.

testing process can bring, and the success of such a process, cannot be underestimated. It is possible for a testing process to fail simply because the results of a successful pilot study were not effectively reported to anyone else in the organization. The availability of an effective champion will be a major channel for spreading the word, but the testing technical staff also have a role to play in publishing articles on the organizations intranet, producing newsletters, holding lunchtime seminars, getting technical papers published at conferences, etc. Setting up a testing special interest group within the organization is another powerful way of ensuring information is shared by everyone involved in the testing process. And last but not least, make sure management is briefed on a regular basis about progress and successes.

13.3 Maintenance of the Testing Process

Almost as soon as it has been implemented, any testing process will be out of date. At the very least, the process will need to change to take account of lessons learned during its use. Other reasons for change can include alterations to the organizational infrastructure (such as the introduction of a new quality group), changes to the implementation technology or approach to software development, introduction of automated testing tools, or as the result of a formal process improvement initiative.

The testing process should be reviewed at key points and where changes need to be made, proposals should be submitted to the *testing manager* (or equivalent should this role not exist in a particular testing process) for appraisal and subsequent action. Mandatory review points should include:

▶ The end of individual testing projects (such as a project close-down meeting) in order to identify any lessons learned during the project
▶ Following changes in the software development process (such as the adoption of a rapid prototyping software development method, see [12])
▶ As a prelude to the adoption/introduction of new testing tools or techniques (such as test automation tools, see [22])
▶ Following changes in the management approach of the organization (such as the adoption of the PRINCE project management methodology, see [3])
▶ As a result of trends observed or as a result of the analysis of metrics collected during a process improvement initiative.

Other desirable review points might include:

▶ At regular dates, such as an annual or biannual review
▶ As and when required by the testing manager (or equivalent)
▶ As and when required by the QA manager (should one exist for a particular organization).

Whatever review points are adopted as part of the review process, they should be documented as part of the testing process. Following such a review, where changes need to be made to the process, or where sections are found to be no longer relevant, the following measures should be taken:

▶ If a part of the process is no longer relevant, it should be removed from the testing process and the process document amended appropriately
▶ If the existing material is only partially relevant (e.g., material that is out of date or superseded by more recent information), this should be updated to reflect the new process view.

Where any part of the testing process is updated, removed, or otherwise changed,[2] the following parts of the testing process document should be checked and, where necessary, modified:

▶ Update the contents of the testing process to reflect any changes
▶ Update Chapter 1, Section 1.4 "Structure and Content..." to reflect any changes
▶ Review embedded chapter, appendix, section, figure, and table references and amend as necessary
▶ Where references to external sources have been added or removed, update the references section to reflect these changes. Where these changes have altered the order (e.g., numbering) of any existing references, those points in the body of the document where they are cited must also be amended
▶ Where terms, phrases, abbreviations, or acronyms have been removed, altered, or introduced, ensure that the glossary is amended to reflect these changes.

Finally, the configuration management details of the testing process document should be amended to reflect the changes.

13.4 A Proposal for a Quick Start Test Process

This chapter and the preceding chapters have provided a great deal of best practice advice and guidance on the how, when, and where of implementing an effective and efficient test process. In Part 2 of the book, Chapters 15–20 provide a series of real world examples of how individual organizations and projects, facing their own unique requirements for effective and efficient testing, have implemented their own customized view of test process. However, what if you have been tasked with delivering quality improvements in your project or organization, but do not have the luxury of sufficient time, resources, or budget to devise, design, implement, and roll out a fully formed and working testing process?

Do you decide that because you don't have the time or resources, perhaps soldiering on with the hope things may spontaneously improve of their own accord is

---

2 This assumes the testing process document has followed a similar content and structure to Part 1 of this book. If this is not the case, the amendments should be made to the analogous sections of the process document.

the best solution? Or do you take the more enlightened view that any small steps made to improve the quality of the delivered software are worth making?

The following sections provide guidance on what can be done to make quick quality management wins when you are short of time, resources, and budget.

First, take a moment to take stock of your current situation:

▶ Try to make an assessment of what you know of the current development process, and of where the most quality issues are introduced. For example, the requirements (their elicitation, management, and maintenance) often have been cited as being responsible for as much as 75 percent of the quality issues found in delivered software (48)

▶ Examine the defects being reported to determine if you can trace them down to a specific aspect of the development process:

   ▷ What are their characteristics? Can you categorize them? For example, are the defects mainly in the user interface, do they occur where logical comparisons are being made, are they due to configuration issues between development, testing, and delivery platforms?

   ▷ Are you able to trace them to a particular step in the development (or even a particular team or individual)?

   ▷ In a large system, are the defects found more frequently in specific modules/areas of the software?

   ▷ Are the defects largely because of interactions with other systems that the AUT has to interface to?

   ▷ Does the testing team have access to completely up-to-date requirements and design information, ensuring that they are designing and executing tests entirely relevant to the current version of the software being tested?

   ▷ Consider taking a risk-based approach to improving the quality; triage the AUT to determine the critical business aspects of the software, in order to focus test efforts on those areas

Using the previous information, decide how and where to introduce the most effective quality management best practices. For example, having analyzed the defects, and having determined that the majority of them are being introduced during the development phase, consider introducing/enhancing the unit testing conducted by the developers. Consider pairing a testing practitioner with the developers to provide advice and guidance on quality issues (54), introducing unit test tool support (44), and/or proposing the introduction of an automated build/continuous integration approach (54).

Be wary about rushing to adopt testing tools (particularly capture-replay testing products, see [49]), as the time and cost overhead associated with the purchase and introduction of such tools will, in the short term, almost certainly outweigh any benefits they may bring.

Don't try to eat the whole elephant in one go.[3] Use the testing process proposed in this book as a framework you can incrementally populate as you identify those areas of the development and testing that can most benefit from the introduction of quality management best practices.

Process improvement (and the metrics that often accompany such approaches) may seem to be an unnecessary overhead when you are already short of time, resources, and budget. However, process improvement will be an invaluable means of fine tuning your testing process. Remember it may be very difficult to obtain historical data from earlier phases of your projects, and there may be benefits from collecting some basic metrics as early as possible (such as defect detection rates) to allow for later comparisons when you have the time to implement process improvement. You also might consider employing tools that automatically collect and store such data (such as quality management tools, see [61]). Also consider holding retrospectives (53) to collect process improvement suggestions from stakeholders during iteration/project close-down meetings.

Finally please read Appendix S which contains valuable real-world advice and guidance on this subject.

---

[3]   Question: How do you eat an elephant? Answer: One bite at a time!

14 Agile Testing

> "Agile is arguably a thirty year old overnight success."
>
> **– Bob Bartlet**

14.1 Introduction

This chapter discusses the "recent" phenomenon of agile approaches to software development and testing, reviews a number of successful agile quality management practices being employed by testing practitioners on real-world projects, and concludes by making a series of recommendations about how to implement an effective and efficient agile testing approach.

Chapter 20 provides a case study that documents the role and use of agile testing best practices within the context of an agile development and testing project.

14.2 Overview of Agile Testing

In recent years[1] new approaches to the development and testing of software and the management of software projects, such as Extreme Programming (XP) and Scrum (50 and 51) have encouraged practitioners to be more agile in the delivery of software systems.

The typical features of such agile approaches include:

▶ Breaking large monolithic software projects down into smaller more easily achieved iterations

▶ The rapid delivery of working elements of the developing system for early testing and to gain feedback from the customer on the suitability of the software

▶ Colocation of the development and testing team with suitably knowledgeable and empowered customer representatives

▶ Employing use cases (8) or user stories (50) to capture customer requirements in a clear and simple manner that enables the customer to understand and agree on the requirements

▶ Being as responsive to customer requests for changes to the developing system as possible

---

[1] Although the agile phenomenon is arguably more than thirty years old now, with early work by James Martin (52) and others (12).

▶ Employing focused and effective project communications including stand-up meetings (51), agile retrospectives (53), and short lines of communications

▶ Working with up-to-date project data (such as estimates and actuals) and having effective solutions to communicate this data to the project team

▶ Staffing projects with well-trained, motivated, and empowered agile practitioners.

Although there are a number of detractors who claim that agile only works for small, well-defined, low-risk projects populated by experienced agile practitioners, there is good evidence (54) that agile can be applied to a range of projects and has been highly successful from a number of perspectives:

▶ Managers like agile because it enables them to manage projects more easily and more successfully, and helps them to manage the expectations of the customer

▶ Customers like agile approaches because they are exposed to initial versions of the software earlier in the project, and are able to request changes and/or improvements to the system, resulting in delivered software that more closely matches their needs

▶ Developers like agile because it gives them a well defined framework in which to develop the code, with clear milestones, as well as the perception that they are empowered to make changes and improvements to the software as needed.

The paradox is that agile brings its own particular challenges to testers. Software developed more quickly, delivered in greater volumes, and within strictly defined milestones still has to be thoroughly tested in order to deliver quality systems.

As a result of the additional pressures that agile projects impose on the testers, they need to find new best practices and processes to be as effective and efficient as possible within such projects.

14.3 Agile Quality Management Practices

Although (54) provides detailed and comprehensive guidance on agile testing, the following sections review a number of the key practices testing practitioners have successfully employed in real-world agile projects. Although individually these practices have been shown to have delivered benefits to the projects where they are used, many deliver additional value when used in combination with each other (as discussed in Section 14.4):

▶ **Agile Meetings and Communications** – arguably, the most significant component in the success of agile methods is the increased focus on effective communication within projects. Strategies for improving communications can include:
  ▷ Effective Meetings – wherever possible short, sharp, focused meetings should be employed, such as stand-up meetings (51)
  ▷ Retrospectives – depending on the size and/or duration of the project, retrospectives (53) should be used at the end of iterations/phases of the project

to identify successful practices suitable for reuse, as well as unsuccessful practices, whose future use may need to be challenged

▷ Effective Workshops – for larger agile projects, the introduction of formal workshop like sessions, such as those used in DSDM Atern (12), should also be considered

▷ Adopting Effective Communications Techniques – Isabel Evans (54) makes a very compelling case for improving general interpersonal project communications, describing successes with such techniques as De Bono's Hats in a Meeting (55), Weaver Triangles (56), and Ishikawa Fish-bones (57)

▶ **Employ Test-Driven Development**[2] – TDD is a key quality assurance best practice employed in a number of agile methods (e.g., 50). Where a TDD approach is being used, developers review the requirements and generate the unit tests before coding begins. In doing so, the developer gains a much clearer understanding of the requirements, resulting in code of higher quality. Interestingly, because of the benefits of gaining a better understanding of the requirements and writing high-quality code, this practice arguably saves time and effort that otherwise might have been spent rewriting and retesting code containing defects

▶ **Involve Test Resources as Early as Possible** – although this has always been a guiding principle in traditional development and test projects, the iterative approach employed in agile projects promotes early and frequent test involvement by providing early delivery of working software. In addition to what is in effect a quality management by-product of iterative approaches, a number of the agile case studies included in Reference 54 document the technique of pair testing. Analogous to the XP practice of pair programming, pair testing brings testers together with developers to work on code quality issues – providing unit test guidance for example. Testers also can be successfully paired with analysts. Reference 54 documents a case study where a tester, paired with an analyst involved in eliciting customer requirements, was able to provide very early guidance on the testability of specific requirements, as well as observations about error, duplications, and omissions in the requirements

▶ **Fix All Defects Immediately** – although there has always been an emphasis on the need to fix defects as quickly as possible, many agile projects enforce an approach in which defects must be fixed as soon as they are detected. There are a number of excellent examples in Reference 54 of projects where development activity is halted until a defect is corrected. This approach works well where continuous integration (58) and build tools (59) are used in combination with automated testing of newly submitted code, so that the cause of a new defect can more easily be identified. Combine this approach with new and effective means of visualizing defects, and testers have a particularly efficient means of driving code quality

▶ **Effective Visualization of Defect Detection** – where continuous integration and build have been automated and combined with automated testing (including unit

---

[2] Also termed test-driven design.

test, code analysis, capture-replay testing), the ability to quickly and effectively draw practitioners' attention to a newly detected defect has been shown to have significant value (54). Solutions can include:

▷ Automated email or SMS (Short Message Service) text messages sent to appropriate team members

▷ Dashboards graphically displaying project progress and issues on the workstations of the team members

▷ Exotic visualization solutions such as red and green lava lamps. One case study from Reference 54 reported a project where the automated detection of a defect (following a new build) would cause a green lava lamp (showing that there were currently no defects) to be turned off and a red lava lamp (announcing a defect) to be turned on. The case study reported that there was a great deal of project pride in fixing the defect before the lamp had warmed up and the red wax had begun to flow

▶ **Test Refactoring** – this quality management technique is analogous to the agile development approach of code refactoring (50) where suitably empowered developers are encouraged to revisit code that they or their colleagues have written earlier in the project to review, and where appropriate, make changes to improve the code. Clearly, this practice must be accompanied by effective configuration management, change management, and regression testing (perhaps using an automated approach) to ensure changes do not introduce deleterious effects to the overall code base, and that if they have, the software can be rolled back to its previous working state as quickly as possible. Test refactoring introduces an analogous testing practice, in which testers are encouraged to revisit the test suite and review it to ensure the tests remain relevant, current, and as effective and efficient as possible

▶ **Identify Targets of Test** – in larger agile projects, and particularly where the code base and associated test suite are large, testers may need to find solutions for focusing test activity on high risk areas of the software system under development. John Tilt (54) describes an approach he termed laser-guided testing, that employs heuristics, knowledge of the structure, quality history of the application under development, and automated statistical calculations to select a subset of the test suite to rerun against the new build or release of the software to ensure thorough and effective regression testing. John reports a remarkable tenfold reduction in testing effort (from ten days to less than one day's testing) to run the regression testing suite prior to a major release of software

▶ **Increased Focus on Automation** – in addition to the universally used unit testing tools (44), it is common for agile projects to use a range of other products to enable testers to cope with higher volumes of code delivered in shorter timescales, such as:

▷ Continuous integration tools (58)

▷ Automated build tools (59)

▷ Code analysis tools (60)

▷ Automated capture-replay tools (13).

▶ **Employ Agile Progress Measurement, Estimation, and Metrics** – in a swiftly moving agile project, with short iterations, and the need to deliver working code as quickly as possible, it is essential to employ an equally fast solution to measuring project progress. Automated solutions such as agile development environments that automatically collect progress metrics as the practitioners undertake their work, and which can report progress in a near-real-time manner (see 61), provide a very powerful tool in the project manager's tool box

▶ **Find Solutions to Employing Agile Practices on Off-Site and Off-Shore Projects** – where you are looking to employ agile best practices on projects where team members may be based in different offices or even different geographies, it will be necessary to find additional solutions to support your approach. In Reference 54, Test Manager Pete Kingston describes how he and his test team did precisely this. Solutions adopted include:

▷ Implement an effective and rich communications infrastructure. In addition to effective email and telephone facilities, ensure real-time messaging technologies are employed across all sites. Consider providing Internet-based, and/or traditional teleconferencing facilities, as well as innovative solutions for supporting team meetings – such as Web 2 technologies like Second Life (62)

▷ Deliver real-time, distributed process guidance; ensure all team members in each office/geography have access to real-time distributed agile best practice guidance. Reference 8 provides one example of a solution delivering effective real-time distributed agile best practice guidance

▷ Consider changing working start and stop times; this solution is applicable to projects distributed across different time zones, and looks to increase the overlap of working hours between the time zones by encouraging practitioners in different time zones to stagger their working hours. For example, in one time zone team members could be encouraged to begin their working day half an hour earlier, whereas those in a second time zone begin their working day half an hour later, thereby increasing the overlap in their working days by an hour

▷ Consider colocating off-shore representatives; in order to deal with the issues of language, idiom, and cultural differences that may be encountered between practitioners in different geographies, consider colocating a member of the off-shore team with the local team. This has been demonstrated (54) to significantly reduce misunderstandings between geographically separate teams, and to increase the efficiency of communications

▷ Consider the adoption of distributed process enactment tools (63); even where geographically distributed projects have adopted all of the previous solutions, it is still possible for the practitioners in different geographies to be using different processes and working practices. Process enactment tools (61) provide a rich real-time distributed environment for software development and testing that drive and encourage the use of particular agile best practices – in effect, using the environment means you are using the agile process. Reference 63 provides an example of such an environment that out-of-the-box allows a project to optionally select Scrum and EclipseWay (51 and 64), or supports the implementation/customization of a bespoke, project-specific, agile practice

▶ **Employ Traditional Best Practices Where Appropriate** – finally, a significant number of the case studies in Reference 54 make a very compelling case for not ignoring the benefits of traditional tried and tested quality assurance best practices. For example, several case studies report success employing a V Model (39) approach to test management, planning, design, and execution, a number of the case studies report the successful use of exploratory testing (65) in identifying and correcting errors, and other case studies, and particularly those dealing with high risk and/or larger projects, report that employing formal start-up and close-down meetings have been of value in ensuring the delivery of quality software.

14.4 A Proposal for an Effective Subset of Agile Best Practices

This section makes a proposal for an effective and efficient subset of the agile practices identified previously and in Reference 54. This subset of agile practices has been formulated while working with numerous real-world projects and practitioners, and provides the maximum QA benefit from the least effort.

The proposed subset of agile practices is as follows:

1. **Employ Test-Driven Development** – encourage developers to adopt this highly effective approach to developing and testing their code (50). This practice can be enhanced by finding opportunities to utilize test practitioners as early as possible during development, such as adopting a pair testing approach (54)
2. **Employ Automation** – at the least, this should include automated unit test, but could also combine code analysis, functional and regression testing tools as your process matures
3. **Employ a Continuous Integration Approach** – combine this approach with a build-management tool and automated testing to immediately identify code that has introduced an error or defect
4. **Employ Innovative Means of Displaying the Results of Testing** – make use of effective solutions for highlighting quality issues such as the red and green lava lamp solution (54), or a project dashboard that alerts project stakeholders that a defect has been detected
5. **Fix All Defects Immediately** – as soon as a defect has been detected, halt all development and focus on identifying the nature of the defect and correcting it before continuing with any further development

6. **Employ Process Improvement** – fine tune the process by holding iteration retrospectives (53) and close-down meetings, and harvesting and reusing the positive aspects of your process, as well as ensuring you don't repeat practices that have not found to be of value.

As discussed previously, each of these agile testing best practices individually provide value when adopted and used by testing practitioners in agile projects. In combination, they deliver far more benefit than the sum of their parts would suggest.

When combined together, the previous practices promote a project environment in which code quality is improved, software is delivered more quickly, with reduced cost and with less resources, and more closely matching the customer requirements. Finally, process improvement drives additional efficiencies into the development and testing process, while helping to eliminate those practices that have failed to deliver value.

14.5 Conclusion

In conclusion, the adoption and use of agile development and testing practices is not a new phenomenon. James Martin and other workers in the field of software process have developed and used agile methods for more than thirty years (52). Even the origins of Scrum and Extreme Programming (XP) (51 and 50) are more than ten years old now.

However, in recent years, with increasing pressure on companies to develop software more quickly, with less resources, and reduced budgets, and still deliver quality products, there has been increasing interest in agile methods.

For those test practitioners looking to obtain agile guidance, approaches such as Scrum and XP (as well as more recent methods such as X-Breed and Evo, see (66) and (67) provide excellent advice on agile best practices. Additionally, (54) documents some fifty-plus agile best practices distilled from more than thirty real-world agile projects, that can be employed on your own agile project to drive effective and efficient testing.

Finally, the agile practices described in Section 14.4, provide a tried and tested subset of agile techniques that can be quickly and easily adopted within software projects, and that will bring a balance of significant quality improvements without excessive cost of implementation.

PART TWO

THE TESTING PROCESS IN THE REAL WORLD: ILLUSTRATIVE CASE STUDIES

This section of the book provides a number of real-world examples of organizations that are involved in testing and who have implemented their own testing processes in collaboration with the author. The organizations are:

▶ The British Library
▶ Reuters Product Acceptance Group
▶ Crown Quality Assurance Group
▶ The Wine Society
▶ Automatic Data Processing (ADP) Limited
▶ Confirmit

These case studies are provided to allow the reader to gain some insight into how they might adapt the classic view of the testing process to more closely match their own specific testing requirements. This will be particularly valuable for those readers who have been given the responsibility of setting up a testing process within their own organizations.

Each case study is presented in a standard manner, which follows the order of the testing process material presented in Part 1 of this book. For each case study, the following sections are provided:

▶ Overview of the organization – providing general information about the organization and the nature of its business
▶ Characteristics of the testing requirement – describing the particular testing requirements and challenges faced by the organization
▶ The management and planning of testing – a discussion of how the organization arranges its testing activities and how it plans and manages the testing process

▶ Roles and responsibilities – describing the testing roles supported by the organization and reviewing their specific responsibilities

▶ Testing phases – describing the specific characteristics of the testing phases employed by the organization in the execution of their testing projects

▶ Artifacts – describing the testing documentation used by the organization in their testing projects, as well as describing how each organization delivers these artifacts to the testing projects

▶ And, where appropriate, process improvement – describing how the organization monitors its testing process, a review of the metrics it collects, and the approach adopted in improving the testing process

The following sections provide brief pen pictures of each of the organizations and the characteristics of their development and testing requirements. This allows the reader to quickly identify a particular case study that most closely reflects the characteristics of their own testing requirements.[1]

British Library

The British Library (BL) can be characterized as a very large organization with a number of geographically separate sites. BL has a requirement to test a wide variety of software developed in-house, produced by third party suppliers, and bought in as *commercial-off-the-shelf* (*COTS*) software. As such, the BL testing process must cover all phases of testing. Typically, the software under test is destined for internal use within BL in support of its business.

Depending on the particular testing project, the BL testing process must address simple to complex data requirements, the need for test harness and simulation software use, as well as test automation tools where appropriate. In order to make their systems easier to use and to reduce the cost of training and help desk support, BL have a particular interest in conducting *usability testing* wherever appropriate.

The BL testing process is administered from within the *information technology* (*IT*) department with strong input from the *quality assurance* (*QA*) group. BL has a strong project management culture based on the PRINCE method, which has implications for the management and organization of testing, as well as for the role of testing process improvement.

Reuters Product Acceptance Group

The Reuters Product Acceptance Group (PAG) can be characterized as a large testing group, which has responsibility for *acceptance testing* a number of Reuters financial dealing products developed by a third-party supplier. Following successful testing,

---

[1]   Although the Wine Society and ADP case studies describe historical testing projects, the present tense is used throughout the pen pictures for the sake of consistency. The correct tense is used within the individual case study chapters.

the AUT is provided to a number of Reuters customers for use in supporting their business practices.

PAG supports a large configurable testing laboratory in order to provide confidence that the software under test will perform successfully on the heterogeneous customer computing platforms as well as to provide a realistic source of test data. Usability testing plays a significant role in the testing process as Reuters believes good usability is one of a number of key characteristics that gives its products an advantage over its competitors. PAG does not use any automated software testing tools in its testing process.

PAG is administered from within the Reuters IT group (and specifically the Reuters Information Division). Although having reviewed and rejected ISO 9000, PAG does follow a number of aspects of the standard. PAG follows a process- improvement approach based on the capability maturity model (CMM, [35]).

Crown Quality Assurance Group

The Crown Quality Assurance Group (Crown) can be characterized as a medium-sized testing group that has responsibility for acceptance and *regression testing* new releases of commercial point of sales (POS) software systems. Following successful testing, the software is released to a number of Crown customers in the hospitality industry.

Crown needs to support a flexible test rig that can be configured to match the specification of various customer installations. Rigorous configuration management is employed to ensure the correct set up of hardware, software, and data for each test (and also to recreate the test rig where it is necessary to reproduce a particular test). Crown is committed to using automated software testing tools in order to reduce testing timescales, effort, and cost, and to improve the quality of testing. This approach is run under the auspices of a European Union process improvement project (EU ESSI, see [27]).

The Crown testing group is administered from within the company QA department. As part of the EU ESSI project, Crown collects and analyzes a comprehensive set of software development and testing metrics, which are fully documented in the case study.

The Wine Society

The Wine Society case study can be characterized as a small testing project with responsibility for acceptance and regression testing new releases of a commercial software product, which supports the major aspects of the Wine Society business process. This software is derived from a standard commercial product that is customized under contract to the Wine Society by a third-party supplier. In addition, there is a supplementary requirement for performance and usability testing within the testing process.

Although the Wine Society is acceptance testing the AUT for subsequent internal use, there is no significant requirement for complex test rig facilities. An interesting feature of the Wine Society testing group is the deliberate policy of resourcing members of the group from the user community. The testing process also makes use of external testing consultants to assist in the management and planning of testing, as well as to provide testing process advice.

The Wine Society testing group is administered from within the information systems (IS) group, and obtains user representatives from the various business areas of the Wine Society as and when required.

Automatic Data Processing Limited

The Automatic Data Processing Limited (ADP) acceptance testing team (ATT) can be characterized as a small testing project with responsibility for acceptance and regression testing incremental releases of a commercial payroll package. Following successful testing, the package is delivered to a number of ADP customers to support their internal payroll processes. Some performance testing is also conducted to provide confidence that the AUT will perform adequately on the customer hardware.

For the majority of the ATT testing activities, there was no particular requirement for test rig hardware or software, except for the performance testing activities, where a small client server rig was set up to perform *load* and *stress testing*. The testing project makes extensive use of automated software testing tools for both functional and regression testing, as well as performance testing.

The ATT is managed from within the ADP QA department.

Confirmit

The Confirmit case study documents an agile software development and testing process involving a medium to large size team of some eighty developers and testers. The Confirmit business intelligence product is delivered to a large community of corporate users via the Web as a software as a service product (68), and has high availability and performance requirements. The Confirmit quality assurance team (of some twenty-four staff) reports to a quality assurance manager, and is based within the Confirmit research and development department.

Within this agile development and testing project, the overall product release cycle lasts some nine months, with the last three months of the project involving rigorous and intensive testing of the software. Weekly iterations are employed, allowing testing to begin early in the project lifecycle and to continue throughout the project. There is extensive use of automation in the project, with the team using unit testing, code analysis, functional, and regression testing tools, as well as automated test management and defect tracking. A continuous integration approach (CI, see [58]) is employed in the project, and supported by a CI tool that also executes automated unit and functional tests during the build process. This highlights any defects introduced into the growing code base from the most recently developed and integrated software. This process has a significant impact on the need for a formal integration testing phase. Finally, frequent exposure of the customer representatives to the incrementally developed software ensures that user feedback is provided at each iteration and that the final delivered product closely matches the customer expectations. This process has significant impact on the need for a formal acceptance testing phase.

15 Case Study 1: The British Library

Ken Eves, British Library IT Quality Manager

15.1 Overview of the Organization

The British Library (BL) is the national library of the United Kingdom. Its work is supported by the expertise of more than 2,000 staff and by links with other organizations worldwide. The library provides:

▶ Internationally important reading room and inquiry services
▶ The world's leading document supply services
▶ Specialist information services in key subject areas
▶ On-line and Web-based services
▶ Essential services for the library, archives, and information world
▶ Library facilities for the general public.

The library's outstanding collection, developed for more than 250 years, contains more than 150 million items and represents every age of written civilization, every written language, and every aspect of human thought.

BL can be seen as the most complete of all the case studies, embodying aspects of each of the process elements described in Part 1 of this book.

15.2 Characteristics of the Testing Requirement

BL has a significant reliance on software systems to support its business for the purposes of:

▶ Maintaining very large quantities of information on document holdings
▶ Maintaining extensive lender personal details
▶ Recording details of document borrowings
▶ Maintaining on-line catalogue searching (involving millions of records)
▶ Supporting large-scale document supply.

The majority of these systems need to interoperate in order to inspect or exchange data and/or to invoke operations on other systems. The systems in use are of various ages, based on a variety of implementation technologies, and frequently supported on different operating systems and hardware platforms.

In terms of the sources of these software systems, BL supports the development of software in-house, by third parties, and acquired from software vendors in the form of *commercial-off-the-shelf* (*COTS*) packages. Additionally, BL operates a number of legacy systems, which need to be extended and maintained. Typically, these systems must be integrated with existing BL software systems leading to a significant systems integration and testing requirement. Additionally, there is a significant requirement for thorough and extensive regression testing.

Software is developed in BL at two separate sites – in Boston Spa, Yorkshire, and at the Saint Pancreas offices in London, each with numerous software development and testing projects. In terms of the quality of their IT development and testing process, the BL Saint Pancreas site has been a previous medalist in the annual British Computer Society Awards for IT.

BL's strong quality culture, the geographically separate development sites and the number of different software development and testing projects have been significant drivers in the development of the British Library testing framework.

15.3   The Management and Planning of Testing

BL follows a comprehensive testing process framework, specifically tailored to its particular testing requirements and documenting all aspects of its testing process.

In terms of software project management, BL follows the PRINCE 2 methodology (3), with the testing process organized and run as a PRINCE 2 program.

It is important to note that the BL view of the organization and management of testing is likely to be more complex than that employed by most organizations engaged in testing. This organizational structure has been adopted because of the size and complexity of BL itself, the number of software development and testing projects with their geographical separation, the strong quality culture, and the adoption of the PRINCE 2 project management method.

Figure 15.1 provides a high-level overview of the organization of the BL software testing program.

The BL testing framework is administered by a PRINCE 2 testing project board, which is responsible for the overall direction of the project management of the testing program and for representing the user and supplier interests within individual testing projects.

The testing manager reports to the testing project board and is responsible for the day-to-day management of the testing program. The precise responsibilities of the testing manager, and the other subordinate roles shown in Figure 15.1, are discussed in detail in Section 15.4.

In terms of the planning of testing, BL employs the *V Model* approach described in Chapter 4. However, because of its particular testing requirements, the BL interpretation of the V Model includes a number of extensions, which are shown in Figure 15.2.

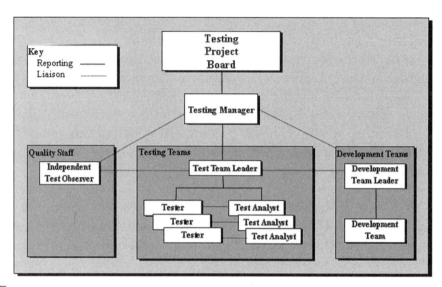

15.1 British Library Software Testing Program Organization

Specifically, BL terms the traditional integration testing phase – link testing – introduces a system integration testing phase between system and acceptance testing termed integration testing, and distinguishes between user and operations acceptance testing. The particular requirements leading to this interpretation of the V Model and the introduction of the additional testing phases are discussed in detail in Section 15.5.

The planning and preparation of tests for use in integration testing takes place during the specification phase of software development.

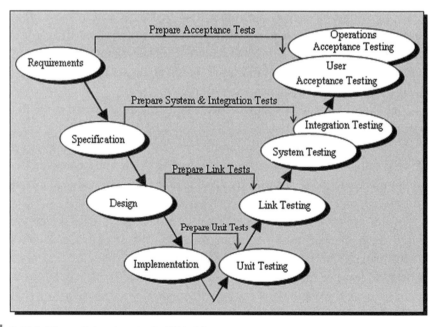

15.2 British Library Extensions to the V Model

The planning and preparation of tests for use in user and operations acceptance testing takes place during the requirements phase of software development.

In all other respects, the role and use of the V Model within the British Library testing framework remains the same as described in Chapter 4.

15.4 Roles and Responsibilities

The testing roles and responsibilities employed in the British Library testing framework closely follow those descriptions provided in Chapter 4 and in Appendix A of this book. The following BL testing roles and responsibilities are described in this section:

▶ Testing manager
▶ Test team leader
▶ Test analyst
▶ Tester
▶ Independent test observer.

It is important to note that within the BL testing framework it is possible for a single person to assume more than one role within a project. The one notable exception to this is the independent test observer, who must maintain complete independence from the project and its progress.

It is also possible for a single person to assume different roles on different projects. For example, a test analyst on one project could perform the role of test team leader on another.

Testing Manager

Within BL, the testing manager is responsible for ensuring that the individual testing projects produce the required products (i.e., the outputs from the testing phases), to the required standard of quality and within the specified constraints of time and cost, and ensuring that they produce a result that is capable of achieving the benefits defined in the PRINCE project initiation document.

The testing manager reports to the testing project board, is reported to by the test team leader(s), and liaises with the independent test observer and the development team(s).

The specific responsibilities of the testing manager include:

▶ Setting up and resourcing new testing projects (project initiation in PRINCE terms)
▶ Ensuring that (where appropriate) the development teams follow the *unit* and *link* (the BL term for *integration*) testing approach documented within the British Library testing framework
▶ Assuring that where bespoke software development is conducted by a third-party organization on behalf of BL, good development and testing practice (e.g.,

following the principles specified in the British Library testing framework) has been adhered to

▶ Formally representing BL during the cosigning of the test certificate (Appendix H) with the representative of a third-party organization responsible for development of bespoke software

Test Team Leader

The test team leader is primarily responsible for the day-to-day running of a testing project. The test team leader reports to the test manager, is reported to by the test analyst(s) and tester(s) within the project, and liaises with the independent test observer and (where appropriate) the development team leader.

The specific responsibilities of the test team leader include:

▶ Generating the test plan and test specification documents (Appendices C and D, respectively) for the testing project
▶ Tasking one or more test analysts and monitoring their progress against agreed plans
▶ Tasking one or more testers and monitoring their progress against agreed plans
▶ Liaising with the independent test observer (e.g., to determine their availability)
▶ Liaising with development teams (e.g., to determine availability date of the AUT)
▶ Set-up and maintenance of the testing project filing system
▶ Reporting testing progress and issues to the testing manager at agreed intervals

Test Analyst

The test analyst is primarily responsible for the design and implementation of the *test cases* and *test scripts* within a testing project. The *test analyst* reports to the test team leader and liaises with one or more testers.

The specific responsibilities of the test analyst include:

▶ Assisting the test team leader in generating the test specification and test plan documents (Appendices D and C, respectively)
▶ Defining the test requirements (with respect to the functional specification for the AUT)
▶ Designing and implementing test cases and test scripts (Appendix E)
▶ Designing and implementing test data sets
▶ Briefing the tester for the AUT prior to testing
▶ The generation of reuse packs (Appendix I)
▶ The back-up and archival of all testing documentation and materials

Tester

The tester is primarily responsible for the execution of the test scripts created by the test analyst. The tester reports to the test team leader and liaises with the test analyst. The tester will also liaise with the independent test observer during testing.

The specific responsibilities of the tester include:

▶ Executing test scripts and observation of test results

▶ Identification and logging of any observed faults (i.e., departures from the expected result)
▶ Documentation of test results on test result record forms (Appendix F)
▶ Cosigning the test result record forms with the independent test observer
▶ Maintenance and retention of test result record forms
▶ Creation of tests for retest of fault fixes
▶ Set-up and initialization of the test bed
▶ Back-up and archival of the test bed
▶ Recovery of the test bed in the event of failure

Independent Test Observer

The independent test observer is principally responsible for assuring the testing process is followed correctly.

The independent test observer reports to the quality assurance manager and liaises with the test team leader. Where the independent test observer witnesses a serious departure from the formal testing process, which cannot be resolved with the test team leader, he or she may also directly report this matter to the attention of the quality assurance manager.

Specifically, the independent test observer is responsible for:

▶ Attending the testing of the AUT
▶ Formally witnessing that the tester correctly completes all test cases within the test script (Appendix E)
▶ Cosigning the appropriate section of the test result record form (Appendix F)
▶ Reporting any problems observed during the testing process to the testing manager

BL has a well-established culture of quality assurance where the notion of peer review and approval is routinely followed. Independent test observers are likely to be selected on the basis of their ability to assure testing projects adhere to the correct testing process.

The independent test observer may also be invited to review the test plan and test specification documents, and test scripts for the testing project they are involved in. Most often, it will be sufficient for the independent test observer to assure him or herself that the correct process has been followed in the development of the documents rather than review the documents in detail.

15.5 Testing Phases

The testing phases supported by the British Library testing framework closely follow those described in Part 1 of this book with the following exceptions:

▶ BL calls the traditional integration testing phase link testing. The choice of the term link testing was made to distinguish it from the BL testing phase that tests the integration between separate and distinct BL software systems – termed integration testing within the BL testing framework. The specific details of the link testing phase are in all other ways the same as described in Chapter 6 with the exception that no test summary report (Appendix J) is produced

▶ The BL testing framework includes an additional testing phase between system testing and acceptance testing, termed integration testing. This testing phase is required because of the particular BL requirement that so many of its software systems interoperate to a greater or lesser degree. Clearly, where there is no requirement for a particular application to interoperate with other systems, the integration testing phase will be omitted. Similarly, if the requirement to interoperate with other systems is weak, then the tests normally conducted in integration testing may be transferred into the system testing phase

▶ BL makes a clear distinction between user and operations acceptance testing, and typically schedules separate tests for both end users and staff responsible for operating and administering the AUT

▶ As a general departure from the testing process described in Part 1 of this book, none of the testing projects produces test summary reports as an output from each testing phase. This is because the underlying PRINCE 2 project management method employed by BL already includes comprehensive reporting of the sort that the test summary report provides.

15.6 Artifacts

The artifacts produced within the British Library testing framework closely follow those described in Appendix C to Appendix I of this book. Specifically, each BL testing project is expected to produce the following standard artifacts:

▶ Test plan document (Appendix C)
▶ Test specification document (Appendix D)
▶ Test script(s) (Appendix E)
▶ Test result record form(s) (Appendix F)
▶ Test log (Appendix G)
▶ Reuse pack (Appendix I)
▶ And for the higher levels of testing (i.e., system, integration, and acceptance testing), and in particular of third-party bespoke applications, signed test certificates (Appendix H).

As discussed previously in this chapter, BL testing projects do not produce a test summary report (Appendix J).

To ensure that all testing projects have access to the testing artifacts and make use of standard testing documentation, BL provides access to testing artifact templates and checklists via its intranet system. In this way, any project manager requiring a particular testing document template can simply download it from a central repository.

15.7   Process Improvement

On completion, testing projects are expected to perform the equivalent of PRINCE 2 post-implementation review for the purposes of identifying those aspects of the project that were successful, and those aspects of the project that could be improved.

It is planned that this information will be provided to testing project staff via the BL intranet system to ensure that future testing projects can benefit from the experiences of previous projects.

16 Case Study 2: Reuters Product Acceptance Group

Paul Goddard

16.1 Overview of the Organization

More than 521,000 users in 52,800 locations access Reuters information and news worldwide. Data is provided on more than 940,000 shares, bonds, and other financial instruments as well as on 40,000 companies. Financial information is obtained from 260 exchanges and over-the-counter markets, and contributed by 5,000 clients.

Reuters services are delivered globally over one of the world's most extensive private satellite and cable communications networks. Typically, Reuters updates 6,000 prices and items of other data per second and handles 65 million changes daily. The information available from Reuters' databases ranges from real-time to greater than 10 years old.

The company's two main business divisions are Reuters Information (RI) and Reuters Trading Systems.[1]

Reuters Information products include real-time information and historical information databases, and focus on four main markets, foreign exchange and money, commodities (including energy), fixed income, and equities. Reuters corporate and media information business includes textual news services for print media, broadcast, and on-line clients. The company prides itself on the diverse content, freedom from bias, accuracy, and speed of supply of information to its customers.

Reuters Trading Systems division groups together Reuters management systems, transaction products, risk management products, and other applications.

The Reuters Product Acceptance Group (PAG) operates within the RI division and is based in Singer Street, London. PAG is responsible for the *acceptance testing* of financial trading products on behalf of its customers, which are implemented under contract by third-party suppliers.

This case study is a snapshot of PAG's testing activities between October 1997 and May 1998 when Paul Goddard was the U.K. PAG manager. Paul now works as VP, database technology group in the data services division in Toronto, Canada.

---

[1] For current information on Reuters visit http://www.reuters.com/aboutreuters/background/

16.2 Testing Requirements

PAG is principally responsible for the acceptance testing of the Reuters 3000 product family.

The Reuters 3000 product family provides integrated access to extensive, high-quality historical reference data and real-time data that supports both pretrading decision-making and posttrade analysis. Data is presented to the user via a series of functionally related and customizable workspaces, allowing the user to navigate to the required information and apply sophisticated analytics. The Reuters 3000 product family includes:

▶ Reuters Treasury 3000 – which allows users to search, analyze, display, and export bond terms, conditions, and price histories. Treasury 3000 is designed to be used by fund managers, portfolio managers, analysts, researchers, brokers, traders, salesmen, and mid- and back-office staff
▶ Reuters Securities 3000 – which performs a similar role for the equity market
▶ Reuters Money 3000 – which performs a similar role for the real-time money markets

All of the Reuters 3000 products are expected to interoperate with each other, exchanging data and services, as well as interoperate with other Reuters systems such as the 2000-series real-time products and data (IDN), Reuters Graphics, and Reuters Terminal products. The Reuters 3000 products also are expected to interoperate with other *commercial-off-the-shelf* (*COTS*) products, such as spreadsheets and word-processing packages, for the purposes of analysis or report writing.

Reuters 3000 products are implemented under contract to Reuters by a third-party supplier, who is responsible for *unit, link, systems, and integration testing*[2] of the *application under test* (*AUT*) before delivery to PAG. Following successful acceptance testing by PAG, the AUT is delivered to the customer site for user testing prior to live use.

Customers deploy Reuters 3000 products on a wide variety of hardware and software platforms with a variety of specifications and configurations. This situation is further complicated by the availability of coresident software products (such as spreadsheet, word processing, and/or communications software).

As a consequence of the heterogeneity of customer computer platforms, PAG must ensure that thorough *interoperability* and *compatibility testing* is conducted as part of the acceptance testing process. In order to support this requirement, PAG maintains a flexible configurable test laboratory, which at the time of this case study, comprised some forty PCs, servers, and networking equipment, plus a wide variety of test software. The PAG lab is a secure facility that can be quickly configured to

---

[2] As with many organizations with a strong requirement for testing the integration of a number of interoperating systems, PAG employs a *systems integration testing* phase (termed integration testing within PAG), with the traditional integration testing phase being termed link testing.

model customer installations in order to perform a variety of realistic acceptance testing activities.

Each Reuters 3000 product delivered to PAG must undertake two separate testing streams:

▶ Reference database (RDB) acceptance testing – verifying that the data service aspects of the AUT are correct
▶ Client-site (or graphical user interface [GUI]) acceptance testing – verifying that the customer aspects of the AUT are correct

The testing requirements for each stream are sufficiently different for the RDB and GUI acceptance tests to be distinct and separate events, conducted by separate testing teams (see Figure 16.1). The principal differences between the RDB and GUI testing teams in terms of skills and experience are:

▶ RDB testing
  ▷ Low-level technical skills including client-server knowledge
  ▷ Thorough knowledge of Reuters information services
  ▷ Thorough knowledge of the Reuters 3000 data requirement
  ▷ Thorough knowledge of the server operations, support environment, and methodology
▶ GUI testing
  ▷ Knowledge of the customer business process
  ▷ Knowledge of the Reuters standards for GUI design
  ▷ Good usability testing skills
  ▷ Knowledge of the user interface design paradigms across the range of Reuters GUI products

The organization of the RDB and GUI testing streams and their position within PAG is discussed in the following section.

16.3 The Management and Planning of Testing

PAG follows a formal testing process, tailored to its particular testing requirements and documenting all aspects of its process. The details of the process are documented in the *PAG Methods of Working* document, which is described in Section 16.6.

Figure 16.1 provides a high-level overview of the organization of PAG, its position within Reuters, and its relationships to third-party developers and to Reuters customers.

PAG is managed by the PAG manager, who has responsibility for the day-to-day running of the group. The PAG manager reports to the U.K. operations manager and is reported to by the managers of the reference database (RDB) acceptance manager and graphical user interface (GUI) acceptance manager.

The RDB acceptance manager is responsible for ensuring thorough testing of the AUT to determine if all RDB application changes are ready for operational release.

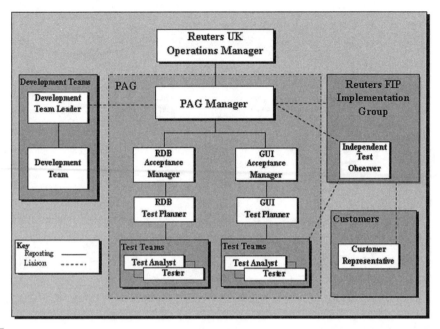

16.1   Reuters Product Acceptance Group Organization

The GUI acceptance manager is responsible for testing the AUT from the customer perspective to determine if the AUT is ready for release to the users.

All of the PAG roles shown in Figure 16.1 are described in detail in Section 16.4.

In terms of test planning, PAG employs the *V Model* approach described in Chapter 4. However, because of its particular testing requirements, the PAG interpretation of the V Model includes a number of extensions, which are shown in Figure 16.2.

As described previously, the third-party supplier is responsible for conducting the early phases of testing, including unit, link, systems, and integration testing.

Employing V Model principles, the planning and preparation of the acceptance test begins within PAG during the requirements phase of software development, and is the responsibility of the respective RDB/GUI test planner. The involvement of these roles in planning and preparation for testing is described in detail in Section 16.4.

PAG routinely worked in close coordination with the product manager/business unit sponsor to ensure what was required at the outset of the development was tested and delivered – or if not, what compromises along the way were acceptable to the product manager. The requirements are recorded in a product requirements specification (PRS) document.

Within the PAG testing process, reuse of existing testing materials, such as test specification documentation, test scripts, and test logs, is a key technique used to ensure acceptance testing is as efficient and effective as possible. In order to support this requirement, access to a Web-based document repository was provided for staff requiring such material.

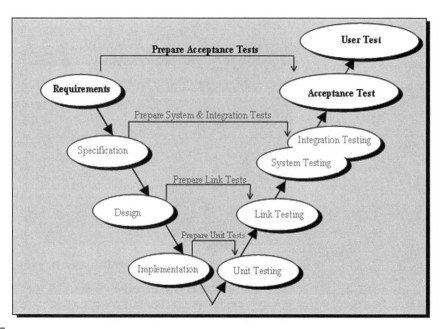

Reuters Product Acceptance Group View of the V Model

Although there was no specific librarian role, the RDB or GUI acceptance managers had responsibility for administering these facilities, with the project deliverables being reviewed by the PAG manager.

Although PAG did not employ formal reuse packs, the acceptance managers were encouraged to make tools and documents generated during testing projects available to subsequent projects.

16.4 Roles and Responsibilities

The testing roles and responsibilities employed in PAG include:

► PAG manager
► RDB/GUI acceptance manager
► RDB/GUI test planner
► Test analyst
► Tester
► Independent test observer

PAG Manager

The PAG manager ensures that the individual testing projects produce the required products (i.e., the outputs from the testing phases, which includes the tested AUT), to the required standard of quality and within the specified constraints of time and cost.

The specific responsibilities of the PAG manager include:

▶ Developing, documenting, and maintaining the PAG testing process
▶ Setting up and maintaining the PAG filing system
▶ Setting up and resourcing new testing projects
▶ Tasking the RDB and GUI acceptance managers and monitoring their progress against agreed plans
▶ Monitoring the quality of acceptance testing against the documented PAG testing process.

The PAG manager reports to the U.K. operations manager, is reported to by the RDB and GUI acceptance managers, and liaises with the development team leader to agree on delivery dates for the AUT, and to verify correct procedures have been employed in the development and testing of the AUT. The PAG manager also will liaise with the FIP implementation group to deliver the acceptance tested AUT for subsequent installation and user testing.

RDB/GUI Acceptance Managers
The RDB and GUI acceptance managers are responsible for determining if the AUT is ready for formal release to the customer.

The RDB acceptance manager has specific responsibility for verifying that the reference database aspects of the AUT (i.e., all areas of the AUTs interaction with the data source for Reuters 3000 products) are correct. This includes aspects of supportability and operability.

The GUI acceptance manager has specific responsibility for verifying that the customer aspects of the AUT (i.e., testing the AUT from a user perspective) are correct. This includes verifying functional requirements, interoperability, and usability.

The specific responsibilities of the acceptance managers include:

▶ Working in conjunction with the test planner to develop the acceptance test plan for a given testing project
▶ Working in conjunction with the testing team to develop the test specification document for a given testing project
▶ Ensuring that the test planner and test analysts are aware of the need to consider reuse of existing testing materials
▶ Tasking the appropriate test planner and monitoring progress against agreed plans
▶ Liaising with the independent test observer (e.g., to determine his or her availability)
▶ Set-up and maintenance of the filing system for each testing project
▶ Reporting testing progress and issues to the PAG manager at agreed intervals

The acceptance managers report to the PAG manager and are reported to by the respective test planners, test analysts, and testers.

RDB/GUI Test Planner

The test planner role incorporates a number of the responsibilities of the test team leader in a traditional testing project. The specific responsibilities of the test planner include:

▶ Developing the acceptance test plan document in conjunction with the acceptance manager (the RDB and GUI test planners must liaise with their counterparts to ensure no contention for PAG lab facilities occurs)
▶ Assisting the respective RDB/GUI acceptance manager in generating the acceptance test specification document
▶ Tasking the test analyst and tester and monitoring their progress against agreed plans
▶ Reporting testing progress to the acceptance manager at agreed intervals
▶ Wherever appropriate, considering reuse of existing testing materials (i.e., acceptance test plans and test specification documents)

The test planner reports to the respective acceptance manager and is reported to by the test analyst and the tester.

Test Analyst

The test analyst is primarily responsible for the design and implementation of the *test cases* and *test scripts* within a testing project.

The specific responsibilities of the test analyst include:

▶ Performing the functional analysis of the AUT and defining the test requirements (with respect to the product requirements specification and the project functional specification)
▶ Assisting the respective RDB/GUI acceptance manager and test planner in generating the acceptance test specification document
▶ Designing and implementing test scripts and test cases
▶ Briefing the tester for the AUT prior to testing
▶ Wherever appropriate, considering reuse of existing testing materials (such as acceptance test scripts and test cases)
▶ Back-up and archival of all testing documentation and materials

The test analyst reports to the respective test planner and liaises with the tester.

Tester

The tester is principally responsible for the execution of the test scripts created by the test analyst. The specific responsibilities of the tester include:

▶ Executing test scripts and observation of test results
▶ Identification and logging of any observed faults (i.e., departures from the expected result)

▶ Documentation of test results on test result record forms
▶ Maintenance and retention of test result record forms
▶ Modification of tests for retest of fault correction
▶ Set-up and initialization of the test bed within the PAG lab for each user configuration to be tested
▶ Recovery of the PAG lab test bed in the event of failure.

The tester reports to the respective test planner and liaises with the test analyst.

Independent Test Observer

The independent test observer is principally responsible for assuring the testing process is followed correctly. Independent test observers are drawn from the product managers of RDB operations managers.

The independent test observer reports to FIP or operations and liaises with the test teams. Where the independent test observer witnesses a serious departure from the formal testing process, which cannot be resolved with the test team leader, he or she may also directly report this matter to the attention of the PAG manager.

Specifically, the independent test observer is responsible for:

▶ Attending the testing of the AUT
▶ Formally witnessing that the tester correctly completes all test cases
▶ Signing the appropriate section of the test result record form
▶ Reporting any problems observed during the testing process to the PAG manager

The independent test observer also may be invited to review the acceptance test plan and acceptance test specification documents and test scripts for the testing project he or she is involved in. Most often, it will be sufficient for the independent test observer to assure him or herself that the correct process has been followed in the development of the documents rather than review the documents in detail.

16.5   Testing Phases

Unit, link, systems, and integration testing of Reuters 3000 products is conducted by the developers on development computers (NCR 5100 series machines) using a representative copy of the *live data*. A copy of Reuters 3000 data is used to ensure testing of the preacceptance test ready software does not corrupt live data.

PAG are responsible for the acceptance testing of new members of the Reuters 3000 product range as well as acceptance testing of new versions/releases of current Reuters 3000 products. In the latter case, PAG also will need to conduct rigorous regression testing of the AUT to ensure the new functionality has not impacted on the correct performance of the existing functionality.

Acceptance testing is conducted in the PAG lab using a range of configurations of hardware and software, which are set up to be representative of the various

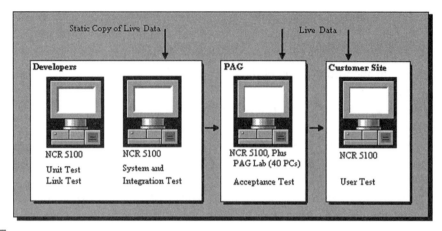

Static Copy of Live Data | Live Data |

| Developers | PAG | Customer Site |

NCR 5100   NCR 5100   NCR 5100, Plus   NCR 5100
                      PAG Lab (40 PCs)

Unit Test   System and   User Test
Link Test   Integration Test   Acceptance Test

16.3   Summary of Reuters 3000 Testing Phases

customer installations. Acceptance testing is conducted against the live Reuters 3000 data source to provide further confidence in the accuracy of the results of testing.

Following successful acceptance testing, the AUT is delivered to the customer where user testing is conducted on the *live environment* using live data.

Figure 16.3 provides an overview of the testing phases, their location, and the data requirements.

Unit, Link, System, and Integration Testing

The developers are responsible for conducting adequate unit, link (the developer term for the traditional *integration testing* phase), system, and integration (the developer term for *systems integration*) testing. System and integration testing take place in a single combined testing phase.

The data used for the developer-managed testing phases is a copy of the live data used by Reuters 3000 products and supplied to the developer by PAG to ensure realistic and representative testing. The developer may augment the live data using handcrafted data for the purposes of testing boundary and error conditions, and any such data will be generated using formal design techniques (i.e., those described in Chapter 3).

Following successful system and integration testing, the AUT is delivered to PAG for acceptance testing. PAG is responsible for verifying that the developer has followed correct procedures during the development and testing of the AUT.

Acceptance Testing

The principal reason for PAG performing acceptance testing of Reuters 3000 products is to provide confidence that they are of suitable quality for delivery to customers. Specific aspects of the products tested include:

▶ Installation testing

▶ Product impact – that is, regression testing to ensure the user continues to see the same level of functionality/performance/quality for all elements of the product that haven't specifically been changed

▶ Interoperability testing

▶ Operability testing – that is, can the operations group manage day to day monitoring and support? For example, do the error messages/info messages make sense – do they fit with existing operations norms/requirements?

▶ Supportability – that is, can the development group support the product over the long term. For example, does it meet standards for naming/DBA conventions, and does it use standard interfaces/common functions?

▶ Usability testing

▶ Benchmarking – that is, performance testing (including performance results monitored over time to observe trends).

Each Reuters 3000 product that undergoes acceptance testing by PAG does so under two separate and distinct testing streams: RDB acceptance testing (verifying that the reference database aspects of the AUT are correct) and GUI acceptance testing (verifying that the customer aspects of the AUT are correct). These testing projects are conducted by two separate testing teams, each possessing skills and experience appropriate to the particular aspect of the AUT they are testing.

Since both RDB and GUI testing for a particular AUT take place in the PAG lab, adequate planning of the tests is required to avoid contention for the testing facilities.

The acceptance test scripts and test cases are designed by the test analyst based on the information provided in the PRS and PFS document, plus any supplementary design material (such as prototype software or user guide documentation).

The test scripts are executed by the tester, who records the results of the test cases and documents any observed errors. Testing takes place in the PAG lab using a number of different arrangements of the lab facilities to accurately represent the possible configurations that different customers may use in their live environments. Similarly, live Reuters 3000 data is used in acceptance testing to provide confidence that the test results will match those expected on the live customer environment.

Following analysis of the test result record forms, any errors are logged using a commercial defect tracking system and are reported to the developers to correct within mutually agreed timescales. The tester is also responsible for retesting the AUT to verify the defects have been corrected and to perform adequate regression testing to ensure the existing functionality of the AUT has not been compromised during correction of the defects.

At the successful completion of acceptance testing, the AUT is released to FIP for subsequent delivery to the customer and user testing.

Regression Testing

Because of the business critical nature of Reuters 3000 products, it was determined that new releases of the products (such as enhancement and defect correction releases) would undergo thorough and rigorous regression testing to provide maximum confidence in the quality of the software.

In order to save time and effort expended in regression testing and to ensure a consistent and thorough approach is maintained, the *PAG Methods of Working* document proposes that regression testing be made as effective and efficient as possible by employing reuse of existing testing materials wherever possible (Appendix I provides further advice on exploiting reuse in testing projects).

At the conclusion of the acceptance test (and following a new release of the AUT), the tester is responsible for making copies of the test scripts, test cases, and any other relevant testing materials (such as the test data), and placing them into a reuse pack that is then filed for potential reuse during the next acceptance test.

At the planning stage of the next acceptance test, the RDB/GUI acceptance manager, test planner, and test analyst will review the existing reuse packs in order to identify appropriate testing materials that can be reused in the current testing phase.

Apart from the obvious benefits in terms of saved time and effort, the testing process also benefits from the reuse of "tried and trusted" testing materials, which the testing staff have confidence in using.

User Testing

User testing was conducted by FIP product/project managers, who are responsible for alpha and beta testing. Output from these tests was typically used as input to the requirements for the next release.

16.6 Artifacts

PAG employs a comprehensive set of testing documents within its testing process. Standard document templates are available for PAG staff to reuse in order to maintain the quality and consistency of the testing process, and to save time, effort, and cost in the generation of testing documents.

The testing artifacts employed within the PAG testing process include:

▶ The product requirements specification (PRS) that is drafted by FIP, and subsequently amended by PAG, to produce a generic PRS to represent the overall user/operations/product requirements for testing purposes
▶ PFS project plan
▶ The *PAG Methods of Working* document – a high-level policy document describing the philosophy and approach to testing Reuters 3000 products, in effect providing the description of the PAG testing process. The *Methods of Working* document contains the following sections:
   ▷ A statement of the scope of testing to be performed by PAG
   ▷ A statement of the approaches and processes to be used in testing
   ▷ The entry criteria to be fulfilled before AUTs will be received by PAG

  ▷ The exit criteria to be fulfilled before AUTs can leave PAG
  ▷ A definition of the various test categories used in acceptance testing
  ▷ Standard templates to support the testing process, such as:
    • Test logs
    • Test scripts
    • Test result record forms
▶ PAG acceptance test plan documents – with sections providing:
  ▷ The project plan and schedule for testing of the AUT
  ▷ The scope of testing (together with any exclusions)
  ▷ A description of the testing approach to be used in testing the AUT
  ▷ Details of any risks, constraints, and assumptions associated with the testing of the AUT
  ▷ Specific entry and exit criteria for the AUT
  ▷ Configuration details for the AUT, test data, and test hardware
  ▷ Any specific project controls to be used in testing the AUT
▶ PAG acceptance test specification documents – with sections providing:
  ▷ A description of what is to be tested and what is not to be tested
  ▷ For each test:
    • A high-level description of the purpose of that test
    • A high-level description of how the test should be performed
    • The test prerequisites that must be satisfied
  ▷ A specification of any specific tools required for testing the AUT
  ▷ A specification of the platform and configurations to be used in testing the AUT
  ▷ A specification of the test environment(s) for the AUT
▶ Reuse packs, to contain:
  ▷ A copy of the test specification document
  ▷ A copy of the test log
  ▷ A copy of the test script (and any revised test cases)
  ▷ A floppy disk of the appropriate format containing the previous
  ▷ A floppy disk copy of any "handcrafted" data (if technically feasible) or a reference to an electronically archived copy of the data
▶ Test logs – as specified within and available from the PAG methods of the working document
▶ Test scripts – as specified within and available from the PAG methods of working document
▶ Test result record forms – as specified within and available from the *PAG Methods of Working* document
▶ A testing summary report delivered to FIP or RDB operations – this could also include the deficient management plan (required for all releases) that documented what was planned in terms of the acceptable deficiencies and specified how they would (or would not) be addressed in future – this was signed off by the product manager

16.7 Process Improvement

PAG reviewed and rejected the ISO 9000 scheme but adopted elements of this in the *PAG Methods of Working* document.

In terms of process improvement, Reuters development federation has adopted the capability maturity model (CMM, [35]). Most of what was the corporate technology group (CTG) is now formally certified at level 2 (including the data services division in Toronto). A number of groups have attained level 3, which is the current global goal.

17 Case Study 3: Crown Quality Assurance Group

James Toon, Crown QA Team Manager

17.1 Overview of the Organization

Crown Management Systems limited (Crown) was established in 1982 to provide software solutions to the hospitality industry.

The company has developed several generations of software products of which InnMaster, InnTrader, and InnTouch are the most current. These products have been designed to provide a business solution to multiple retailers in the hospitality sector.

Crown's services have been developed over the years so that a full turnkey solution can be offered to new clients, in conjunction with its business partners, including systems, hardware, services, support, and maintenance.

Crown's services also include the provision of outsourcing services. For example, it runs and manages Head Office IT systems for a number of clients. Crown also provides site deployment and training outsourcing for larger clients with hundreds of sites.

Since 1997 Crown has been involved in a European Union (EU) project intended to investigate the benefits of using automated testing tools in software development and testing. The project, sponsored by the EU as part of the European Software Systems Initiative (27), uses the IBM Rational Functional Testing tool (13) with the objective of quantifying the amount of time and effort that can be saved during the testing phase of the software development process. The IBM Rational product was selected over other competitive products due to its wide platform support (including Crown's platforms of choice including Delphi and SQL Server), its reputation as a world leader in software development and testing, and the broad range of functionality and integration offered, above and beyond that of its competitors.

At the time this case study was written, James Toon was the quality assurance team manager for Crown and was responsible for all aspects of Crown's testing process.

17.2 Testing Requirements

Crown trades in a highly competitive market, with a number of other companies offering similar products and services. In order to maintain its market share, Crown is constantly responding to requests for modifications to existing features or for the introduction of new functionality to the software systems it distributes. Thorough testing and the associated increase in the quality of the products Crown delivers to its customers is also perceived as key to Crown's continued business success.

This case study focuses on the testing activities of the Crown QA team, which is responsible for performing the *system* and *acceptance testing* of all software products that Crown delivers to its customers.

The need to test the latest functionality of new releases of the software and the need to ensure the existing functionality is unaltered, combined with the commercial cycle of changes to the underlying hardware platforms and operating systems, also means that Crown's products must undergo frequent and thorough *regression testing*. As a consequence, it is key to Crown's commercial success that its software development and testing process is as effective and efficient as possible.

Adoption of a formal testing process has provided Crown with the means of achieving this goal, allowing different testing projects to follow a common testing process with well-defined testing roles and responsibilities, standard templates and documentation, and the opportunity to improve efficiency through reuse.

In addition to adopting a formal approach to testing, the Crown testing process also incorporates the use of automated software testing tools, with the aim of reducing the time, effort and cost of testing, and improving the quality of the delivered systems.

Crown selected its testing tool solution through a rigorous review and evaluation of the testing tool market and the testing products that were available (see Appendix O for an illustrative testing tool evaluation scheme and criteria). The tool selected by Crown was the IBM Rational Functional Testing product, which is being used successfully on a number of Crown testing projects. In particular, Crown believes that test automation will:

▶ Reduce project testing time from 60% to 35% of the project duration
▶ Reduce the number of errors detected in the later phases of testing by 30%
▶ Lead to an increase in employee motivation through the automation of the repetitive elements of testing
▶ Reduce project delivery times by 20%
▶ Increase the reliability and robustness of the *applications under test (AUTs)*.

In selecting an automated software testing tool solution, Crown has carefully managed the rollout and adoption of the tool. Specifically, Crown planned and managed the acquisition of the tool, ensuring sufficient funds were available for on-site training and mentoring from IBM Rational technical staff, as well as expert process consultancy for the purposes of integrating the use of the tool into its existing testing method.

Testing automation plays a major role in supporting Crown's system and regression testing requirements, whereas acceptance testing follows a more traditional manual approach.

Crown supplies a number of different customers with point-of-sale systems, each with slightly different hardware and software requirements. As a consequence, Crown has a challenging requirement for accurately simulating the *live environments* of each of its customers to ensure that the test environment accurately reflects the conditions that the live system will operate under. Because of this requirement, Crown has developed a well-equipped and flexible *test rig* facility that allows it to simulate the live environments of its customers for the purposes of system testing. Acceptance testing typically takes place on the live customer system.

17.3 The Management and Planning of Testing

Crown follows a comprehensive testing process, specifically tailored to its particular testing requirements and documenting all aspects of its testing process. The process incorporates the role and use of automated software testing tools, which are employed at appropriate points in the process to make testing as effective and efficient as possible.

Crown has a strong quality culture, and the individual testing teams are administered under the auspices of the quality assurance (QA) team. This contrasts with those organizations (such as British Library – Chapter 15) where the testing projects are administered within an information technology (IT) group.

The Crown approach to managing its testing projects is heavily influenced by the PRINCE project management methodology (3), and many of the principles of this method are employed in the supervision of the QA team activities. The Crown QA team is managed on a day-to-day basis by the QA team manager, who reports to the Crown development director.

Figure 17.1 provides a high-level overview of the organization of the Crown QA team and its relationships to the other entities involved in the testing process.

The precise responsibilities of the QA team manager, and the other subordinate roles shown in Figure 17.1 are discussed in detail in Section 17.4.

In terms of the planning of testing, Crown follows the *V Model* approach described in Chapter 4. However, because of its particular testing requirements, the Crown view of the V Model is biased toward the higher levels of testing, as shown in Figure 17.2.

At the requirements phase the QA group is involved in reviewing the business specification document (BSD) for the AUT. This document forms the basis of the planning, design, and resourcing of the acceptance testing phase. The document is reviewed to identify any omissions or duplication of requirements, as well as any requirements that are specified in such a manner that they will be difficult to verify during testing for subsequent clarification or restatement.

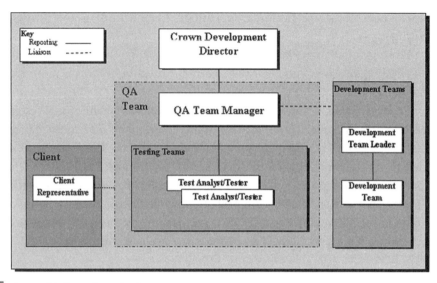

17.1 Crown QA Team Organization

A functional specification document (FSD) is produced by the developers describing how the development work will be carried out. In the FSD, the QA team includes a section on how the application will be tested and how the customer will know that the development has been a success. A client representative will formally review the FSD prior to development commencing.

When the FSD is agreed, the test scripts are created in preparation for system testing. Care is taken in the design of these scripts, because they will also be used for regression testing later versions of the AUT.

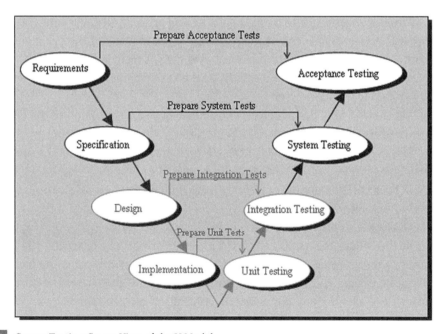

17.2 Crown Testing Group View of the V Model

The testing team will only accept the application for system testing when all defects raised during unit and integration Testing of the AUT by the developers have been cleared and it can be installed on a specially configured test computer from a delivery digital optical disk. In addition to testing the new functionality of the AUT, thorough and rigorous regression testing is performed using the automated testing tool.

For minor releases (such as defect fixes) a technique termed crash testing is used to verify overall quality of the AUT before allowing the software to proceed to more complete testing on the test rig. This approach reduces the problems with scheduling a test, setting up the test rig, and installing the test data, only to find that the AUT is not of sufficiently good quality to test. In practice this approach reduces wasted time and effort, making the testing process more effective and efficient.

When system testing of a major release is complete Crown carries out the user acceptance test at the client site. With upgrade releases, Crown performs the acceptance test internally on behalf of the client.

17.4 Roles and Responsibilities

The roles and responsibilities defined for the Crown QA team directly reflect the nature of the testing requirement for the organization. The relatively small number of staff involved in the testing process has a number of implications for overlap of responsibilities, with individual members of staff performing more than one role within the project. In effect, the QA team manager role also incorporates most of the traditional test team leader responsibilities, and the test analyst and tester roles are combined into a single function.

The QA group testing teams also work closely with the developers of the AUT, hence the inclusion of the developer role in this section (in this sense, developers could refer to both internal development teams, as well as any third-party organization supplying software to Crown). Similarly, the client plays a close part in the acceptance testing of the AUT, with a client representative participating in the "independent" observation of testing.

The following testing roles and responsibilities are described in the following sections:

▶ QA team manager
▶ Test analyst/tester
▶ Developer representative
▶ Client representative.

QA Team Manager

Within Crown, the QA team manager is responsible for ensuring that the individual testing projects produce the required products (i.e., the outputs from the testing phases, which includes the tested AUT), to the required standard of quality and within the specified constraints of time and cost. This is achieved by means of the PRINCE project management approach (3).

The testing manager reports to the Crown development manager is reported to by the test analyst/testers and liaises with the developer and client representatives.

The specific responsibilities of the QA team manager include:

▶ Developing test strategy and test planning
▶ Set-up and maintenance of the QA team project filing system
▶ Resource planning and allocation of testing projects
▶ Writing the test strategy section of the functional specification document
▶ Ensuring that each testing project produces a result that is capable of achieving the benefits defined in the functional specification document (see Section 17.6)
▶ Tasking one or more test analysts/testers and monitoring their progress against agreed plans
▶ Assuring that where bespoke development is conducted by a third party on behalf of Crown, that good development and testing practice (such as, the principles specified in the Crown testing process) have been adhered to
▶ Reporting testing progress and issues to the Crown development director at agreed intervals
▶ Process improvement, and QA metrics measurement and reporting.

Test Analyst/Tester

The test analyst/tester is principally responsible for the design and implementation of the test cases within a testing project, and reports to the test team leader.

The specific responsibilities of the test analyst/tester include:

▶ Assisting the QA team manager in generating the test strategy material for the FSD and the test plans
▶ Defining the test requirements (with respect to the FSD)
▶ Performing the functional analysis of the AUT for the purposes of the design of test scripts and test cases
▶ Designing and implementing the test procedures and test cases
▶ The design and specification of the test rig and test data sets
▶ Implementing the test rig and test data sets prior to testing
▶ The set-up and initialization of the test rig and test data, and recovery of the test rig and data in the event of failure during testing
▶ Back-up and archival of the test rig specification and test data sets
▶ Executing test scripts and observation of test results
▶ Documentation of test results on test result record forms and their subsequent maintenance
▶ Identification and logging of any observed faults (i.e., departures from the expected result)
▶ Design and implementation of tests for fault fixes (or reuse of existing tests if appropriate)

▶ The generation of reuse testing packs for each testing phase
▶ Back-up and archival of all testing documentation and materials.

Developer Representative

Because of the close working arrangement that has been established by Crown with respect to the developers of the AUT, the role of developer representative is formally defined within the Crown testing process.

Specifically, the developer representative is responsible for:

▶ Providing the AUT specifications (that is the business specification and functional specification documents, plus any supplementary design material)
▶ Providing build information on each delivered build/release of the AUT
▶ Providing confirmation of the correct execution of unit and integration testing
▶ Providing supporting information regarding AUT data requirements
▶ Providing baseline information for setting up the test rig, such as operating system details or the need for supporting or interoperating software
▶ Providing formal sign-off of the delivered AUT.

This formal definition of the developer responsibilities with regard to the testing process forms an effective contract ensuring the correct and timely delivery of the system test-ready AUT and supporting information required for testing. Such an approach is highly recommended for those organizations who receive test-ready software developed by a third-party organization for the purposes of system and/or acceptance testing.

Client Representative

The Crown QA team works closely with its clients to ensure that the delivered point of sale systems are of appropriate quality, and specifically that they meet their functional requirements, are reliable and robust, and provide adequate performance.

As part of this close relationship, the role of client representative is formally defined within the Crown testing process. The role carries an unusual mix of traditional user representative responsibilities (such as formal acceptance of the AUT), as well as some of the responsibilities of an "independent" test observer (such as formally witnessing the testing process to ensure correct procedures are followed).

Specifically, the client representative is responsible for:

▶ Formally attending the acceptance testing of the AUT (typically at the client site)
▶ Formally witnessing that the tester correctly completes all test cases
▶ Signing the appropriate section of the test result record form
▶ Cosigning the acceptance test certificate at the completion of a satisfactory acceptance test (or following an unsatisfactory acceptance test, after all outstanding defects in the AUT have been demonstrated to be corrected)
▶ Reporting any problems observed during the acceptance testing process to the QA team manager.

The client representative is also likely to be involved in the day-to-day monitoring of the progress of the software development and testing process with the QA team manager.

17.5 Testing Phases

As described earlier in this chapter, Crown obtain the test-ready software from developers who will have completed unit and integration testing on the AUT prior to delivery to Crown's QA group on digital optical disk.

The AUT undergoes a cycle of enhancement and release in response to change requests from the applications customers as well as the need to periodically update the software (e.g., to take account of hardware or operating system changes).

The release schedule is demanding, with a major release twice a year and minor releases every quarter. Combined with the need to ensure the AUT will perform correctly on each of the customer sites, the QA team faces a challenging testing load. In order to address the heavy testing load as well as the need to conduct rigorous regression testing, Crown employs an automated testing solution.

Each system test involves manual testing of the new functionality for the AUT as well as regression testing to ensure the existing functionality has not been compromised. As the manual tests are run, the automated testing tool is used to create scripts recording the steps and verifications employed in the test. These scripts can subsequently be replayed against later releases of the AUT for the purposes of regression testing and can even be run in an unattended manner overnight or over the weekend.

Crown is responsible for the following testing phases:

▶ System testing
▶ Acceptance testing
▶ Crash testing
▶ Regression testing.

The specific interpretation of each of these testing phases as a result of Crown's particular testing requirements is described in the following sections.

System Testing

Crown conducts system testing of the delivered software to ensure it is fit for purpose and of suitable quality to pass its acceptance test. System testing is conducted in-house by Crown's QA team using its test rig facilities to simulate the customer's live environment.

The system tests are designed by the test analyst/tester with reference to the business specification and functional specification documents, as well as any other supplementary design information. The automated testing tool is used to record the system tests as they are implemented. In this way, a library of previously recorded tests is assembled, from which selected automated tests can be compiled into a larger regression testing suite and executed. The recorded tests can also be used at a later date to reproduce the results of running a particular system test.

System testing also incorporates any *systems integration testing* that the AUT needs to undergo. This is a pragmatic testing solution to the problem of the complexity of the test rig used in system testing, because it would be very time-consuming to have to reconstitute an identical test rig for a subsequent testing phase.

The data used for system testing is a copy of that used on the live system, extended by the introduction of handcrafted data for the purposes of boundary testing and stimulating error conditions. The design of such data is based upon the testing techniques (such as boundary value analysis and equivalence partition methods) described in Chapter 3.

On completion of system testing (i.e., when the exit criteria specified in the FSD have been satisfied), the AUT is ready to proceed to acceptance testing.

Acceptance Testing

Following successful system testing, the AUT will undergo acceptance testing at the customer site as part of the formal process of delivering the application to the customer (minor releases of the AUT will be acceptance tested on behalf of the customer by Crown at its offices).

Although an automated testing tool has been used during system testing and for regression testing, the acceptance test is conducted using manual testing techniques.[1] The client representative performs *thread testing* of the AUT using scenarios designed with reference to the BFD and in the presence of one or more members of the QA team.

Crown does not run separate user and operations acceptance testing, but incorporates elements of both into a single acceptance test. This is a pragmatic solution to the problem of convening and setting up separate user and operations acceptance tests at the customer site. In practice, running a single acceptance test has been shown to be both effective and efficient.

On the successful completion of the acceptance test, the client representative and a representative of the Crown QA team cosign an acceptance certificate to show formal acceptance of the AUT.

In the event that defects are observed during testing that prevent the AUT from being accepted, the client representative and QA team representative will discuss and agree to timescales for remedial work on the AUT, and agree to a maximum period within which the acceptance test will be repeated.

Crash Testing

For the minor releases of the AUT (i.e., for releases incorporating minor enhancements or bug fixes), the Crown QA group performs a testing technique termed crash testing. In effect, the software is loaded from the delivery digital optical disk

---

[1] Crown has considered the benefits of its customers using automation for acceptance testing – with the customer in effect rerunning the automated tests on the live environment. At present, this solution has not been adopted due to the difficulties in convincing each of Crown's customers to invest in the automated technology.

onto a standalone workstation for the purposes of conducting a series of high-level tests to verify that the release is of sufficient quality for it to proceed with system testing.

In practice, this approach has saved Crown significant time and effort in terms of setting up the test rig and test data only to discover that the AUT was not really ready for testing (Crown estimates that crash testing can save enough effort to allow up to 33% additional testing time for the AUT, providing additional confidence in the quality of the application).

Regression Testing

Regression testing of the AUT is conducted using the IBM Rational Functional Tester automated testing tool (13). As described previously, the test analyst/tester designs a series of test scripts to verify the additional functionality incorporated into a new release of the AUT. At the tester executes these test scripts, the testing tool is used to record the steps involved in the test as well as any verification points.

In subsequent system tests, these recorded tests can be rerun against the latest release of the AUT in order to ensure that the existing functionality of the AUT has not been compromised by the new enhancements/modifications.

Typically, Crown runs these regression tests unattended (either overnight or over the weekend) to maximize the efficiency of the testing process. The results of regression testing are automatically written to a test log file, which can be inspected to determine the outcome of testing.

17.6 Artifacts

The following artifacts are employed in the Crown testing process:

▶ The test plan document (e.g., see Appendix C)
▶ The business specification document (which is equivalent to the traditional functional specification document). The purpose of the BSD is to specify the business requirements in such a way that they are unambiguous and can be readily interpreted by development and support staff. The principal sections covered in this document include:
  ▷ An overview of the function(s) covered by the specification
  ▷ A statement of the business or technical function that is to be satisfied by a module or object and the key features that are to be incorporated.
▶ The functional specification document (which contains a section written by the QA manager that is analogous to the traditional test specification document described in Part 1 of this book and in Appendix D). The purpose of the FSD is to specify the requirements in such a way that they are unambiguous and can be readily interpreted by development and support staff. The principal sections covered in this document include:
  ▷ An overview of the function(s) covered by the specification

    ▷ A detailed breakdown of each function into its constituent parts (e.g., file layouts, screen templates, report layouts, calculations, process characteristics and logic)

    ▷ An analysis of the impact the development will have on other areas of the system

    ▷ Any special conditions to be taken into consideration during testing

▶ Automated test scripts and verification points

▶ Manual test scripts and test cases (where required)

▶ Test log – detailing the day-to-day events of each testing project

▶ Reuse pack

▶ Acceptance test Certificates.

To ensure that all testing projects have access to the same testing artifacts and to ensure the use of standard testing documentation, Crown controls all testing artifacts using the Visual SourceSafe system, which is used as a repository for all QA documents.

17.7 Process Improvement

Crown is committed to striving continually to improve its software testing process. There are two principal reasons for this commitment; Crown is keen to take advantage of the commercial advantage it gives them, and because of their involvement in the EU process improvement project (27).

Crown collects and utilizes the following metrics as part of its process improvement initiative:

▶ Total effort expended in testing. An important use of this information is in the analysis of the benefits of the use of automated testing

▶ Total number of test procedures or scripts run against the AUT at system, acceptance (and optionally, regression) test. Useful for estimating how many automated scripts can be created for a given amount of effort

▶ Number of defects detected versus time in testing (and optionally, in use by the client). Analysis of this information is useful in determining when to stop testing (by plotting the rate of detection of defects and looking for this rate to level out), as well as for showing defect trends across the duration of the testing project. Defects are categorized as either significant or minor bugs to simplify analysis

▶ Defect detection effectiveness (percentage) or DDE. This metric provides an indication of how effective the Crown testing process is over time, and is a good metric to use in improving the process (i.e., the DDE percentage should increase the more effective the testing process becomes). DDE is calculated as follows:

$$DDE = (TDFT / (TDFC + TDFT)) * 100, \text{ where}$$

    TDFT = Total Defect Found by Testing (i.e., by the testing team)

$$\text{TDFC} = \text{Total Defects Found by Client (measured up to some standard point after release} - 6 \text{ months, for example)}$$

▶ Defect Removal Effectiveness (percentage) or DRE. This metric provides an indication of how effective the testing task is at removal of defects. DRE is calculated as follows:

$$\text{DRE} = \text{TDCT/TDFT} * 100, \text{ where}$$

$$\text{TDCT} = \text{Total Defects Closed during Testing}$$

$$\text{TDFT} = \text{Total Defects Found during Testing}$$

▶ Test Design and Test Development Coverage (i.e., the degree to which the test requirements have been addressed and tests planned, designed, implemented, and run). This information is easily obtained from within the IBM Rational Functional Tester tool as part of its standard reporting facilities.

The process of collecting and analyzing testing project metrics is simplified by the use of the reporting facilities provided in the automated testing tool. For example, it is very straightforward to run predefined coverage reports that show how many tests have been planned, designed, run, and passed.

Case Study 4: The Wine Society

David Marsh, Morag Atkins, and Annette Phillips

18.1 Overview of the Organization

The Wine Society is a co-operative owned by its shareholder (its "members"). It was founded in 1874 to serve its members rather than be run for profit. This ethos still holds true today. An elected body of members oversees the Wine Society and represents the interests of more than 85,000 active members.

The objective of the society is to offer its members wines and spirits of good quality from a wide range of sources, at the best prices possible, which it has consistently managed to achieve, with a list of more than 800 different wines available either by the bottle, in unmixed dozens, or in mixed cases of the members' own selection. Preselected mixed cases are also available and come with comprehensive tasting notes. The Wine Society organizes delivery of member purchases to any address in the United Kingdom.

The Wine Society has extensive storage facilities with temperature-controlled warehouses in Stevenage. The longer-lived wines are allowed to mature gently and reach their optimum potential. It is also possible for members to take advantage of the society storage facilities by storing wines bought from the society in the designated members' reserve section of the cellars. Updated drinking dates are provided to the members taking advantage of this facility annually to appraise them of the state of maturity of their stock.

The wines are selected by a team of experienced and highly knowledgeable buyers led by a master of wine.

The Wine Society has a significant reliance on information technology (IT) systems for much of its business requirements, including:

▶ Holding members details
▶ Holding current and historical stock details
▶ Holding information on stock held in the members' reserve and its age
▶ Assisting in picking, packing, dispatch, and delivery of goods
▶ Supporting the invoicing of members
▶ Sales order entry facilities.

Traditionally, these diverse business requirements had been supported using a number of different IT systems as well as manual facilities. In 1997, the Wine Society began the process of replacing these IT and manual systems with a single integrated software solution – Maginus. This case study describes the details of the project (Project 2000), which was set up for the purposes of acquiring this software, and more specifically, for *acceptance testing* the application.

David Marsh is currently the IS manager for the Wine Society, and at the time of this case study was one of the members of the program board responsible for directing the Project 2000 Task Force (see Section 18.3). Morag Atkins is currently working as an analyst in the Wine Society IS department, and at the time of the case study was a user representative tester on the Project 2000 team. Annette Phillips is currently working as a QA analyst in the Wine Society IS department, and at the time of the case study was also one of the user representative testers (Section 18.4 contains descriptions of these testing roles).

18.2 Testing Requirements

This case study deals specifically with a testing project set up by the Wine Society to acceptance test the Maginus software system (the *application under test [AUT]*) from MANCOS Computers Limited (the supplier), which took place between March and August 1998.

The AUT is a *commercial-the-shelf (COTS)* product, which is intended to support the majority of the wine societies business processes in a single comprehensive software system. For the software to more closely match business processes, the supplier undertook customization of the AUT under contract to the Wine Society.

The customization of the AUT employed a *rapid application development (RAD)* approach (e.g., [12]), which involved a number of Wine Society user representatives in regular reviews of prototype graphical user interfaces (GUIs). Rigorous configuration and change management were employed to ensure that there was no confusion regarding the version of the GUI delivered for testing and the earlier prototype versions.

The AUT was delivered to the Wine Society in a phased manner, with three major deliveries over a four-month period. It was planned that some interim testing would take place of the first two deliveries of the AUT, but given the rapid release cycle it was decided to perform the full acceptance test following the final delivery.

For the purposes of planning and managing the testing process, the following characteristics of the AUT were identified:

▶ The AUT represents a business critical system because it will support the majority of the Wine Society business processes
▶ The AUT comprises five major business modules (stock, sales, purchase, database, and finance) plus an administrative module, each of which will require rigorous subsystem testing

▶ Testing to verify the communications between modules will also be required as and when business processes demand

▶ The AUT will need to interface to a number of "external" systems, and each of these interfaces must be tested

▶ The AUT stores and processes large volumes of data, including:
  ▷ Records on more than 200,000 members
  ▷ Details on Wine Society stock, with granularity down to a single bottle
  ▷ Member transaction data for more than 1,000 orders per day.

▶ Because of the large data storage and processing requirements, thorough *performance testing* is required, including *volume, load,* and *stress testing*

▶ The AUT runs on Sun hardware under the Unix operating system

▶ The AUT will follow a regular planned release schedule following delivery of the customized software to the Wine Society, for the purposes of incorporating user change requests, defect resolution, and to keep abreast of commercial changes to the underlying hardware and operating system. These releases will undergo thorough *regression testing* by the Wine Society prior to installation on the *live system* to ensure that existing functionality has not been compromised.

The Wine Society proposed the following high-level approach to testing the AUT:

▶ Testing would be resourced from and conducted within the Wine Society IT Taskforce group

▶ External testing consultants would be employed in the testing process as and when required to provide *test analyst* skills and to assure the correct adoption and use of the testing process (e.g., at acceptance testing)

▶ The testing process would involve nominated user and supplier representatives with specified formal roles and responsibilities within the process

▶ Because there would be regular releases/upgrades of the AUT, reuse of testing materials/tests for the purposes of regression testing would be a major goal.

The Wine Society is an interesting case study because although ostensibly dealing with the acceptance testing of a COTS software product, the testing process in fact encompasses many of the elements of a more complete software development and testing project, including:

▶ Traditional acceptance testing

▶ Elements of *integration testing* between the subsystems

▶ Extensive *nonfunctional testing* including:
  ▷ Load, stress, and volume testing
  ▷ Usability testing

▶ *Systems integration testing* involving external software systems

▶ Rigorous regression testing.

Section 18.5 describes the details of the individual testing phases.

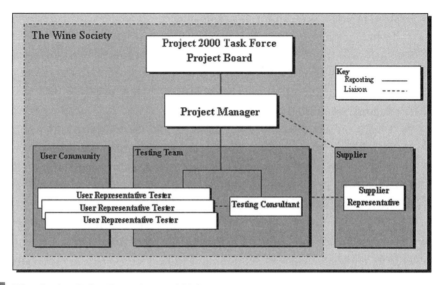

18.1 Wine Society Roles, Reporting, and Liaison

18.3 The Management and Planning of Testing

Prior to the decision to acquire the customized Maginus system, the Wine Society IT group had little direct experience of testing an application of the size and complexity of the AUT.

In acceptance testing the AUT, the Wine Society understood the need to follow a formal testing process. With the assistance of a number of testing consultants, the Wine Society developed a testing process specifically tailored to its particular testing requirements as well as to the society's internal organizational structure.

The Project 2000 Task Force (the project) was created in October 1997 specifically to formally manage the acquisition of the AUT, with members being drawn from across the Wine Society organization. The day-to-day management of the project was conducted using the PRINCE project management methodology (3), and the overall direction of the project activities was managed by means of a project board, which contained technical, user, and director-level representatives. (Appendix A provides information on the composition and responsibilities of a typical project or program board).

In setting up the project organization, a management decision was made to closely involve the user community. A number of user representatives were co-opted onto the project to perform the role of testers (or user representative testers) and worked closely with the testing consultant to form an effective testing team.

Figure 18.1 provides a high-level overview of the organization of the roles of the staff involved in the Wine Society testing process and their interrelationships.

The Wine Society Testing Team was managed on a day-to-day basis by the project manager, who reports to the Project 2000 Task Force Project Board. The detailed responsibilities of the staff shown in Figure 18.1 are discussed in detail in Section 18.4.

The planning of testing followed a pragmatic approach, based upon the delivery dates for the AUT and the final live date for the software to be installed, tested, and in use. Within these hard milestone dates, the testing had to be as effective and efficient as possible, and the testing consultant and project manager employed their previous experience of the software development and testing process in combination with the Prince methodology to create plans for the individual testing tasks. Contingency time was allowed in the plan to accommodate any retesting that might be necessary.

Within the context of the Prince methodology, the testing consultant conducted a risk analysis of the project, and specifically of the issues associated with the testing tasks. This activity was key to identifying particular areas of risk that needed to be explored during testing and to assist in the planning process by prioritizing the order of testing of the AUT. This was particularly important given the challenging fixed timescales involved in the delivery of the AUT and its go live date.

The specific details of the testing plan were enshrined in a test plan document. Low-level planning and design of the test scripts and test cases was based on the requirements for the AUT as listed in the requirements specification document (Section 18.6 contains details of the artifacts associated with the project).

The human resources for testing were drawn from within the Project, which had been set up to accommodate such resource requirements. Details of resourcing were recorded in an acceptance test specification document.

The business specification for the customizations was obtained by the supplier in discussion with the members of the project, and specifically with the user representatives. This information was recorded in a formal requirements specification document.

18.4 Roles and Responsibilities

For the purposes of acceptance testing the AUT, it was determined that the following roles and responsibilities were needed:

- ▶ Project manager
- ▶ User representative tester
- ▶ Testing consultant
- ▶ Supplier representative.

Each of these roles is described in the following sections.

Project Manager

The project manager was responsible for day-to-day running of the project and testing associated with the AUT and had to ensure that outputs from the project (which includes the tested AUT) were fit for purpose. With respect to the testing aspects of the project, the project managers' responsibilities included:

▶ Managing the set-up and resourcing of the acceptance test
▶ Managing set-up of the acceptance test filing system
▶ Managing the planning of the acceptance test
▶ Ensuring the production of the acceptance test plan document
▶ Ensuring the production of the acceptance test specification
▶ Tasking the user representative testers and testing consultant and monitoring their progress against agreed plans
▶ Liaising with the supplier representative to agree to delivery dates for the test-ready AUT and to agree to the time and date for attendance at the acceptance test
▶ Assuring that the supplier followed good testing practice during development and testing of the AUT, and reviewing the supplier unit, link (as the supplier term integration testing), and system test documentation
▶ Formal attendance at the acceptance test for the purpose of cosigning the acceptance test certificate at the conclusion of a successful acceptance test.

The project manager reports to the project board, is reported to by the user representative testers and testing consultant, and liaises with the supplier representative.

User Representative Tester

The user representative tester is responsible for the execution of the steps specified within the test scripts. The user representative tester should be a representative of the Wine Society who is familiar with using the business processes supported within the AUT. Specifically, the user representative testers are responsible for:

▶ Discussing the extent and scope of testing for the AUT with the testing consultant
▶ Reviewing the test scripts and test cases produced by the testing consultant for errors or omissions
▶ Executing test scripts and observation of test results
▶ Maintenance and retention of test result record forms
▶ Set-up and initialization of the test bed
▶ Back-up and archival of the test bed
▶ Recovery of the test bed in the event of failure
▶ The creation and maintenance of test reuse packs (see Appendix I)
▶ Reporting testing progress to the project manager at agreed intervals.

The user representative tester reports to the project manager and liaises with the testing consultant. In practice, the use of IT naive staff in a testing role proved to be very effective because the testers were entirely familiar with the goals and operation of the AUT and had no preconceptions about what was possible or even expected of technically oriented testing staff. Such an approach was made possible because of the availability of the testing consultant, who was able to advise and assist the user representative testers.

Testing Consultant

The testing consultant is appointed by the project manager and is responsible for verifying that the acceptance test is conducted as per the documented test process, and that the results of testing are interpreted and recorded correctly. Specifically, the testing consultant is responsible for:

▶ Assisting the project manager in the development of the acceptance test plan document
▶ Assisting the project manager in the development of the acceptance test specification document
▶ Discussing the extent and scope of testing for the AUT with the user representative tester
▶ Analyzing the functional requirements specification document to design test scripts and test cases to acceptance test the customizations to the AUT
▶ Reviewing the test scripts and test cases with the user representative tester to check for error or omission
▶ Creation of test scripts and test cases for retest of defects where necessary
▶ Determining the need for handcrafted test data for the acceptance test, and its subsequent design and implementation using formal design techniques (see Chapter 3)
▶ Developing the standard documentation to be used in the acceptance test (such as test script templates, test result record forms, and acceptance test certificates)
▶ Attending the acceptance test and observing the results of executing the test Scripts and test cases, interpreting the result, and assigning it to one of the test result categories
▶ Formal attendance of the acceptance test for the purpose of providing "independent" observation of the execution of the test scripts and the results of the test cases
▶ Reporting testing progress to the project manager at agreed intervals.

At the end of the acceptance test, the testing consultant is responsible for agreeing to any remedial work that may need to be performed on the AUT and the timescales involved in discussion with the supplier representative.

Supplier Representative

The supplier representative is responsible for attending the acceptance test on behalf of the supplier and has the authority to sign the acceptance test certificate on behalf of the supplier.

The supplier representative is also responsible for agreeing to any remedial work that may be required to be performed on the AUT and the timescales involved in discussion with the testing consultant.

18.5 Testing Phases

As discussed in Section 18.2, although the Wine Society process for accepting the AUT is ostensibly a traditional acceptance test of a COTS product, in fact the process addresses a number of other testing issues, including integration, performance, usability, and systems integration testing.

In addition to acceptance testing, the AUT was expected to undergo further releases (for the correction of defects and/or the inclusion of enhancements due to user change request), and so rigorous regression testing would be necessary against new releases to ensure that the existing functionality and performance of the system would not be compromised by any changes introduced for a new release.

Acceptance Testing

Based on the functional specification document for the AUT, the project manager and the testing consultant scoped out the high-level testing requirements and produced the test plan and test specification documents. These documents provided information on how to approach the acceptance test, its duration, the resources necessary to perform the testing, and the scope of the acceptance test.

Specifically, the acceptance test needed to verify the following areas of the AUT:

▶ The functional aspects of the AUT implemented for the Wine Society as customizations by the supplier
▶ The existing functionality provided by the AUT to ensure it had not become unstable due to the customizations
▶ The correct operation of each of the five main modules plus the administrative module
▶ The correct operation of the business processes supported between the subsystems
▶ The correct operation of the AUT with respect to the external systems it needed to interoperate with
▶ The adequate performance of the AUT with respect to its business processes under conditions of load and stress
▶ The suitability of the user interface in terms of simplicity, consistency, and intuitiveness, and appropriate levels of online help available to assist the user in successfully completing business tasks.

The specific test cases required to test the previous areas were based on analysis of the functional specification and business process documents by the testing consultant.

Regression Testing

Because of the business critical nature of the AUT, it was determined that the scheduled releases of the software would require thorough and rigorous regression testing.

To save time and effort expended in regression testing and to ensure a consistent and thorough approach was maintained, it was decided to maximize the efficiency of the regression testing process by the use of reuse packs (see Section 18.6 for details on the components of the reuse pack, whereas Appendix I provides further examples of the contents and use of such a pack).

At the conclusion of the acceptance test (and following a new release of the AUT), the user representative tester is responsible for making copies of the test scripts and test cases and any other relevant testing materials (such as the test data) and placing them into the reuse pack, which is then filed for reuse during the next acceptance test.

At the planning stage of the next acceptance test, the project manager and user representative tester will obtain the reuse pack and review its contents to identify testing materials (such as test scripts) that can be reused in the current testing phase.

Apart from the obvious benefits in terms of saved time and effort, the testing process also benefits from the reuse of "tried and trusted" testing materials, which the testing staff have confidence using.

18.6 Artifacts

The artifacts employed in the Wine Society testing process include:

▶ The supplier software testing approach document – a formal document produced by the supplier to record the approach to testing the AUT during development and customization. The role of this document within the Wine Society testing process is to provide confidence in the rigor of the supplier approach to testing.
▶ The AUT functional specification document – this document contains details of the specific customizations to be implemented in the AUT as specified by the user community via the user representative
▶ The business process document – in essence an annotated flow chart describing the business threads or scenarios that the AUT must support. This document was used heavily for risk analysis, prioritization, and planning of the testing process
▶ The Wine Society acceptance test plan – this document is equivalent to the traditional test plan document described in Part 1 of this book and in Appendix C and contains the following sections:
  ▷ Introduction (giving the background, structure of the document, and references)
  ▷ Test approach and constraints (describing the approach to be adopted in testing the AUT and any constraints the testers should consider)
  ▷ Risks and dependencies
  ▷ Test assumptions and exclusions
  ▷ Entry and exit criteria
  ▷ Testing project controls

     ▷ The test plan (recording tasks, durations, milestones and deliverables, and any dependencies)
- ▶ Wine Society acceptance testing specification document – this document is equivalent to the traditional test specification document described in Part 1 of this book and in Appendix D, and contains the following sections:
  - ▷ Introduction (background, scope, structure of document, and references)
  - ▷ Acceptance test requirements (introduction, test philosophy, test environment, and test requirements)
  - ▷ Acceptance test procedure (introduction, pre-test activities, conducting the acceptance test, post-test activities)
- ▶ Acceptance test scripts and component test cases
- ▶ Acceptance test certificates
- ▶ Test result record forms
- ▶ Reuse packs, containing both hard and soft copies of:
  - ▷ Guidance on the use of the pack
  - ▷ Acceptance test plan template
  - ▷ Test scripts templates
  - ▷ Test result record form templates
  - ▷ Acceptance test certificate template
  - ▷ Sets of previously conducted tests (test scripts and test cases).

18.7 Process Improvement

No specific process improvement approach was adopted within the project because of the fixed term of the acceptance testing task. However, at the completion of each testing task, a PRINCE post-implementation review was conducted to identify the positive aspects of the task as well as any aspects that could be improved. Wherever possible, this information was used to improve subsequent tasks in the testing process.

In August 1998, the customized Maginus system entered live operation; shortly thereafter, the project was closed. In practice, the testing process adopted by the Wine Society for acceptance testing of the AUT proved to be successful, with the project meeting its planned timescales and with the AUT being accepted into operation on time and to an acceptable level of quality.

Following the successful completion of the project and the dissolution of the task force, the staff returned to their original jobs. One positive result of bringing staff from different areas of the Wine Society (such as the user representative testers) into the project was that following its dissolution, a great deal of experience of testing and the testing process has become devolved into the different groups within the organization. For example, members of the user community now have much greater empathy with staff involved in testing and a greater understanding of what is involved in accepting software systems. Similarly, members of the marketing department now have more realistic expectations about what testing can do for them (in terms of testing timescales and the quality of the software they use).

New versions of the Maginus software continue to be delivered by the supplier following an ongoing release schedule. The testing of these new releases of the AUT is now the responsibility of staff in the Wine Society IT department, who were formally members of the Project 2000 Task Force, using the testing process, techniques, and experience gained on that project.

19 Case Study 5: Automatic Data Processing Limited

Martin Kemble, Senior QA Analyst

19.1 Overview of the Organization

Automatic Data Processing Limited (ADP) is the leading provider of employer services in the world. Employer services in the past was simply a synonym for payroll, but nowadays it has a significantly wider definition, embracing human resources, expense management, time and attendance, recruitment services, and employer solutions based on Internet technologies. As each of these service extensions has matured, ADP has been in the vanguard of technical and business innovation, consistently redefining the market and expanding the value its services deliver to clients.

Founded in 1949, ADP has been an astonishing success story for more than half a century. Its unrivaled record of profitable growth over more than 150 consecutive quarters bears witness to the extraordinary stability of ADP, making it the partner of choice in critical aspects of a vast number of businesses. Through a single-minded commitment to providing high-quality, employment-related services such as payroll, ADP has grown steadily and now serves a client community of more than 450,000 organizations worldwide.

ADP Employer Services began its United Kingdom (U.K.) operations in 1965 and these are now available throughout the United Kingdom via ADP's purpose-built client, sales, and support centers in Staines, Manchester, Birmingham, and Chessington.

ADP's business strategy is based on the need to grow through consistent improvement and innovation in the provision of employer services and where appropriate to exploit new and emerging technologies to assist in this goal.

ADP offers a broad spectrum of employer services, including:

- ▶ Surepay – a complete suite of facilities and tools to enable payroll offices to produce accurate and timely payrolls
- ▶ Managed payroll service – an outsourced payroll solution in which ADP takes responsibility for the preparation and delivery of the client payroll

▶ Teledata payroll service – a semimanaged payroll solution that is appropriate to clients with smaller numbers of employees

▶ International payroll service – a unique fully managed payroll and tax filing service designed for the particular needs of overseas organizations with satellite operations in the United Kingdom.

This solutions-oriented approach has helped ADP become the world's leading provider of computerized transaction processing, data communications, and information services.

This case study deals with a relatively small-scale testing project set up to perform *acceptance testing* of the software element of a payroll application prior to its delivery to a number of ADP clients as part of a managed payroll solution. At the time of this case study, Martin Kemble was the senior quality assurance analyst within the ADP software development department based in Staines, Middlesex, and was responsible for the day-to-day management of the acceptance testing team.

19.2 Characteristics of the Testing Requirement

Although ADP is a large organization with diverse requirements for software development and testing, this case study focuses on the testing process adopted by the software development department of the employer services division in the United Kingdom for the purposes of acceptance testing a payroll management application (the *application under test* or *AUT*). Following successful acceptance testing, the AUT was to be delivered by ADP to its clients as part of a managed payroll solution.

The software requirements for the application were provided by members of the client implementation team at ADP, which employed their knowledge and experience of the prospective client business processes to specify details of the system. These requirements were recorded in a *software requirements specification* document (the ATT requirements specification document – see Section 19.6).

The AUT underwent an iterative development process with incremental releases of the software delivered to the ADP acceptance testing team (ATT). As a result of the incremental release cycle, the ATT was responsible for both acceptance testing the new functionality for a particular release as well as rigorous *regression testing* of the previously accepted functionality.

A *thread testing* technique was employed to test functional aspects of the AUT (see Chapter 3) based on a business thread document produced by the testing team QA analyst (details of the QA analyst role and ATT business thread document are provided in Sections 19.4 and 19.6, respectively). In addition to the functional aspects of the software, the ATT was tasked with verifying some usability issues (such as "ease of use") of the AUT from a client perspective.

Because the AUT was planned to be delivered to each client as a distributed system with up to twenty users, the AUT also required *performance testing* to provide confidence that the software would execute with adequate speed under a variety of different conditions of *load, volume, and stress*.

In conjunction with its formal testing process, the ATT also incorporated the use of an automated software testing tool for both *functional and performance testing* of the AUT. The decision to employ an automated testing solution was based on the goal of providing ADP with a commercial advantage over its competitors by reducing the timescales, effort, and cost of testing, and improving product quality. The need to provide rigorous and complete automated regression testing of each incremental release of the AUT was another important factor in the selection of a testing tool.

ADP's approach to the selection of a tool involved the release of a formal invitation to tender (ITT) to a short list of leading testing tool and consultancy companies. The principal requirements stated in the ITT were:

▶ To provide an effective testing tool suite capable of matching the characteristics of the software development and testing process
▶ The availability of functional and performance testing facilities seamlessly integrated with the ability to represent test requirements and provide rigorous defect tracking
▶ The availability of effective training, mentoring, and consultancy in the use of the testing tool suite from the selected vendor
▶ The financial stability of the tool vendor and a commitment to continue to support and update the testing tool suite in line with industry and technology trends
▶ The availability of, and continued commitment to, "thought leadership" from the tool vendor who should be involved in researching and developing industry-leading technologies and techniques and delivering these to their customers
▶ The availability of testing process consultancy to extend their existing manual testing process to fully integrate the automated testing approach.

Following a rigorous review and evaluation of the proposals, ADP selected the IBM Rational functional testing solution (13).

Chapter 3 of this book gives additional information on the role and use of automated testing tools, whereas (17) provides a comprehensive treatment of automated software testing tools and their application. Appendix O contains a scheme and criteria for use in evaluating automated testing tools.

The ATT project can be characterized as a small testing project with relatively few staff involved in the testing process. ADP has a strong culture of quality, and the testing project was organized under the auspices of the quality assurance group. Acceptance testing of the AUT took place between 1997 and 1998, and this case study describes the project structure and organization during this period.

19.3 The Management and Planning of Testing

The acceptance testing team project followed a rigorous testing process, specifically tailored to its particular testing requirements and documenting the principal aspects

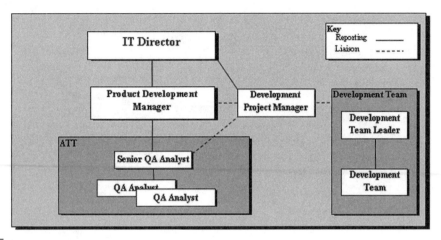

19.1   ADP Testing Process Organization

of its testing process. The ATT testing process was formally recorded in the ATT testing procedures document (see Section 19.6).

Figure 19.1 provides a high-level overview of the organization of the ATT and its reporting and liaison links to senior management and the third-party company developing the AUT.

The ATT is managed by the product development manager, who reports to the IT director. The ADP development project manager provides the interface to the development team for the IT director, product development manager, and the testing team members. The precise responsibilities of the product development manager and the other subordinate roles are discussed in detail in Section 19.4.

Because of its particular testing requirements, the ATT view of the V Model (see Chapter 4 and Figure 19.2) focuses on the acceptance phase of testing, with the earlier testing phases being conducted by third-party developers during implementation of the AUT.[1] In addition to acceptance testing, ATT also has a responsibility to regression test the AUT.

Following the V Model approach, the senior QA analyst and QA analysts are involved in planning and early test design of the acceptance test during the requirements phase of development. These activities are described in detail in the following section.

Defect management within the ATT was performed using the built-in defect tracking facilities within the IBM Rational products. This approach allowed defect tracking to be integrated with the automated testing process, with defect reports being created by the QA analyst following inspection of the automated test logs. Defects were then automatically relayed to the developers by means of an integrated email facility. The same system was used to track and report on the progress of

---

[1] Even though the development of the AUT follows an iterative approach, the V Model (which traditionally applies to the waterfall style of development) is equally relevant to the planning of the ATT acceptance testing. This is possible because each iteration can be considered analogous to a small-scale waterfall.

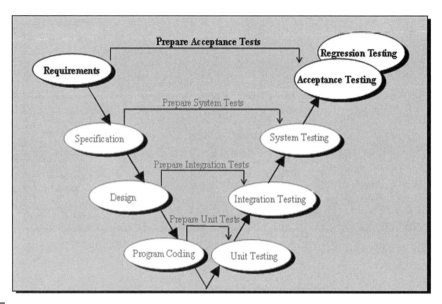

19.2 The ATT View of the V Model

defect correction, and ultimately, following successful retest (in effect, rerunning the original automated test), the defect could be closed.

19.4 Roles and Responsibilities

The roles and responsibilities defined for the acceptance testing team directly reflect the nature of the testing project. The relatively small number of staff involved in the testing process has a number of implications for overlap of responsibilities, with individual members of staff in effect performing more than one role within the project.

Because of the strong quality culture supported within ADP, the ATT was set up and administered by members of the quality group. This contrasts with those organizations (such as British Library – Chapter 15 or Reuters – Chapter 16) where the testing projects are administered from within an IT group.

The following ATT testing roles and responsibilities are described in the subsequent sections:

▶ Product development manager
▶ Development project manager
▶ Senior quality assurance analyst
▶ Quality assurance analyst.

Product Development Manager

The role of product development manager is analogous to the role of testing manager in a traditional testing project (see Chapter 4 and Appendix A). Where there are differences between the roles, this is mainly due to the position of the ATT within the quality group combined with the small number of staff involved in the testing process.

The product development manager is responsible for ensuring that the ATT produces the required products (including the fully acceptance tested AUT), as well as any incidental artifacts (such as the *test plan* and *test specification* documents) to the required level of quality and within acceptable timescales (as specified in the ATT testing procedures and ATT test plan documents, respectively).

The product development manager is also responsible for reviewing the *requirements specification* document for the AUT to determine the resources required for testing and to identify specific risks that may affect the testing process (such as possible late delivery of the AUT), and for producing the ATT test plan document. The product development manager is also responsible for ensuring that the ATT testing procedures document is produced by the senior QA analyst, and for ensuring that the process described in the document is followed by the ATT.

Due to the relatively small size of the ATT, the product development manager also performs the role of "independent test observer." In effect, the product development manager quality assures all aspects of the testing project, being involved in the review of testing artifacts and reviewing the results of the acceptance test to ensure correct procedures were followed (this also involves assuring the suitability of the development and test process employed by the developers of the AUT). The use of an automated testing tool by the ATT further reduces the need for independent observation of testing, because the testing tool does not suffer from human error during testing and the results of testing are logged with complete fidelity for subsequent analysis.

The product development manager reports to the IT director and is reported to by the senior QA analyst. The product development manager also liaises with the development team leader via the development project manager for the purpose of determining the timescales for delivery of the AUT for acceptance testing, as well as to verify that the development team employs appropriate quality procedures in the development and testing of the AUT.

Development Project Manager

The development project manager is responsible for managing the development aspects of the AUT from an ADP perspective and for monitoring the progress of the development team against agreed plans. In effect, the development project manager provides an interface between the developers and other ADP staff involved in the acceptance testing project.

The development project manager reports to the IT director, is reported to by the developers, and liaises with the product development manager and the ATT.

Senior Quality Assurance Analyst

The senior quality assurance analyst is responsible for the day-to-day activities of the testing team. The specific responsibilities of the senior QA analyst include:

▶ Set-up and maintenance of the testing project filing system
▶ Reviewing the ATT requirements specification document for the AUT in conjunction with the QA analysts to determine the testability of the software requirements

and to identify any errors and/or omissions and specific resources needed for testing

▶ Producing the ATT testing procedures document, ensuring that the other members of the ATT are aware of the document and its contents, and follow the defined test process

▶ Tasking the QA analysts and monitoring their progress against agreed plans

▶ Reporting testing progress and issues to the product development manager at agreed intervals

▶ The installation, maintenance, and update of the test automation tools

▶ Liaison with the test automation tool vendor for requests for support, training, mentoring, and consultancy

▶ The planning and organization of training, mentoring, and consultancy services from the test automation tool vendor.

The senior QA analyst reports to the product development manager, is reported to by the QA analysts, and liaises with the development project manager for the purposes of determining the likely dates for delivery of the AUT for testing.

Quality Assurance Analyst

The QA analyst role within the ATT combines aspects of the traditional *test analyst* and *tester* roles as described in Part 1 of this book (see Chapter 4 and Appendix A).

Because of the use of a testing tool to support the testing process, the QA analyst is primarily responsible for the design, implementation, and execution of the *automated test scripts* and their component *verification points* (analogous to *test cases* in traditional manual testing). Where it is necessary to perform manual testing, the QA analyst also has responsibility for the design and implementation of manual *test scripts* and *test cases*.

The specific responsibilities of the QA analyst include:

▶ Reviewing the ATT requirements specification document in conjunction with the senior QA analyst

▶ Assisting the senior QA analyst in generating the ATT testing procedures and ATT performance testing specification documents

▶ Producing an ATT business thread document describing the business functionality of the AUT for the purposes of thread testing

▶ Designing and implementing the automated test scripts and verification points

▶ Designing and implementing manual test scripts and test cases as required

▶ Designing and implementing test data sets as required

▶ Setting up and performing the *skim test* on new releases of the AUT to ensure that it is of sufficient quality to undergo full acceptance testing

▶ Setting up the hardware, software, and data required to conduct the testing as specified by the ATT testing procedures document (for functional testing) and the ATT performance testing specification document (for performance testing)

▶ Setting up the automated software testing tool prior to testing and executing the automated test scripts and subsequently reviewing the test results[2]

▶ Executing the manual test scripts (most capable automated tools provide facilities to support the integration of manual and automated testing – e.g., [25])

▶ Reviewing the automated *test log* to identify any defects and generating a defect report for each observed defect

▶ Rerunning the appropriate automated tests to verify the correction of defects

▶ The generation of the reuse testing pack (this is largely accomplished by the routine use of the automated testing tool, which allows tests to be recorded against one release of the AUT and then simply rerun against a later release to identify any defects in the new release)

▶ The recovery of the test bed in the event of failure (again, the testing tool provides facilities for automatically recovering from system failure and allowing testing to continue)

▶ The back-up and archival of all testing documentation and materials including the automated test repository (containing all of the automated testing artifacts, such as test scripts and verification points and test logs), and the test bed (i.e., a copy of the hardware configuration, test data, and a copy of the AUT).

The QA analyst reports to the senior QA analyst.

19.5 Testing Phases

As described earlier in this chapter, the development of the AUT followed an incremental approach (e.g., see [8]). Although iterative development methods typically produce software systems of appropriate quality within acceptable timescales, the more frequent build and release cycle has serious consequences for the testing process in terms of a much higher volume of testing; in addition to testing the most recently implemented functionality, it is also necessary to conduct thorough regression testing to ensure that the functionality implemented in earlier releases has not been adversely affected by the development completed for the current release.

The result is that the ATT was faced with a very challenging testing load, both for acceptance testing the frequent releases and for ensuring that thorough regression testing was performed. Furthermore, as development of the AUT proceeded, the regression testing load would grow at each release because of the need to test the cumulative functionality of the AUT from earlier releases.

To keep up with the demanding incremental release schedule and the challenging testing load, the senior QA analyst proposed the adoption of an automated software testing solution. The use of automation in the acceptance and regression testing is

---

[2] One of the major advantages of automated testing tools is that they can perform unattended testing of the AUT, allowing tests to be run overnight or over the weekend and allowing the complete set of results (recorded in a test log file) to be inspected after testing has finished.

the principal difference between the ATT interpretation of these testing phases and the classic view presented in Part 1 of this book.

To maximize the efficiency of the acceptance testing process, a skim testing approach was employed to verify the suitability of a new release of the AUT to undergo acceptance testing.

The following testing phases are described in the subsequent sections:

▶ Skim testing
▶ Acceptance testing
▶ Regression testing.

Skim Testing

At each incremental delivery of the AUT, to ensure that the developers had provided a version of the software of sufficient quality to undergo full regression testing, the ATT performed skim testing. This pre-test activity ensured that time, effort, and cost were not wasted setting up and conducting a full acceptance test against a copy of the AUT, which was of unacceptable quality.

The skim testing process involved an initial installation of the AUT on a specially configured PC containing test data. A standard set of manual tests stored in a reuse pack (see Appendix I) was executed against the AUT to verify the correct operation of a number of key business threads (or business scenarios).

If the skim test was successful, the AUT would proceed to full acceptance testing. If not, the AUT would be rejected and returned to the developers with a defect report documenting problems identified during the test.

ADP's skim testing is analogous to the Crown Management Systems Limited technique of crash testing (see Chapter 17 – Case Study 3: Crown Quality Assurance Group). In practice this simple pre-testing check of the AUT has been consistently proven to save time and effort on the part of the testing team and to make the testing process more effective and efficient.

Acceptance Testing

Using the IBM Rational functional testing product (13), the ATT was able to conduct acceptance testing to verify the suitability of the functionality implemented in the most recent release of the AUT while recording the steps performed in the test. In subsequent releases, the existing functionality of the AUT could be rigorously tested by simply replaying the tests recorded in previous acceptance tests.

The functional aspects of the acceptance tests were based on the ATT business thread document, which specified a number of business scenarios that users would employ in their normal use of the AUT (see Section 19.6). Traditional design techniques were used in the design of the acceptance tests, including:

▶ Thread testing and *state transition techniques*, which were employed in designing the test scripts and test cases (which were subsequently implemented as test scripts and verification points in the testing tool)

▶ *Boundary value analysis* and *equivalence partition techniques*, which were employed in the design of handcrafted data for exercising boundary conditions and error handling functionality.

The performance testing aspects of the acceptance tests were based on the functional test scenarios. During performance testing, a simulation technique was employed that used a number of virtual users to represent the higher demand for system resources that would occur in the live system. The automated testing tool provided integrated support to allow the functional test scripts to be reused in performance testing and to be assigned to the virtual users, who concurrently executed the business threads. The results of performance testing were automatically written to a test log, which detailed the load on system resources such as processor utilization, network loading, and memory utilization, allowing subsequent analysis of the results of the performance test. In addition to ensuring the acceptable performance of the AUT with realistic numbers of users, performance testing was used to provide estimates of the minimum acceptable specification for the client computers to support the AUT.

Acceptance testing also verified the correct operation of the database aspects of the AUT and included explicit tests for checking record locking and deadly embrace.

Following completion of successful acceptance testing of each incremental release, a process of formal sign-off of that version of the AUT was performed with the developers.

Regression Testing

Because the AUT dealt with the business critical application of payroll management and was to be delivered to ADP clients as a managed solution, it was essential that the software be reliable, robust, and fit for purpose. Because of these requirements, the ATT had to ensure rigorous regression testing of each new release was performed.

For maximum confidence, it was decided it would be necessary to completely regression test the AUT at each release. In a traditional regression test, because of the drive for efficiency in the testing process, the test analyst will design the tests by considering the scope of the changes to the AUT and analysis of the likely impact on other areas of the functionality of the application. However, using such an approach, there is always risk that changes to the AUT will have some unforeseen effect on the software that selective testing will miss.

The regression testing employed by the ATT was achieved by reuse of automated test scripts that had been created during the earlier acceptance tests. This approach provided an elegant solution to ensuring thorough and rigorous testing of the AUT, as well as managing the demanding testing load that the incremental development of the AUT caused.

Additionally, the ability of the automated testing tool to perform unattended testing meant that the tests could be executed overnight or over a weekend – saving time and effort but also allowing more testing to be conducted in the same time that

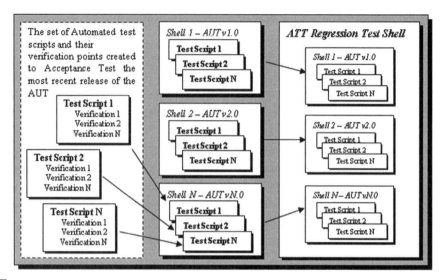

19.3 Organization of ATT Regression Testing Suite

a manual approach would have permitted – increasing the quality of the testing and resulting in greater confidence in the correctness of the AUT.

In order to manage the complexity of the regression test suite,[3] the ATT exploited the "shell" facility provided within the Rational functional testing tool. This allowed all the automated test scripts (and their component verification points) associated with a particular release of the AUT to be assembled into a test shell to be executed together. Each test shell was then assembled into a larger regression test shell, which allowed each of the component shells (and their test scripts) to be executed sequentially, providing a simple and effective means of scheduling and executing the complete regression test (see Figure 19.3).

Following execution of the regression test shell, the automated test tool creates a comprehensive test log detailing the results of testing, and highlighting defects and areas for further investigation. The test log is structured in a hierarchical manner reflecting the hierarchy of test shells and test scripts. This allows defects to be tracked down quickly and easily by the QA analyst responsible for reviewing the results of testing.

19.6 Artifacts

The following artifacts are employed by the acceptance testing team in the process of testing the AUT:

▶ The ATT requirements specification document – generated by the ADP client implementation team, which employed its knowledge and experience of prospective clients business processes to specify the requirements of the system

---

3 In this context, test suite refers to the total collection of test scripts produced as a result of acceptance testing. As a direct consequence of the incremental development approach for the AUT, the test suite would grow in size each time there was a new release of the software.

▶ The ATT test plan document – describing the testing tasks, their timescales, milestones, dependencies, and risks

▶ The ATT testing procedures document – this document is equivalent to the traditional test specification document described in Part 1 of this book and in Appendix D. The sections covered in this document include:

> Introduction – providing a description of the background and purpose of the functional testing and a list of references to related documents (such as the ADP QA responsibilities manual)

> QA testing strategy – providing a description of the purpose of testing, an overview of the roles and responsibilities, testing approach, scope of functional testing

> Responsibilities – providing the list of tasks to be completed by the ATT during acceptance testing and the member of ATT responsible

> Functional testing – providing a specification of the functional areas of the AUT to be tested

> Acceptance criteria – specifying the criteria for delivery of the AUT for testing, defining the categories of severity of defects and priority for correction of defects, and the levels of severity and priority under which the AUT will be deemed to be acceptable following testing and review of the results

▶ The ATT performance testing specification document – this document is an adjunct to the acceptance test team testing procedures document that provides the specification for the performance testing aspects of the acceptance testing project. The sections provided in this document include:

> Introduction – providing a description of the background and purpose of the performance testing and a list of references to related documents (such as the ADP QA responsibilities manual)

> Test hardware – specifying precise details of the hardware required to conduct the performance testing of the AUT, and of the networking infrastructure

> Test software – providing a specification of the operating system, networking software, and details of the AUT, as well as a list of additional software required for the purposes of conducting stress and interoperability testing (such as email or word-processing software that could be resident in memory at the same time as the AUT)

> Test data – describing the need for adequate volumes of data representative of the live data to be used by the AUT, and specific handcrafted data required for exercising boundary and error conditions

▶ ATT business thread document – a document created by analysis of the software requirements for the system and knowledge of the manner in which the end users employ the AUT to support their business requirements. The business thread document describes scenarios to be used in thread testing the AUT (see Chapter 3)

▶ Automated test scripts and verification points – planned, designed, and created using the IBM Rational functional testing tool

▶ Manual test scripts and test cases (where required)

▶ Test log – automatically generated by the testing tool during the process of executing the automated tests and available after testing for the QA analyst to review

▶ Reuse pack – for skim testing as well as any manual tests required during acceptance and regression testing.

The use of an automated testing tool meant that there was no need for the ATT to produce test result record forms because in effect these were provided within the tool. Similarly, it was not necessary to produce a test summary report because the testing tool provided extensive facilities to automatically generate a wide variety of management reports.

19.7 Process Improvement

Because of the size and short duration of the testing project, the ATT did not adopt a formal process improvement program.

However, information on certain aspects of the testing process was collected and used to improve efficiency of testing during the course of the project:

▶ During the testing process, data were collected on the numbers of defects detected and the rate at which they were corrected and signed off. This enabled the ATT to ensure that correction of defects was being completed effectively and that there would be no retesting bottlenecks

▶ Testing coverage metrics were also collected, showing what percentage of the AUT had been covered during testing. This information was used to help plan and refine subsequent testing tasks.

20 Case Study 6: Confirmit

Tom Gilb and Trond Johansen

20.1 Overview of the Organization

Confirmit supplies software that enables organizations to conduct customer feedback, employee feedback, and market research programs.

The Confirmit customer base is drawn primarily from global 5000 companies and worldwide market research agencies Its customers rely on Confirmit's wide range of products for feedback/data collection, panel management, data processing, analysis, and reporting.

Confirmit takes pride in providing innovative, superior technological solutions that are scalable, secure, and flexible to support its clients' constantly evolving needs. The company is committed to understanding and meeting the needs of its multinational customer base and developing strategic relationships that support this. Confirmit's adoption and use of Tom Gilb's evolutionary project management (67) approach to agile product development and testing is a key factor in achieving these goals.

Confirmit was established in 1996 and rapidly became the leading provider of software-as-a-service (68) feedback and research solutions. In 2007, Confirmit merged with leading market research software provider Pulse Train. Since the merger, Confirmit has evolved its product portfolio to offer a range of best-of-breed solutions based on the combined forty years of software expertise and market knowledge of the two companies. In 2009, this evolution led to the launch of Confirmit Horizons, the world's first fully on-demand, multimode platform for market research, customer feedback, and employee feedback.

Confirmit now employs more than 260 people and has offices in Oslo, Norway (headquarters); Guildford and London in the United Kingdom; New York and San Francisco in the United States; and Moscow and Yaroslavl in Russia. Confirmit's software is also distributed through partner resellers in Barcelona, Kuwait City, Madrid, Milan, Pattaya, Sydney, and Tokyo.

This case study focuses on the rollout, adoption, and use of the agile Evo method in the development of the Confirmit product portfolio. Specifically, this case study examines the role and use of Evo in reducing the integration effort and timescales for developments and enhancements made to the *Confirmit*[1] product, as compared with the previously used Waterfall-based (69) development process.

20.2 Characteristics of the Testing Requirement

Confirmit is a powerful Web-based software package that enables organizations to gather, analyze, and report on key business information across a broad range of commercial applications.

Delivered to its customers via a Web-based interface, *Confirmit* is a complex product with numerous screens and rich functionality. The product has rigorous requirements for high availability and rapid response to customer requests (in practice, 99.7% product availability is guaranteed via a service-level agreement). In use, the product supported more than 30 million completed surveys in its On Demand environments in 2009, which displayed 1.5 billion pages. Confirmit customers globally have acquired more than 550 million questionnaires since *Confirmit*'s launch.

Some eighty staff (including a quality assurance team of twenty-four) work in the Confirmit research and development department and have responsibility for developing the core *Confirmit* functionality, as well as for developing custom bespoke modules for specific clients. *Confirmit* follows a challenging release cycle, with a new version of the product being delivered every nine months.

Early in the company's history, when Confirmit had just a few clients, the development process was fairly ad-hoc and customer driven. Changes to the software were made on an almost daily basis driven by client feedback, and although this delivered stakeholder value quickly, the process also resulted in numerous defects, long working hours, and poor control of the software development and testing process.

As the *Confirmit* client base grew, Confirmit was faced with the need to become more effective and efficient in its development and testing of the product; it was clear that a more formal process was needed.

Initially, Confirmit looked to adopt a Waterfall approach, incorporating process improvement via the Capability Maturity Model (35). After following a Waterfall approach for a number of years, the following issues were observed:

▶ Risk discovery and mitigation was delayed until the later stages of the project
▶ Document-based verification was postponed until the later stages of the project
▶ There was dissatisfaction with the need to stipulate unstable requirements too early; requirements change is perceived as a bad thing in Waterfall
▶ Operational problems were discovered far too late in the process (typically at acceptance testing)
▶ There were lengthy modification cycles and unnecessary rework and retesting

---

[1] Confirmit produces the *Confirmit* product. To avoid and confusion the company name will be shown in plain text while the product will be shown in italics throughout this case study.

▶ Most importantly, the requirements were nearly all focused on functionality, not on the quality attributes of the system.

With increasing dissatisfaction with its Waterfall approach, Confirmit began to work closely with Tom Gilb to roll out and adopt an Evo approach to improve its development process for *Confirmit*. In particular, three key goals were identified:

▶ **Reducing the integration effort** – that is, the amount of effort for each developer to get the latest build to work on his/her workstation so that he or she is able to code against the latest code platform
▶ **Reducing the time to upgrade** – from a previous code platform to the most recent code platform from the past figure of three hours to a goal of two minutes
▶ **Improving the reliability of builds** – which historically had been an area where there had been significant quality issues.

Historically, the Confirmit development process for the *Confirmit* product had focused mostly on functional requirements, but with Evo the requirements process changed with the realization that it is the product quality requirements that provide Confirmit with a competitive advantage over its rivals.

Other Evo principles[2] embraced by the Confirmit development and testing team included:

▶ Real results, of value to real stakeholders, will be delivered early and frequently
▶ The next Evo delivery step must be the one that delivers the most stakeholder value possible at that time
▶ Evo steps deliver the specified requirements, evolutionarily
▶ We cannot know all the right requirements in advance, but we can discover them more quickly by attempts to deliver real value to real stakeholders
▶ Evo is holistic systems engineering – all necessary aspects of the system must be complete and correct – and delivered to a real stakeholder environment. It is not only about programming – it is about customer satisfaction
▶ Evo projects will require an open architecture – because we are going to change project ideas as often as we need to to really deliver value to our stakeholders
▶ The Evo project team will focus its energy, as a team, toward success in the current Evo step. The team will succeed or fail in the current step, together. The team will not waste energy on downstream steps until it has mastered current steps successfully
▶ Evo is about learning from hard experience, as fast as we can – what really works, and what really delivers value. Evo is a discipline to make us confront our problems early – but which allows us to progress quickly when we probably have got it right
▶ Evo leads to early and on-time product delivery – both because of selected early priority delivery and because we learn to get things right early
▶ Evo should allow us to prove new work processes and get rid of bad ones early.

2   With sincere thanks to Tom and Kai Gilb for allowing me to reproduce this information.

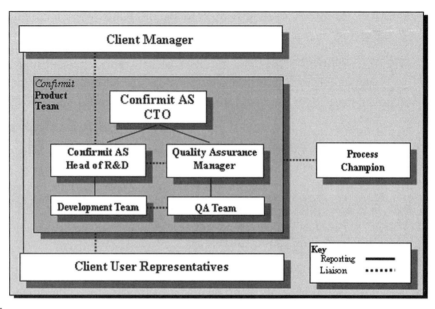

20.1 Confirmit Development and Test Process Organization

20.3 The Management and Planning of Testing

As described previously, development of the *Confirmit* product is performed by a core team of some eighty developers and quality assurance practitioners.

The development team is managed by the Confirmit head of research and development (R&D), who in turn reports to the Confirmit chief technical officer (CTO). The quality assurance (QA) team is managed by the Confirmit quality assurance manager, who like the head of R&D, reports to the Confirmit CTO. Process guidance is provided by an external process champion (see Figure 20.1).

As described previously, Confirmit adopted an agile approach to software development and testing to address a number of quality issues associated with the historical use of the Waterfall model of software development.

A key aspect of the planning and managing of the *Confirmit* was the adoption of a short, well-bounded weekly iteration cycle; the benefits of this included:

▶ A well-defined, regular, and predictable iteration cycle time. The project stakeholders easily and naturally adopted a project rhythm in which they automatically knew what their project responsibilities were on a day-by-day basis
▶ The weekly iteration cycle time provided an effective solution to managing the project, providing a level of task granularity that helped ensure project progress was kept on track
▶ The weekly iteration cycle time helped manage the customer expectations, providing a regular and predictable means of exposing the customer to the weekly delivery of incremental product features

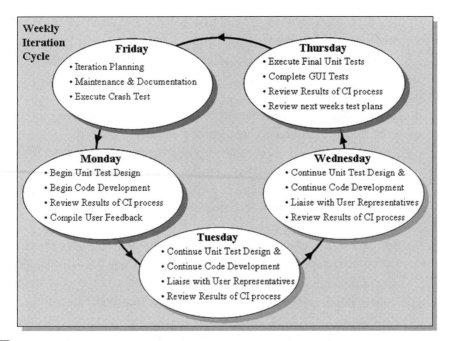

Weekly Iteration Cycle

Friday
• Iteration Planning
• Maintenance & Documentation
• Execute Crash Test

Thursday
• Execute Final Unit Tests
• Complete GUI Tests
• Review Results of CI process
• Review next weeks test plans

Monday
• Begin Unit Test Design
• Begin Code Development
• Review Results of CI process
• Compile User Feedback

Wednesday
• Continue Unit Test Design &
• Continue Code Development
• Liaise with User Representatives
• Review Results of CI process

Tuesday
• Continue Unit Test Design &
• Continue Code Development
• Liaise with User Representatives
• Review Results of CI process

20.2 The Weekly *Confirmit* Iterative Lifecycle

The planning of the next weekly iteration takes place across the previous week, culminating with the delivery, by the Confirmit head of R&D, of the detailed plan for the next week's iteration, to the client manager for review and approval on the Friday. Following review of the plan, the client manager meets with the Confirmit head of R&D to discuss the next week's iteration plan and to record any comments and observations.

The plan is executed throughout the next week's iteration, with the development team providing regular feedback on progress to the head of R&D, to allow for mid-iteration correction to the plan or to allow for deployment of additional resources to address issues that may jeopardize the successful execution of the plan.

Figure 20.2 provides a graphical overview of the Confirmit weekly iteration cycle, whereas the following sections provide further details of the activities involved in the cycle.

Within each weekly iteration, the following key activities are completed:

▶ **On the Friday:**
  ▷ The Confirmit head of R&D delivers the detailed plan for the next week's version of the software to the client manager prior to attending a weekly project management meeting
  ▷ The client manager reviews and approves/rejects the design and records their comments
  ▷ The head of R&D and client manager attend the weekly project management meeting to discuss the detailed plan for the next week's iteration and review the client manager's comments

▷ The developers focus on general maintenance and documentation tasks
▷ The QA team runs the final build and set-up for the current week's developed version, installs set-up on test servers, and performs initial crash test[3] of this version prior to its release.
▶ **On the Monday:**
▷ The developers first generate the tests required to validate the current week's code, and then begin development of the code
▷ The QA team reviews the results of the continuous integration (58) process and reviews test plans and tests for the current week's iteration
▷ The client user representatives begin to use the software delivered in the previous week's iteration and compile feedback for the developers.
▶ **During Tuesday to Wednesday:**
▷ The developers continue to design and implement the tests required to validate the current week's software and continue to develop the associated code
▷ The developers meet with the user representatives to discuss the feedback from using the software delivered in the previous week's iteration
▷ Incorporating the feedback from the users, the developers continue to generate the tests required to validate the software developed during the current week's iteration, and continue to develop the associated code
▷ The QA team reviews the results of the CI process, and reviews test plans and tests for the software developed during the current week's iteration.
▶ **On the Thursday**
▷ The developers complete the designs for the final tests for the software developed during the current week's iteration, code and execute the tests. The developers also complete the graphical user interface (GUI) tests for the software developed during the previous week's iteration
▷ The QA team reviews the results of the CI process and reviews test plans and tests for the following week

The Confirmit development and testing process makes extensive use of automation. Software development takes place within an integrated development environment (IDE – 63), which in addition to facilitating the software development also provides automated support for unit testing and continuous integration.

The quality assurance team also employs tools to support automated testing, including automated test management (e.g., 61), code analysis (e.g., 60), functional and regression testing (e.g., 13), and defect tracking (e.g., 21).

The Confirmit development and testing process makes use of project metrics stored in the various automated tools used on the project for a variety of purposes, including:

▶ Monitoring project status

---

[3] A testing technique used to determine the fitness of a new build or release of the software to undergo more thorough testing (11).

- Supporting the Confirmit process improvement strategy and monitoring the impact of changes to the process
- Generating a number of standard reports employed on the project (such as a graph of currently open defects versus time, in order to gauge software quality as the software nears delivery).

20.4   Roles and Responsibilities

This section documents the roles employed in the *Confirmit* development and testing process, and their responsibilities (as summarized in Figure 20.1).

With its focus on agile development and testing, and the goal of focusing on the rapid and frequent delivery of value to the client base, the roles and responsibilities emphasize close working and good communications between the project stakeholders (including the client representatives).

The roles (with their responsibilities described in the following sections) include:

- Client manager
- Confirmit head of research and development
- Quality assurance manager
- Development team
- Quality assurance team
- Client user representatives
- Process champion

Client Manager

The client manager provides the executive-level customer viewpoint into the development and testing process.

The client manager liaises with the Confirmit head of research and development (head of R&D) and is reported to by the client user representatives.

Within the context of the *Confirmit* project, the specific project tasks of the client manager include:

- Receiving the detailed weekly iteration plan from the head of R&D for review
- Reviewing the detailed weekly iteration plan to determine its suitability and documenting detailed comments as appropriate
- Attending the weekly project management meeting to discuss the detailed weekly iteration plan with the head of R&D and to review any comments on the plan that may have been documented
- Receiving feedback from the client user representatives on the suitability of the delivered software from the previous week's iteration

Confirmit Head of Research and Development

In the context of the *Confirmit* project, the head of R&D is responsible for managing the day-to-day aspects of the development and testing of the *Confirmit* product.

The Confirmit head of R&D reports to the Confirmit CTO, is reported to by the development team, and liaises with the client manager and the quality assurance manager.

Within the context of the *Confirmit* project, the specific project tasks of the head of R&D include:

▶ Working with the project stakeholders to compile the detailed plan for each weekly iteration, and delivering a copy to the client manager for review
▶ Convening a weekly project management meeting to review the weekly iteration plan and to discuss the client manager's comments
▶ Monitoring project progress, and where necessary taking remedial action, such as deploying additional project resources
▶ Liaising with the quality assurance manager to ensure appropriate quality assurance procedures are being followed during the *Confirmit* project
▶ Scheduling, chairing, and documenting the results of the end of release-cycle process-improvement retrospective-meeting, and where appropriate, modifying the *Confirmit* software development and testing process in response to the lessons learned
▶ Seeking process advice and guidance from the process champion as and when appropriate
▶ Reporting project progress to the Confirmit CTO.

Quality Assurance Manager

The quality assurance manager is responsible for ensuring that the project stakeholders follow software best practices, as defined by the Confirmit software development and testing process.

The QA manager reports to the Confirmit chief technology officer, and is reported to by the quality assurance team. The QA manager liaises with the Confirmit head of research and development.

Within the context of the *Confirmit* project, the specific project tasks of the QA manager include:

▶ Working with the QA team to confirm that the development team is following appropriate quality assurance procedures
▶ Liaising with the head of R&D to ensure appropriate quality assurance procedures are being followed
▶ Attending the end of release-cycle process-improvement retrospective-meeting to provide input from the QA perspective
▶ Seeking process advice and guidance from the process champion as and when appropriate
▶ Scheduling and administering the final *Confirmit* system test.

Development Team

The development team is responsible for the day-to-day development activities for the *Confirmit* product.

The development team reports to the Confirmit head of R&D, and liaises with the quality assurance team and the client user representatives.

Within the context of the *Confirmit* project, the specific project tasks of the development team include:

- ▶ Providing input to the head of R&D for the purposes of iteration and overall project planning
- ▶ Reporting project progress to the head of R&D, as well as highlighting any project risks that might jeopardize the ability to deliver the software on time, to budget, or with acceptable quality
- ▶ Developing, using a test-driven development approach (50), the tests required to validate the code that will form the current iteration deliverable
- ▶ Developing the code that will form the current iteration deliverable
- ▶ Meeting with the client user representatives to obtain and discuss feedback on the previous week's deliverable, and where appropriate, to incorporate their feedback into the current week's iteration (or a subsequent iteration)
- ▶ Completing and executing (on the last day of the weekly iteration cycle) the final tests for the current iteration deliverable
- ▶ Completing and executing (on the last day of the weekly iteration cycle) the graphical user interface tests for the previous week's iteration deliverable
- ▶ Conducting general development-environment maintenance and documentation tasks (typically at the end of the weekly iteration cycle)
- ▶ Attending the end of release-cycle process-improvement retrospective-meeting to provide input from the development team perspective
- ▶ Seeking process advice and guidance from the process champion as and when appropriate

Quality Assurance Team

The quality assurance team is responsible for ensuring that the development team follows software best practices, as defined by the Confirmit software development and testing process. The quality assurance team is also responsible for the design and execution of the weekly product crash test, functional, and regression test. The quality assurance team also has responsibility for the maintenance of the automated test management and functional testing tools employed on the project.

The quality assurance team reports to the quality assurance manager and liaises with the development team.

Within the context of the *Confirmit* project, the specific project tasks of the quality assurance team include:

- ▶ Reviewing the results of the continuous integration and test process executed by the development team, and where appropriate, highlighting any issues to the development team and quality assurance manager
- ▶ Reviewing the test plan (and any tests already available) for the following week's iteration cycle, and highlighting any issues to the development team and quality assurance manager

▶ On the last day of the weekly iteration cycle, running the final build and set-up for the current week's iteration deliverable, installation and set-up on the test servers, and performing an initial crash test on the deliverable prior to its release

▶ Updating and maintaining the test plan, and functional and regression testing suite within the automated test management and functional testing tools

▶ Attending the end of release-cycle process-improvement retrospective-meeting to provide input from the quality assurance team perspective

▶ Seeking process advice and guidance from the process champion as and when appropriate.

Client User Representatives

The client user representatives are drawn from the *Confirmit* user community and are selected to provide a realistic cross-section of the users of the software.

The client user representatives report to the client manager and liaise with the development team.

Within the context of the *Confirmit* project, the specific day-to-day tasks of the client user representatives include:

▶ Performing a range of typical business activities using the version of the software delivered at the end of the previous week's iteration cycle to assess the suitability of the delivered software

▶ Formally documenting their observations on using the software delivered at the end of the previous week's iteration cycle

▶ Meeting with the development team to provide feedback on the observations compiled while using the software delivered at the end of the previous week's iteration cycle

Process Champion

The process champion liaises with the *Confirmit* product team to provide guidance and mentoring on the role and use of the Evo software development and testing method. The process champion is knowledgeable about the general aspects of the software development and testing lifecycle, has detailed knowledge of the Evo process employed within Confirmit, and is able to provide comprehensive advice and guidance on aspects of process improvement.

Within the context of the *Confirmit* project, the process champion is not a full-time role, but may be consulted as and when required.

20.5 Testing Phases

This section contains a description of the testing phases used in a Confirmit development and test project.

Adoption of an iterative agile approach to development, testing, and delivery of the *Confirmit* product has a number of significant implications for the organization of testing in comparison with the Waterfall project previously used by Confirmit:

▶ Breaking the traditional Waterfall view of the project lifecycle into short, well-defined, and well-bounded iterations has supported the QA best practice of moving testing earlier into the development cycle and encouraging more frequent testing
▶ The adoption of a short, well-bounded iteration cycle has had significant implications for the V Model (39) testing view of the project lifecycle, introducing a series of repeating testing phases synchronized specifically with the weekly iteration cycle, rather than the rigid linear progression of V Model-driven test phases
▶ The adoption of a continuous integration approach throughout the iterative development cycle has implications for the integration test phase typically employed in traditional V Model projects. There is no explicit integration test phase, but instead integration testing occurs implicitly throughout the CI approach, with automated testing being conducted through tool support as the code base grows
▶ Repeated exposure of the customer to the incrementally developed system, with frequent opportunities to provide feedback to the development team resulting in the delivery of software that closely matches the client expectations and needs.[4] In practice, this has meant that the vast majority of acceptance testing for the *Confirmit* product has been done during the development lifecycle, rather than as a single large testing phase at the end of the project.

The testing phases employed within a Confirmit project are as follows:

▶ **Weekly Iteration Unit Test** – test scripts produced during the weekly iteration cycles by the development team (employing a partial test driven development approach (50) are run against the developed code. These are executed both manually by the development team as well as using an automated unit test tool (70). The automated unit tests can also be rerun later for regression testing purposes within the automated continuous build process
▶ **Weekly Iteration Crash Test** – crash test scripts produced during the weekly iteration cycle by the quality assurance team are run against the current week's iteration deliverable to provide confidence that it is robust and reliable enough for release
▶ **Weekly Iteration GUI Test** – members of the development team design and execute a series of GUI tests that will provide confidence that the *Confirmit* product user interface still performs correctly following development completed during the current weekly iteration. Specifically, the navigation through the GUI will be tested to ensure no links between screens have been broken, as well as ensuring

---

[4] Contrast this with industry metrics that suggest that as many as three quarters of software projects fail to deliver software that matches the customer requirements (48).

that it is still possible to invoke all aspects of the functionality of the system. The GUI test phase is supported by an automated Web teesting tool (71)

▶ **System Test** – following completion of the final iteration of a particular *Confirmit* project, and prior to release to the client base, thorough system testing is performed against the final software release candidate. This testing typically takes place over the final three months of the nine-month project lifecycle and makes significant time and cost savings through the rerunning of a selection of unit, functional, GUI, and manual tests compiled during the earlier iterations. A number of specific tests designed to exercise the business logic of the *Confirmit* product are also executed. Much of the system test is supported through the use of the automated testing tools employed throughout the earlier iterations.

Finally, it should be noted that there is no formal acceptance testing because senior customer and business users of the Confirmit product have been closely involved in reviewing, using, and providing feedback throughout the previous iterations. Additionally, the Confirmit clients will have been invited to attend and observe the Confirmit system test.

20.6 Artifacts

This section describes the testing artifacts used and/or created within the Confirmit software development and testing process. As described in Section 20.3, a high degree of reliance is placed on automated tool support for the development and testing of the *Confirmit* product.

The following artifacts are employed in the course of a *Confirmit* project:

▶ **Weekly Iteration Test Plan** – created by the quality assurance manager and designed and implemented using an automated test management tool
▶ **Weekly Unit Test Scripts** – designed by the development team following a test driven development approach, and implemented using an automated unit test tool
▶ **Weekly Crash Test Scripts** – designed by the quality assurance team, and implemented as a series of manual test scripts
▶ **Weekly Functional Test Scripts** – designed by the quality assurance team, and implemented using an automated capture-replay testing tool. Where necessary,[5] some functional tests are implemented using manual test scripts
▶ **Weekly GUI Test Scripts** – created by the development team, and implemented using an automated Web testing tool
▶ **Weekly User Representative Feedback** – compiled by the client user representatives in a word processor document

---

[5] In order to test some aspect of the *Confirmit* product that would be difficult or impossible to implement using an automated tool – such as the visual verification that a report had been printed correctly, for example.

▶ Regression Tests – reusable manual tests compiled during previous iterations. The manual test scripts are also stored and backed up electronically as word processor files

▶ System Test Plan – created by the quality assurance manager, and designed and implemented using an automated test management tool

▶ System Test Suite – a collection of automated test scripts sourced from tests previously created during earlier iterations, as well as a number of test scripts specifically created for the *Confirmit* system test

▶ Test Log – automatically generated by the testing tool during the process of executing the automated tests, and highlighting the results of the testing (such as detected defects or other issues). Available after testing for the quality assurance team and development team to review

▶ Defect Reports and Notifications – information available from an automated defect management tool used to manage the resolution of defects, including automated email notification of defects to specified members of the *Confirmit* team

▶ Standard Project Reports – a number of standard reports are published using automated tool support:

▷ Open Defects – a report showing graphically the number of open defects (closely monitored by the head of R&D and the quality assurance team, with the expectation that this will decline as the release date approaches)

▷ Code Churn – a report showing the rate of code churn (closely monitored by the head of R&D and the development team, with the expectation that this will decline as the release date approaches)

▷ Test Code Coverage – a report showing test script coverage versus the code base (closely monitored by the development and quality assurance teams to ensure that all aspects and all areas of the growing code base have associated tests)

▶ Ad-Hoc Reports – generated as and when needed using automated tool support.

20.7 Process Improvement

Evo coauthor Tom Gilb makes the observation that a valuable lesson to learn is that there are always new lessons to be learned! The Confirmit approach to development and testing embraces this view, and employs a formal process improvement scheme.

Toward the end of each nine-month release cycle, the Confirmit head of R&D convenes a post release retrospective meeting (53). During this meeting the project stakeholders, including the quality assurance and development teams, head of R&D and quality assurance manager discuss a number of aspects of the recently completed project, and document:

▶ What aspects of the project and associated process went well

▶ What aspects of the project and associated process could be improved upon

▶ What aspects of the project and associated process might need to be challenged before being used again in future release cycles.

The findings of the post release retrospective meeting are documented and acted upon in subsequent release cycles.

Unlike many agile projects, there are no formal end of iteration retrospectives, although proposals for improving the development and testing process can be made to the head of R&D on an ad-hoc basis.

To support process improvement, formal metrics, such as defect detection and defect resolution rates, can be obtained from the automated testing tools employed on the *Confirmit* project. For example, defect data are automatically stored by the test management tool for previous iterations and release cycles, and can be compared with observed values following the implementation and adoption of a proposed improvement.

20.8 Acknowledgment

I am very grateful to Trond Johansen (Norwegian head of research and development for Confirmit), his manager CTO Peter Myklebust, and Tom Gilb (independent testing consultant and coauthor (with Kai Gilb) of the evolutionary development method) for their assistance and encouragement in documenting the details of the *Confirmit* software development and testing process.

THE APPENDICES

Part 3 of this book contains a set of standard testing document templates, proformas, and checklists, and a number of appendices that expand on topics described in passing in the main body of the book.

The standard testing document templates, proformas, and checklists are also available from the following link: http://www.cambridge.org/9780521148016, so that they can be used immediately without modification or customized to reflect the particular requirements of any organization (such as a corporate style, branding, or documentation standard).

Specifically, the appendices contain:

- ▶ Appendix A – Terms of Reference for Testing Staff (one-page summary sheets documenting the terms of reference for staff involved in the testing process)
- ▶ Appendix B – Testing Guides (one-page summary sheets documenting the key aspects of each testing phase)
- ▶ Appendix C – Test Plan Document Template
- ▶ Appendix D – Test Specification Document Template
- ▶ Appendix E – Test Script Template
- ▶ Appendix F – Test Result Record Form Template
- ▶ Appendix G – Test Log Template
- ▶ Appendix H – Test Certificate Template (for those testing activities that require formal demonstrable proof of the acceptance of the tested software)
- ▶ Appendix I – Reuse Pack Checklist (to help set up and manage testing reuse packs)
- ▶ Appendix J – Test Summary Report Template

▶ Appendix K – Equivalence Partition Example (providing a worked example of equivalence partition analysis)

▶ Appendix L – Boundary Value Analysis Example (providing a worked example of boundary value analysis)

▶ Appendix M – State Transition Example (providing a worked example of state transition analysis)

▶ Appendix N – Pairwise Testing Example (providing a worked example of pairwise analysis)

▶ Appendix O – Automated Testing Tool Selection Criteria (providing a list of criteria to be used in the evaluation of automated testing tools and a scoring scheme)

▶ Appendix P – Usability Testing Overview

▶ Appendix Q – Testing Process Health Check (providing a set of criteria and a process for auditing testing projects)

▶ Appendix R – The Testing of Object-Oriented Software (discussing the particular challenges facing staff involved in the testing of object-oriented software).

Terms of Reference for Testing Staff

A1 Introduction

This appendix provides recommendations for the terms of reference (TORs) for the following staff involved in software testing:

▶ Testing manager
▶ Test team leader
▶ Test analyst
▶ Tester
▶ Independent test observer.

For each TOR, the following information is documented:

▶ Responsibilities
▶ Reporting and liaison
▶ Typical characteristics
▶ Appropriate references for further information.

Each TOR appears in the following pages of this appendix.

This appendix also describes the role of a typical *testing programme* board (see Chapter 4) for those organizations interested in introducing such an entity into their testing programme.

Individual TORs can be provided to the appropriate staff on testing projects, either as photocopies or electronically, as memory aids.

Testing Manager

Responsibilities

The testing manager is responsible for:

1. Setting up and resourcing new testing projects

2. Tasking one or more *test team leaders* and monitoring their progress against agreed-on plans
3. Ensuring that (where appropriate) development teams follow the *unit* and *integration* testing approach documented within the testing process
4. Assuring that (where appropriate) software development conducted by a third party follows good development and testing practice
5. Formally representing the organization during cosigning of the test certificate (Appendix H) with the representative of a third party responsible for developing bespoke software
6. Maintenance of the testing programme filing system
7. Reporting progress and issues to senior management at agreed-on intervals
8. Liaising with independent test observers to ensure good practice has been followed in testing.

Reporting and Liaison

Figure A1 shows the lines of reporting and liaison for the testing manager:

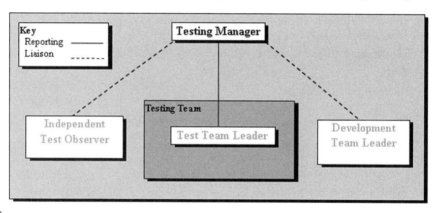

A1 Lines of Reporting and Liaison for the Test Manager

Characteristics of a Testing Manager

The characteristics of a testing manager include:

1. Good project management skills
2. Good communications skills including negotiation and diplomacy
3. Good appreciation of the software development lifecycle and the need for testing
4. Excellent project planning and monitoring skills across multiple projects and staff
5. Capability of working under pressure and being able to motivate staff.

References

1. Chapter 4 – The Management of Testing.
2. Reference 3 (PRINCE 2 Manual).

Test Team Leader

Responsibilities

The test team leader is responsible for:

1. Generating the test plan (Appendix C) and test specification documents (Appendix D)
2. Tasking one or more *test analysts* and monitoring their progress against agreed plans
3. Tasking one or more *testers* and monitoring their progress against agreed plans
4. Liaising with development teams (e.g., to determine availability date of the *application under test [AUT]*)
5. Liaising with the independent test observer, user and operations representatives
6. The set-up and maintenance of testing project filing system
7. Reporting progress and issues to the *testing manager* at agreed intervals
8. Performing other ad-hoc tasks as specified by the testing manager
9. (Potentially) managing multiple concurrent test plans across multiple AUTs.

Reporting and Liaison

Figure A2 shows the lines of reporting and liaison for the test team leader:

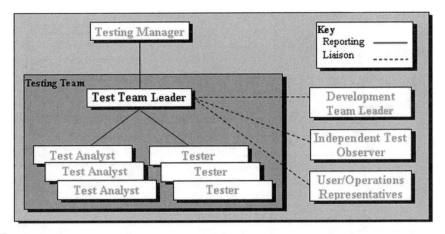

A2 Lines of Reporting and Liaison for the Test Team Leader

Characteristics of a Test Team Leader

The characteristics of a test team leader include:

1. Good communications skills including negotiation, diplomacy, and a sense of humor
2. Good appreciation of the software development lifecycle and the need for testing
3. Good project planning and monitoring skills
4. A pragmatic and practical approach

5. Capability of working under pressure and being able to motivate staff
6. Experience with automated test management tools is desirable.

References

1. Chapter 4 – The Management of Testing.
2. Reference 3 (PRINCE 2 Manual).

Test Analyst

Responsibilities

The test analyst is responsible for:

1. Helping the test team leader generate test specification and test plan documents
2. Performing testing tasks as specified by the test team leader
3. Helping the test team leader with functional analysis of the *AUT*
4. Defining the test requirements (with respect to the functional specification)
5. Designing and implementing *test cases* and *test scripts* (Appendix E)
6. Designing and implementing test data sets
7. Briefing the *tester* for the AUT prior to testing
8. The generation of reuse testing packs (Appendix I)
9. Back-up and archival of all testing documentation and materials
10. Completion of the test summary report (Appendix J).

Reporting and Liaison

The following Figure A3 shows the lines of reporting and liaison for the test analyst:

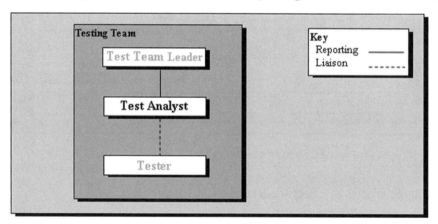

A3 Lines of Reporting and Liaison for the Test Analyst

Characteristics of a Test Analyst

The characteristics of a test analyst include:

1. Good team player with good communications skills

2. Good appreciation of the software development lifecycle and the need for testing
3. Good experience of testing and the testing process
4. A concise and structured way of working
5. Capability of completing tasks independently to an agreed plan
6. Capability of working under pressure
7. Experience with automated testing tools is desirable.

Reference

1. Chapter 4 – The Management of Testing.

Tester

Responsibilities

The tester is responsible for:

1. Performing testing tasks as specified by the *test team leader*
2. Executing *test scripts* (Appendix E)
3. Observation and documentation of test results on test result record forms (Appendix F)
4. Maintenance and retention of test result record forms
5. Identification and logging of any observed faults
6. Creation of tests for retest of fault fixes
7. Set-up and initialization of the test bed
8. Back-up and archival of the test bed
9. Recovery of the test bed in the event of failure.

Reporting and Liaison

The following Figure A4 shows the lines of reporting and liaison for the tester:

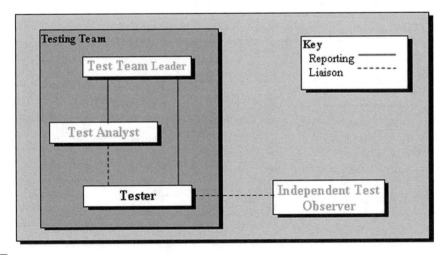

A4   Lines of Reporting and Liaison for the Tester

Characteristics of a Tester

The characteristics of a tester include:

1. Good team player
2. Good appreciation of the need for testing
3. A concise and structured way of working
4. Capability of completing tasks independently to an agreed plan
5. Capability of working under pressure
6. Experience with automated testing tools is desirable.

Reference

1. Chapter 4 – The Management of Testing.

Independent Test Observer

Responsibilities

The independent test observer should be a member of staff capable of providing independent observation of the testing project (such as a member of a quality assurance (QA) group if one exists in the organization). The independent test observer is responsible for:

1. Attending testing of the *AUT*
2. Formally witnessing that the *tester* correctly completes all *test cases*
3. Signing the appropriate section of the test result record form (Appendix F)
4. Liaising with the testing manager to report any problems observed during the testing process (or testing project board if appropriate).

Reporting and Liaison

The following Figure A5 shows the lines of reporting and liaison for the independent test observer:

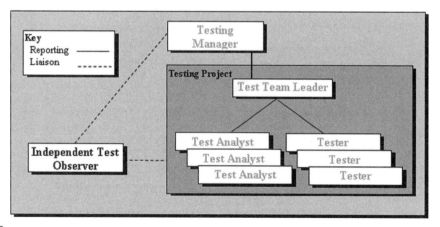

A5 Lines of Reporting and Liaison for the Independent Test Observer

Characteristics of an Independent Test Observer

The characteristics of an independent test observer include:

1. Capability to independently assess the testing project and testing activities
2. Good communications skills including assertiveness, diplomacy, and negotiation
3. Good appreciation of the need for testing
4. Good appreciation of the need for independent validation of the testing process
5. Good understanding of quality and the quality process.

References

1. Chapter 4 – The Management of Testing
2. Reference 3 (PRINCE 2 Manual)
3. Reference 14 (ISO 9001 & 9003)

Testing Programme Board

Responsibilities

Some organizations (such as those following the PRINCE project management approach) may decide to introduce the notion of a testing programme board into their testing process.

A testing programme board represents the user and developer interests of individual testing projects at senior managerial level (3). The testing programme board is likely to be composed of senior decision-makers within the organization and is responsible for the commitment of resources to the project (such as user representatives).

The seniority level of manager required to fill the roles will depend on such factors as the budget and importance of the testing programme. The testing programme board members' responsibilities will be in addition to their normal tasks, and the use of "management by exception" (i.e., keeping the board members informed of events but only requiring joint decision-making at key points in the project) is recommended.

The members of the testing programme board typically fulfill the following roles:

▶ The executive, who is ultimately accountable for the success of the testing programme, and who is responsible for ensuring that individual testing projects are conducted efficiently, balancing the demands of the business, user, and developers/suppliers

▶ The senior user, who is responsible for ensuring that the results of the testing projects yield a system that is fit for purpose, meets the user needs, and falls within the constraints of the business case for the AUT. This role represents the interests of all those staff (including operators) who will use the AUT and who has the authority to commit user resources (such as user representatives for acceptance testing)

▶ The senior supplier, who is responsible for ensuring that proposals for testing (such as test plans and the scope of testing) are realistic in terms of achieving the results required by users within the cost and time parameters for which senior management are accountable. This role represents the interests of those staff designing, developing, procuring, or maintaining the AUT.

The term testing Programme board is synonymous with the PRINCE 2 term project board (see [3] for further details).

Reporting and Liaison

The following Figure A6 shows the lines of reporting and liaison for the testing programme board:

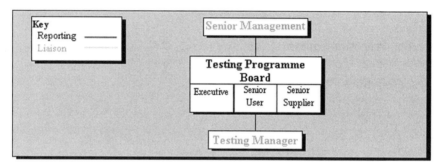

A6 Lines of Reporting and Liaison for the Testing Programme Board

Reference

1. Reference 3 (PRINCE 2 Manual).

Testing Guides

B1 Introduction

This appendix contains a number of one-page testing guides that can be used as an aide memoir for staff involved in the various phases of software testing. Full details of each of the testing phases covered in this appendix are provided in Chapters 5 to 11.

In particular, the guides are intended to be used by the *tester* (whether they be a member of the *development team* (in *unit* and *integration testing*), a member of the *testing team* or the *quality assurance group*.

This appendix contains the following testing guides:

▶ Unit testing guide
▶ Integration testing guide
▶ System testing guide
▶ Systems integration testing guide
▶ User/Operations acceptance testing guide
▶ Regression testing guide.

For each testing phase, the following summary information is provided:

▶ Purpose – a brief description of the purpose of this testing phase
▶ Approach – listing the high-level approach to conducting this testing phase
▶ Inputs – listing the inputs to this testing phase
▶ Testing techniques – listing the testing techniques appropriate to this testing phase
▶ Outputs – listing the outputs from this testing phase
▶ Quality considerations – listing a number of quality issues that should be considered within this testing phase
▶ References – further sources of information on this testing phase.

The individual testing guides should be provided to appropriate staff on testing projects, either as photocopies or electronically for reference purposes.

Unit Testing Guide

Purpose of Unit Testing

The purpose of *unit testing* is to produce reliable program units that meet their requirements. The process is primarily intended to identify errors in program logic.

Approach

1. Review unit test plan.
2. Execute and check all unit test scripts and complete the test result record form (Appendix F).
3. Ensure that each completed test result record form is countersigned by the *independent test observer*.
4. Complete unit test log during the course of the testing phase (Appendix G).
5. On completion of unit testing, provide the *development team leader* with completed test result record forms, unit test log and unit test summary report (Appendix J).

Inputs

1. Unit testing plan (from the development team leader).
2. Unit test scripts and test cases (as designed by the test analyst).
3. Blank test result record forms (from Appendix F of the testing framework document).
4. Any relevant reuse packs from previous unit testing (from the project file).

Testing Techniques (see Chapter 3)

1. *Functional testing* against the requirements for the unit under test.
2. *Static testing* (such as code review and code walkthrough).
3. *White box testing* (the structure of the unit should be known to the developer).
4. *State transition testing* (particularly where it is possible for the unit to be in a number of different states and for negative testing of the unit).
5. *Nonfunctional testing* (where appropriate, e.g., for performance, stress or reliability testing of the unit).

Outputs

1. Fully tested units.
2. Revised test cases (where appropriate).
3. Archived test data.

4. Completed test result record forms.
5. Completed unit test log.
6. Completed unit test reuse pack (Appendix I).
7. Completed unit test summary report.

Quality Considerations

1. The use of independent observation of unit tests and traceability of testing documentation (such as signed off test result record forms) is essential.
2. Where a particular unit demonstrates serious defects on testing (and on retesting), consider deleting the existing unit and rewriting it (statistics show that units [and modules] that have demonstrated poor quality during unit and integration testing are extremely likely to continue to demonstrate defects in live running).
3. Ensure adequate contingency is included in the development plans for both testing and retesting.

References

1. Chapter 5 (Unit Testing).
2. Chapter 3 (Testing Techniques).
3. Chapter 4 (The Management and Planning of Testing).
4. Glossary.

Integration Testing Guide

Purpose of Integration Testing

The purpose of *integration testing* is to demonstrate that modules that comprise the *application under test (AUT)* interface and interact together in a stable and coherent manner prior to *system testing*.

Approach

1. Review integration test plan.
2. Execute and check all integration test cases and complete the test result record form (Appendix F).
3. Ensure that each completed test result record form is countersigned by the *test observer*.
4. Complete integration test log (Appendix G).
5. On completion of integration testing, provide the *development team leader* with completed *test result record* forms, *integration test log* and *integration test summary report* (Appendix J).

Inputs

1. Integration testing plan (from the development team leader).
2. Integration test script and test cases (as designed by the test analyst).
3. Blank test result record forms.
4. Reuse packs from the unit testing phase (from the project file).

Testing Techniques (see Chapter 3)

1. *Functional testing* using *black box testing* techniques against the interfacing requirements for the module under test.
2. *Nonfunctional testing* (where appropriate, e.g., for performance or reliability testing of the module interfaces).
3. Where appropriate, some functional testing against relevant intermodule functionality (again using black box testing techniques).

Outputs

1. Fully tested and integrated modules.
2. Revised test cases (where appropriate).
3. Archived test data.
4. Completed test result record forms.
5. Completed integration test log.
6. Completed integration test reuse pack (Appendix I).
7. Completed integration test summary report.

Quality Considerations

1. Where a particular module demonstrates serious defects on testing (and on retesting), consider rewriting the module. (Statistics show that modules that have demonstrated poor quality during integration testing are likely to continue to demonstrate defects in live running.)
2. For reliability testing, consider how representative the test environment is of the live system (e.g., has the volume of background network traffic been simulated accurately).

References

1. Chapter 6 (Integration Testing).
2. Chapter 3 (Testing Techniques).
3. Chapter 4 (The Management and Planning of Testing)
4. Glossary.

System Testing Guide

Purpose of System Testing

The purpose of *system testing* is to establish confidence that the system will be accepted by the users (and/or operators) and to avoid errors in the live system that will have an adverse impact on the business from a functional, financial, or image perspective.

Approach

1. Review system test plan.
2. Execute and check all system test cases and complete the test result record form (Appendix F).
3. Ensure that each completed test result record form is countersigned by the *independent test observer*.
4. Complete system test log (Appendix G).
5. On completion of system testing, provide the *test team leader* with completed test result record forms, system test log and system test summary report (Appendix J).

Inputs

1. System testing plan (from the test team leader).
2. System test script and test cases (from the test analyst).
3. Blank test result record forms.
4. Reuse packs from the unit and integration testing phases (from the project file).

Testing Techniques (see Chapter 3)

1. *Black box testing* against high-level system requirements.
2. *Thread testing* against the high-level business requirements for the AUT.
3. *Nonfunctional testing* (such as volume, stress, and performance testing).
4. *Static testing* (e.g., review of system documentation, such as user manuals).

Outputs

1. The tested system.
2. Revised test cases (where appropriate).
3. Archived test data.
4. Completed test result record forms.
5. Completed system test log.

6. Completed system test reuse pack (Appendix I).
7. Completed system test summary report.

Quality Considerations

1. What development methodology has been used for the system under test?
2. Is the hardware/operating system/network software mature and robust?
3. Is the quality of the test data adequate?
4. Where appropriate, has it been possible to simulate appropriate load/stress/volume that the live system will be exposed to?

References

1. Chapter 7 (System Testing).
2. Chapter 3 (Testing Techniques).
3. Chapter 4 (The Management and Planning of Testing).
4. Glossary.

Systems Integration Testing Guide

Purpose of Systems Integration Testing

The purpose of *systems integration testing* is to provide confidence that the *application under test (AUT)* is able to successfully interoperate with other specified systems and does not have an adverse affect on other systems that may also be present in the live operating environment or *vice versa*.

Approach

1. Review systems integration test plan.
2. Execute and check all systems integration test cases and complete the test result record form (Appendix F).
3. Ensure that each completed test result record form is countersigned by the *test observer*.
4. Complete systems integration test log (Appendix G).
5. On completion of systems integration testing, provide the *test team leader* with completed test result record forms, systems integration test log, and systems integration summary report (Appendix J).

Inputs

1. Systems integration testing plan (from the test team leader).

2. Systems integration test script and test cases (from the *test analyst*).
3. Blank test result record forms.
4. The reuse packs from the *unit, integration, and system testing phases* (from the project file).

Testing Techniques (see Chapter 3)

1. *Black box testing* against high-level system requirements (and specifically, those requirements addressing interoperability issues).
2. *Thread testing* against the high-level business requirements for the AUT (again, focusing on interoperability requirements).
3. *Negative testing* and *error guessing* to uncover unanticipated problems (such as contention for system resources).

Outputs

1. The integrated system.
2. Revised test cases (where appropriate).
3. Archived test data.
4. Completed test result record forms.
5. Complete systems integration test log.
6. Complete systems integration test reuse pack (Appendix I).
7. Complete systems integration test summary report.

Quality Considerations

1. Systems integration testing must take place on the live environment. (Using a separate test environment should only be considered if there are pressing reasons not to use the live system, and if the alternate environment can accurately represent the live system.)
2. Consider tool use to monitor system resource usage (e.g., to identify contention for resources).
3. Ensure test analyst is both experienced and knowledgeable about the AUT and the live system (this is particularly valuable in the negative testing).

References

1. Chapter 8 (Systems Integration Testing).
2. Chapter 3 (Testing Techniques).
3. Chapter 4 (The Management and Planning of Testing).
4. Glossary.

User/Operations Acceptance Testing Guide

Purpose of Acceptance Testing

The purpose of *acceptance testing* is to confirm that the system meets its business requirements and to provide confidence that the system works correctly and is usable before it is formally "handed over" to the user(s) (either the *end user* or the *operations user*).

Approach

1. Review acceptance test plan.
2. Execute and check all acceptance test cases and complete the test result record form (Appendix F).
3. Ensure that each completed test result record form is countersigned by the *test observer*.
4. Complete acceptance test log (Appendix G).
5. On completion of acceptance testing, provide the *test team leader* with completed test result record forms, acceptance test log, and acceptance test summary report (Appendix J).

Inputs

1. System testing plan (from the test team leader).
2. System test script and test cases (from the *test analyst*).
3. Blank test result record forms.
4. The reuse pack from the *system* and *integration testing phases* (from the project file).

Testing Techniques (see Chapter 3)

1. *Black box testing* against high-level system requirements.
2. *Thread testing* against the high-level business requirements for the AUT.
3. Static testing (e.g., review of system documentation, such as user manuals).

Outputs

1. The user accepted system.
2. Revised test cases (where appropriate).
3. Archived test data.
4. Completed test result record forms.
5. Completed acceptance test log.

6. Completed acceptance test reuse pack (Appendix I).
7. Completed acceptance test summary report.

Quality Considerations

1. Reuse of system test materials (e.g., system test cases) wherever possible.
2. It is essential that user representatives be chosen with appropriate experience and skills.

References

1. Chapters 9 (User Acceptance) and 10 (Operations Acceptance).
2. Chapter 3 (Testing Techniques).
3. Chapter 4 (The Management and Planning of Testing).
4. Glossary.

Regression Testing Guide

Purpose of Regression Testing

The purpose of *regression testing* is to ensure that the *application under test (AUT)* still functions correctly following modification or extension of the system (such as user enhancements or upgrades or following new builds or releases of the software).

Approach

1. Review regression test plan.
2. Execute and check all regression test cases and complete the test result record form (Appendix F).
3. Ensure that each completed test result record form is countersigned by the *test observer*.
4. Complete regression test log (Appendix G).
5. On completion of regression testing, provide the *test team leader* with completed test result record forms, regression test log, and regression test summary report (Appendix J).

Inputs

1. Regression Testing Plan (from the test team leader).
2. Regression test script and test cases (from the *test analyst*).
3. Blank test result record forms.
4. Reuse packs from previous testing phases (from the project file).

Testing Techniques (see Chapter 3)

1. *Black box testing* against high-level system requirements.
2. *Thread testing* against the high-level business requirements for the AUT.
3. *Nonfunctional testing* (such as volume, stress, and performance testing), where appropriate.

Outputs

1. The regression tested system.
2. Revised test cases (where appropriate).
3. Archived test data.
4. Completed test result record forms.
5. Completed regression test log.
6. Completed regression test reuse pack (Appendix I).
7. Completed regression test summary report.

Quality Considerations

1. Reuse of test cases from earlier testing phases (and in particular from system testing) is key.
2. Test expertise must be employed to anticipate the impact of the effect of enhancements/extensions to the AUT and its existing functionality.
3. Consider the role of automated testing tools in performing regression testing.

References

1. Chapter 11 (Regression Testing).
2. Chapter 3 (Testing Techniques).
3. Chapter 4 (The Management and Planning of Testing).
4. Glossary.

Test Plan Document Template

C1 Introduction

This appendix contains a template for a *test plan document*, guidance on its use, and where appropriate, examples of the typical contents of such a document. This template may be used as the basis of a test plan document for a particular test phase.

An electronic version of this template can be downloaded from the following link: http://www.cambridge.org/9780521148016 (or, assuming the role has been implemented, a copy can be obtained from the *testing manager* or equivalent role).

As described in Chapter 4 (The Management and Planning of Testing), each testing project must generate a test plan as one of the documents produced prior to the commencement of testing activities.

Where text appears within the body of the template in angle brackets ($<$ $>$), this denotes a place marker, which must be replaced with the appropriate information for a particular testing phase.

Text that appears in *italic* is provided for information only (such as illustrative examples) and should not appear in the final test plan document.

Where references to "Appendices" appear within this appendix, these refer to other appendices in this book. The term "Annex" is used to refer to supplementary sections within this template.

The principal approach to be used in writing a test plan document is to keep it brief and simple. Make best use of the supporting information presented in this book (such as other relevant template appendices), as well as pertinent material from the appropriate testing phase chapters.

Test Plan Document Front Sheet

Document Information {to <Client> Doc Standard}	
Project ID:	<Project ID> *the unique ID for this testing project*
Document Ref:	<Doc Ref> *a unique document reference for this document*
Testing Phase:	<Testing Phase> *the testing phase (e.g., unit test)*
AUT Title:	<AUT Title> *the definitive title of the application under test*
Date:	<Date> *the date this document was completed*

Distribution	
Copy Number	**Recipient**
1.	<activity leader> *i.e., development team leader for unit and link testing, test team leader for system test.*
2.	<Test Analyst> *i.e., the person designing and developing the test cases*
N.	Project File

Review & Approval	
Issue:	<issue status> *issue status of the document, e.g., draft, 1.0.*
R&A Number:	<R&A reference> *the reference to the final approving review*
Author	<name of the author>
Author Signature	<signature of author> *the person who wrote this document*
Approval (PM)	<name of the project manager>
Approval (PM) Signature	<signature of the project manager >
Approval (QA)	<name of the quality assurance representative>
Approval (QA) Signature	<signature of the quality assurance representative>

Contents

1 Introduction

    1.1 Background
    1.2 Structure of the Document
    1.3 References

2 Test Approach and Constraints

    2.1 Introduction
    2.2 Test Objectives
    2.3 Test Constraints

3 Risks and Dependencies

    3.1 Introduction
    3.2 Risks
    3.3 Dependencies

4 Test Assumptions and Exclusions

    4.1 Introduction
    4.2 Assumptions
    4.3 Exclusions

5 Entry and Exit Criteria

    5.1 Introduction
    5.2 Entry Criteria
    5.3 Exit Criteria

6 Testing Project Controls

    6.1 Introduction
    6.2 Roles and Responsibilities
    6.3 Training Requirements
    6.4 Problem Reporting
    6.5 Progress Reporting

Annex A Test Plan

1 Introduction

1.1 Background

This document provides the plan for completing testing activities required for the <Testing Phase> testing of the <AUT Title>.

This section should contain a brief background and history of this testing project, which should include:

a) *a brief description of the purpose of the AUT*
b) *definitive version information for the AUT*
c) *any other relevant supporting information.*

1.2 Structure of the Document

This document is structured in the following manner:

1) Chapter 2 describes the approach to testing including the objectives of the project and any constraints
2) Chapter 3 describes the risks and dependencies associated with the testing project
3) Chapter 4 lists the test assumptions and exclusions
4) Chapter 5 documents the entry and exit criteria for testing
5) Chapter 6 lists the project controls to be employed in the testing project
6) Annex A provides a <type of plan> plan of the testing project {such as a man power and milestone plan or a Gantt chart. If a project management or planning tool is used on the project, it may be possible to obtain a hard copy of the plan to insert into the annex}.

1.3 References

A numbered list of documents referenced within this document, e.g.,

    <list of references to overall project documents>

      1) <Project authorization document>
      2) <Overall project plan>
      3) <Quality assurance plan>
      4) <Configuration management plan>
      5) <Relevant policies referenced within this document>
      6) <Relevant standards referenced within this document>

    <list of references to items specific to this testing project>

      7) <AUT Title> Functional specification (version N.N), <date>
      8) <AUT Title> Design specification (version N.N), <date>
      9) <AUT Title> Users guide (version N.N), <date> (if appropriate)

10) <AUT Title> Operations guide (version N.N), <date> (if appropriate)

11) <AUT Title> Installation guide (version N.N), <date> (if appropriate).

2 Test Approach and Constraints

2.1 Introduction

This chapter describes the overall approach to be used in testing the AUT and constraints that may apply. These will be used at a high level to support planning of the testing project.

This chapter also documents the use of any particular testing tool (such as an automated record/playback tool) and its details (version number, release information, etc.), or project support tool (such as a project planning or project metrics tools).

2.2 Test Objectives

This section lists the high-level objectives of the testing project. *For example, in regression testing a particular AUT, the objectives might include – "the regression testing process will specifically consider just the functionality of the AH51 module modified during the extensions to the system and any interfaces between this module and other related modules."*

It will also be appropriate to list any exclusions. For example, in regression testing a particular AUT, the objectives might include – "the regression testing will not address any load or performance issues."

2.3 Test Constraints

This section lists constraints that may apply to the testing project. *For example, in regression testing a particular AUT, the objectives might include – "Regression testing must be complete (including correction of errors and retesting) by the Nth of October 2005 for scheduled release to beta test client site."*

3 Risks and Dependencies

3.1 Introduction

This chapter documents the risks and dependencies that apply to this testing project. These will be used at a high level to support the planning of the testing project.

3.2 Risks

This section documents risks that may have a deleterious impact on the testing project. The occurrence, impact, and likelihood of these risks must be reviewed during the testing project, and procedures for mitigation/recovery must be documented.

The level of rigor employed in the process of identifying risks will depend on a number of factors including:

1) the business criticality of the AUT
2) safety criticality of the AUT
3) whether the AUT is to be used "in-house" or supplied to a client.

Although typically the process of identifying risks to the testing project is conducted in an informal manner, relying on the experience of the testing staff (and in particular the test team leader/development leader), a number of tools and methods are available (e.g., see Reference 11).

For example, in regression testing a particular AUT, the following risk might have been identified – "It is possible that the latest version of the operating system, which was planned to be used for testing the AUT, will not be available from the manufacturer in time for the planned testing start date. In the event that this occurs, testing will proceed using the current version of the operating system software, with a subset of regression tests to be rerun as and when the new version of the operating system becomes available."

3.3 Dependencies

This section documents events that must take place as a prerequisite to any planned events within the testing project. The progress of these dependencies must be reviewed during the testing project to determine their impact on the testing project timescales.

Dependencies can be categorized as:

1) internal – that is, a dependency originating within the testing project
2) external – that is, a dependency originating outside of the testing project.

For example, in regression testing a particular AUT, an internal dependency might include – "The start of the testing process by the tester is dependent on receipt of the test script and test cases from the test analyst."

For example, in regression testing a particular AUT, an external dependency might include – "The testing start date is dependent on the delivery by the software development team of version N.N of the AUT."

4 Test Assumptions and Exclusions

4.1 Introduction

This chapter provides greater detail about the testing process, and in particular assumptions that have been made for the purposes of the testing project, precisely what issues will be addressed by the testing, and what issues will not be addressed.

4.2 Assumptions

This section lists assumptions that have been made for the purposes of the testing project. It also lists specific aspects of the AUT to be tested.

For example, in regression testing a particular AUT, the following assumptions have been made:

1) the testing project will test:
    ▷ the functionality of the AH51 module
    ▷ the interface between module AH51 and AH52
    ▷ the interface between module AH51 and AH53
2) the database server will be live during the entirety of the testing process
3) access will be available to the test rig outside of normal working hours.

4.3 Exclusions

This section lists items not to be included in the testing project.

For example, in regression testing a particular AUT, the following exclusions have been made:

1) the testing project will not test:
    ▷ performance aspects of the AH51 module
    ▷ load aspects of the AH51 module
    ▷ the interface between the AH51 module and the AH50 module
2) it is not necessary for a user representative to be present during testing
3) testing tool support will not be necessary for this testing project.

5 Entry and Exit Criteria

5.1 Introduction

This chapter documents criteria that must be satisfied before testing can begin as well as criteria to be satisfied for testing to finish. This information is recorded to provide a clear and unambiguous means of determining whether to start or stop testing.

5.2 Entry Criteria

This section lists entry criteria for the testing project.

For example, in regression testing a particular AUT, the following entry criteria have been specified:

1) the test environment has been set up (and tested)
2) the amended (to reflect changes to the AUT) requirements specification document has been received
3) the final copy of the amended AUT has been received from the development team and has been installed on the test environment

4) the latest version of the operating system required for testing has been installed on the test environment
5) the test project has been appropriately resourced.

5.3 Exit Criteria

This section lists exit criteria for halting the testing process.
For example:

1) there are no outstanding defects
2) the observed defects are below an agreed profile, such as:
    ▷ no critical defects, and less than N severe defects
    ▷ N hours testing time without observing a defect
    ▷ a complete run (or rerun) through the test script with no defects
3) some budgetary criterion, such as:
    ▷ the assigned testing budget has been exceeded
    ▷ the assigned testing effort has been exceeded
4) some scheduling criterion, such as:
    ▷ testing must stop to allow planned delivery of AUT
    ▷ testing must stop to allow planned development of AUT (e.g., unit testing must be complete by a certain date to allow integration of the AUT to begin)
5) testing must stop because the AUT is unfit for this level of testing, that is, the AUT is of such poor quality that further testing would be a waste of effort.

6   Testing Project Controls

6.1 Introduction

This chapter documents the staff involved in the testing project, roles and responsibilities, and the manner in which problems and progress will be reported.
The precise details for each of the following sections will need to be tailored to match the particular testing phase (see appropriate chapter of this testing framework document) and the specific testing requirements for the AUT (see test specification document – Appendix D).

6.2 Roles and Responsibilities

This section specifies the names, roles, and responsibilities of the staff involved in the testing project.
For example, for a system test project, the following roles would need to be documented:

1) Test team leader – Carol Jenkins

2) Test analyst – Martin Stemp
3) Tester – Chris Dodsworth
4) User representative – Angela Jones
5) Independent test observer – Lesley Williams.

6.3 Training Requirements

This section documents any particular training needs for the staff involved in the testing.

For example, the test analyst and tester may require training with the AUT to gain familiarity with the user interface to improve effectiveness during the design and execution of the tests.

6.4 Problem Reporting

This section documents the manner in which defects observed during testing are recorded and reported to the appropriate staff.

For example, all defects observed during system testing will be recorded on the appropriate test result record form (see Appendix F). All such defects will be reviewed during the post-test review meeting, where the test team leader and the development team leader shall discuss the scope of remedial work to the AUT, timescales for correction, and any test case(s) that need to be rerun as a result of the remedial work.

If a test management tool or defect reporting tool is being used within a particular testing project, the tool information and the process by which it will be used should also be documented here.

6.5 Progress Reporting

This section documents the frequency, scope, and detail of testing project progress reporting and describes the staff involved in the process.

For example, the test team leader shall issue a weekly progress report. This report will include:

1) planned versus actual progress
2) revised estimates and their justification
3) any outstanding problems and issues.

The report will be issued to:

a) the testing manager
b) test analyst
c) tester
d) independent test observer.

The test team leader will convene a fortnightly progress meeting to report on the testing project progress. The following staff should be invited:

a) Testing manager
b) Development team leader
c) User representative
d) Independent test observer.

A Test Plan

This annex contains a <type of plan> plan of the testing project *{such as a man power and milestone plan or a Gantt chart. If a project management or planning tool is being used on the project, it may be possible to obtain a hard copy to insert into the annex}.*
   As a minimum, the <type of plan> should include the following items:

1) timescales for each task
2) milestones
3) dependencies
4) ...

The V Model (Chapter 4) can be used to provide useful guidance during planning aspects of the testing project.

Test Specification Document Template

D1 Introduction

This appendix contains a template for a test specification document, guidance on its use, and where appropriate, examples of the typical contents of such a document. This template may be used as the basis of a test specification document for a particular test phase.

An electronic version of this template can be downloaded from the following link: http://www.cambridge.org/9780521148016 (or, assuming the role has been implemented, a copy can be obtained from the testing manager or equivalent role).

As described in Chapter 4 (The Management and Planning of Testing), each testing project must generate a test specification as one of the documents produced prior to commencement of testing activities.

Where text appears within the body of the template in angle brackets (< >), this denotes a place marker, which must be replaced with the appropriate information for a particular testing phase.

Text appearing in *italic* is provided for information only (such as illustrative examples) and should not appear in the final test specification document.

Where references to "Appendices" appear within this appendix, these refer to other appendices in this book. The term "Annex" is used to refer to supplementary sections within this template.

The principal approach to be used in writing a test specification document is to keep it brief and simple. Make best use of the supporting information presented in this book (such as other relevant template appendices), as well as pertinent material from the appropriate testing phase chapters.

Test Specification Document Front Sheet

Document Information {to <Client> Doc Standard}	
Project ID:	<Project ID> *the unique ID for this testing project*
Document Ref:	<Doc Ref> *a unique document reference for this document*
Testing Phase:	<Testing Phase> *the testing phase (e.g., unit test)*
AUT Title:	<AUT Title> *the definitive title of the application under test*
Date:	<Date> *the date this document was completed*

Distribution	
Copy Number	**Recipient**
1.	<activity leader> *i.e., development team leader for unit and link testing, test team leader for system test*
2.	<Test Analyst> *i.e., the person designing and developing the test cases*
N.	Project File

Review & Approval	
Issue:	<issue status> *issue status of the document, e.g., draft, 1.0*
R&A Number:	<R&A reference> *the reference to the final approving review*
Author	<name of the author>
Author Signature	<signature of author> *the person who wrote this document*
Approval (PM)	<name of the project manager>
Approval (PM) Signature	<signature of the project manager>
Approval (QA)	<name of the quality assurance representative>
Approval (QA) Signature	<signature of the quality assurance representative>

Contents

1 Introduction

1.1 Background

This document provides the specification for the testing activities required for the <Testing Phase> testing of the <AUT Title>.

This section should contain a brief background to this testing project, which should include:

a) a brief description of the purpose of the AUT
b) definitive version information for the AUT
c) any other relevant supporting information.

1.2 Scope

This document contains both the requirement for and the specification of the <AUT Title> <Testing Phase> test.

This section should contain any specific information on the scope of this testing (e.g., if the testing activity does not address nonfunctional testing of the AUT, this should be stated).

1.3 Structure of the Document

This document is structured in the following manner:

a) Chapter 2 documents the <Testing Phase> test requirement for conducting <Testing Phase> testing on the <AUT Title> system
b) Chapter 3 describes the high-level activities comprising the <Testing Phase> test
c) Annex A contains a list of the Test Cases to be employed in testing <AUT Title>.

1.4 References

A numbered list of documents referenced within this document. For example:

<list of references to overall project documents>

1) <Project authorization document>
2) <Overall project plan>
3) <Quality assurance plan>
4) <Configuration management plan>
5) <Relevant policies referenced within this document>
6) <Relevant standards referenced within this document>

<list of references to items specific to this testing project>

7) <AUT Title> Test plan document (version N.N), <date>
8) <AUT Title> Functional specification (version N.N), <date>
9) <AUT Title> Design specification (version N.N), <date>
10) <AUT Title> Users guide (version N.N), <date> (if appropriate)
11) <AUT Title> Operations guide (version N.N), <date> (if appropriate)
12) <AUT Title> Installation guide (version N.N), <date> (if appropriate).

2 Test Requirement

2.1 Introduction

This chapter documents the test requirement for conducting <Testing Phase> testing on the <AUT Title> system.

Testing will be against the functional specification (1), plus any other test instructions specified within this document.

The structure of this chapter is as follows: Section 2.2 describes the philosophy behind the <Testing Phase> test process, Section 2.3 describes the requirements for the <Testing Phase> test environment, and Section 2.4 describes the test procedures to be used during the <Testing Phase> testing.

2.2 Test Philosophy

2.2.1 Overview

This section provides a brief overview of the purpose and goals of this testing activity.

The author should consider cutting and pasting selected sections from the "Overview" section of the appropriate testing phase chapter of this framework document (e.g., Chapter 5 unit testing, etc.).

The overview should also contain a statement describing what the basis of developing the tests will be. For example, the individual <Testing Phase> tests will be derived from the functional specification document (1).

Finally, the overview should state on what version of the AUT the testing will take place. For example, acceptance testing will be performed on the final delivered system (vN.N).

2.2.2 Functional Areas

This section describes the general areas of functionality tested as part of the <Testing Phase> test: For example:

a) user interface, including help system
b) on-line query and maintenance facilities
c) error handling
d) remote operation of the system.

2.2.3 Test Result Categories

This section describes the test result categories assigned as the result of conducting individual test cases. For example:

There are five categories of test result, of which four represent an error state (i.e., a deviation of the observed result from the expected result). The categories are as follows:

a) Pass – the observed test result conforms to the expected result
b) Test error – the observed result is correct, but the expected result is incorrect (e.g., a typographical error in the test script)
c) Acceptable – the observed result indicates that the system differs from the agreed specification but is acceptable, requiring no change to the AUT but requiring a change to the functional specification
d) Tolerable – the observed result is incorrect, the AUT is workable and shall be accepted, but the fault must be rectified within an agreed time
e) Intolerable – the observed result is incorrect and the fault must be corrected before the AUT passes this testing phase.

On completion of each test, one of the previous test result categories shall be assigned to the test case by the tester.

2.2.4 Exclusions

This section lists any areas or aspects of the AUT that will not be considered for testing within this testing project. For example:

The user acceptance test will exclude testing of the system administration functions, because these will be testing during operations acceptance testing.

2.3 Test Environment

2.3.1 Overview

This section provides a brief overview of the test environment and should include:

a) where the testing is to take place (i.e., which <Client> site/department)
b) which computer facilities (e.g., standalone PCs, <Client> network)
c) any other relevant supporting information.

2.3.2 Hardware

This section provides definitive information on the hardware to be used for this testing activity. For example:

The acceptance test will be conducted using the following hardware:

a) a twin node DEC VAX cluster consisting of:
   i) VAX 6410 of 32Mbytes memory
   ii) VAX 8550 of 48Mbytes memory.

b) VT220 terminal
c) HP Laserjet 4Si printer.

2.3.3 Software

This section provides definitive information on the software to be used for this testing activity (including operating system details and any ancillary system details, such as networking software). For example:

The acceptance test will be conducted using the following software:

a) <AUT Title> (<version information>)
b) VAX VMS operating system (v 5.4)
c) Oracle RDBMS (v 6.0).

2.3.4 Test Data

This section specifies the data that will be used for purposes of the testing, as well as any exceptions or exclusions. For example:

The acceptance test will be conducted using live data. No items of "handcrafted" data will be used during the test.

2.4 Staff Roles and Responsibilities

This section specifies the staff who will be expected to attend the <Testing Phase> test, the roles they will perform, and their responsibilities.

Unless there are significant departures from the roles and responsibilities outlined in the appropriate testing phase chapter of this book (such as Chapter 5 – Unit Testing), "cutting and pasting" that section or providing a reference to the appropriate section will be sufficient.

If there are any exceptions or exclusions to the standard roles and responsibilities, these should be stated. For example:

During the user acceptance test, the user role will be represented by a committee of five users.

2.5 Test Identification

2.5.1 Test Scripts

Each individual test case shall have a script that will describe how the test shall be conducted and the expected result. (Annex A provides a list of the individual test cases.) In particular, the script shall contain the following information:

a) a unique test identifier
b) a description of the purpose of the test
c) a brief description of the state of the AUT prior to the test (e.g., for the purposes of this test, the tester shall begin the test with the AUT in the start up screen.

The working database shall be loaded, and the cursor shall be in the login name field of the login dialog box).

d) the precise and unambiguous steps required to execute the test

e) a brief description of the expected results.

See Appendix E for a test script template. An electronic version of this template is available from the following link – http://www.cambridge.org/9780521148016.

2.5.2 Result Reporting

The test results shall be recorded on a test result record form. This form will record the following information:

a) the AUT title and version

b) the testing phase (e.g., unit test)

c) the date of the test

d) a unique test identifier

e) the time of execution of each test case

f) the observed test result

g) the assigned test result category (as documented in Section 2.3.3 of this document)

h) a test error description (in the event that the assigned test result category is test error)

i) the signature of the tester and test observer (plus any other signatures appropriate to the particular testing phase).

See Appendix F for a test result record form template. An electronic version of this template is available from the following link – http://www.cambridge. org/9780521148016.

2.5.3 Acceptance Criteria

This section documents the frequencies of the test result categories (see Section 2.3.3) considered acceptable for the AUT to pass this testing phase. For example:

The AUT shall be deemed acceptable and the <Testing Phase> test certificate signed when:

a) there are no outstanding intolerable faults

b) there are fewer than five tolerable faults.

This section may also consider a number of general criteria that could be satisfied to accept the AUT:

a) Test requirements – has it been demonstrated that all the requirements for the AUT have been verified?

b) Test coverage – has it been demonstrated that all "parts" of the software have been exercised during testing (including exception handling and error handling routines)?

c) Test case metric – how many test cases have been planned, designed, implemented, executed, and passed or failed? This is a useful metric to collect to measure progress of the testing activity

d) Defect detection metric – has the rate of defect detection been plotted and has the rate of detection of defects leveled off? A reasonable indication that the majority of the defects have been detected (however, caution must be exercised, because tester fatigue could also produce a similar result).

2.5.4 Test Error Clearance

Where errors have been observed and recorded during testing, this section specifies the process by which the scope and mechanism for rectifying the errors is to be achieved. For example:

For each observed error that requires further work to the AUT or the functional specification, the user representative, test team leader, and development team leader shall formally agree to the following:

a) the scope of rework and timescales for correction

b) the test case (or test cases) required to be rerun following correction.

Any such rework made to the <AUT Title> system shall be made under strict change management procedures.

2.5.5 Test Documentation

This section describes the documents that shall be generated in support of the test activity. These documents are as follows:

a) the test script and component test cases

b) test results in the form of completed test result record forms

c) a test report briefly summarizing the test results and any outstanding actions

d) a test certificate to formally record that the AUT has passed the testing *(see Appendix H for a test certificate template).*

3 Test Procedure

3.1 Introduction

This chapter describes how the <Testing Phase> test will be performed.

This chapter is structured as follows: Section 3.2 describes those activities that must be completed before testing can begin; Section 3.3 describes those activities that take place during the <Testing Phase> test; Section 3.4 describes those activities that take place after the <Testing Phase> test.

3.2 Pre-test Activities

This section describes the activities that must be completed prior to the testing of the AUT.

3.2.1 Test Environment

This section describes what must be done in setting up the test environment for the testing. For example:

> *The test team leader will contact the system manager to ensure that the live system will be available for the testing and that live system data is available for the acceptance test.*

3.2.2 Test Timescales

The <AUT Title> <Testing Phase> test start date will be agreed in consultation with <staff involved in the testing> *(see the Roles and Responsibilities section of the appropriate testing phase chapter for further details).*

The period allowed for the completion of the test will be <time period> (as determined from the Testing Plan).

It may also be appropriate to specify how much time will be allowed for retest following correction of errors. Although it may be difficult to provide an estimate, one rule of thumb would suggest that retest should take less time than the original testing period.

3.2.3 Test Liaison

This section documents the requirements for liaison with other staff. For example:

> *The test team leader shall liaise with the development team leader to agree to the delivery date of the AUT for testing.*

> *The test team leader shall liaise with the test observer to ensure that they can attend the testing.*

> *The test team leader shall liaise with the user representative to ensure that they can attend the testing.*

3.2.4 Test Script Preparation

The test analyst shall, with reference to the functional specification for the AUT and any other specific instructions, prepare a test script and component test cases.

3.3 Conducting the Test

3.3.1 Test Execution Procedure

The tester shall execute the individual test cases comprising the <Testing Phase> test in the order in which they appear in the test script.

For each test case, the tester shall follow the instructions specified in the test script for executing that test case.

Following the completion of each test case, the tester shall complete a test result record form, assigning a test result category for that test case by observation and interpretation of the test result, and signing the test result record form for each test case.

The independent observer shall observe this process to ensure the tester follows the correct procedure, and to witness this fact by signing the test result record form for each test case.

3.3.2 Filing of Completed Test Result Record Forms

Completed test result record forms shall be provided to the test team leader for filing and subsequent review at the post-testing review.

3.4 Post-test Activities

This section describes the activities that must be completed following the testing. For example:

> *Following the completion of the <Testing Phase> test, a review meeting shall be convened with the objective of:*
>
> a) reviewing the test result record forms
> b) determining whether the AUT passes the <Testing Phase> test.
>
> *If any test observations require further work on the AUT or its functional specification, the following shall be agreed:*
>
> a) the scope of further work and the timescales for correction
> b) the test case (or test cases) that need to be rerun.
>
> *A test certificate will be issued to formally show that the AUT has passed its <Testing Phase> test.*
>
> *Back-up and archival of the test assets (AUT, test data set(s), testing procedures, test cases, description of test rig).*
>
> *Lessons Learned.*

Annex A Test Cases

This annex contains a list of the test cases to be designed, implemented, and executed during testing of <AUT>.

For each test case, the following information is documented:

1) the unique identifier for the test case
2) a reference to the requirements this test case will test
3) a brief description of the test case
4) any other supporting information.

Test Script Template

E1 Introduction

This appendix contains a test script template that may be copied and used to record the information necessary for conducting each test comprising a particular testing phase. An electronic version of the template can be obtained using the following link: http://www.cambridge.org/9780521148016/.

A completed example of a test script (Figure E1) is also included at the end of this appendix for guidance.

For each test, a separate test script will need to be completed by the *test analyst*. Each test script contains the following sections:

▶ Project ID – the unique project identifier
▶ AUT title – the definitive title of the *application under test* (front sheet only)
▶ AUT version – the definitive version information for the AUT (front sheet only)
▶ Testing phase – the title of the phase of testing being conducted (e.g., *unit test*, *integration test*, *system test*, etc.) (front sheet only)
▶ Date of test – the planned start date of testing (front sheet only)
▶ Test ID – the unique identifier for the test
▶ Purpose of test – a brief description of the purpose of the test including a reference where appropriate to the requirement that is to be tested (consider providing references to the requirements specification, design specification, user guide, operations guide, and/or installation guide), as well as any dependencies from or to other test scripts/test cases
▶ Test environment – a brief description of the environment under which the test is to be conducted (may include a description of the state of the AUT at the start of this test, details regarding the platform or operating system, as well as specific information about data used in this test)
▶ Test steps – concise, accurate, and unambiguous instructions describing the precise steps the tester must take to execute the test, including navigation through the AUT as well as inputs and outputs

▶ Expected result – a brief and unambiguous description of the expected result of executing the test.

Where text appears in angle brackets (< >), this denotes a place marker, which must be replaced with the appropriate information for a particular testing phase. For example <Client> should be replaced by the name of your own company or organization.

Where the test script template provided in this appendix does not precisely match the requirements of a particular testing project, the *test team leader* should obtain an electronic copy of this template and modify it as required.

<Client> Test Script		*(front sheet)*
Project ID		
AUT Title	**Version**	
Testing Phase	**Date of Test**	

Test ID	
Purpose of Test	
Test Environment	
Test Steps	
Expected Result	
	Page 1 of Pages

	\<Client\> Test Script		*(continuation sheet)*
Project ID			

Test ID	
Purpose of Test	
Test Environment	
Test Steps	
Expected Result	
	Page of Pages

Lime Telecoms Test Script			(*front sheet*)
Project ID	P1234A		
AUT Title	Market*Master (M*M)	**Version**	v1.1
Testing Phase	User Acceptance	**Date of Test**	31/8/2000

Test ID	P1234A/PM5.5/1
Purpose of Test	To ensure that: • M*M can be run • the user can log in successfully.
Test Environment	Windows 2000 Start Up window. No other applications should be running. Hand crafted "login data" is held in C:\test-dir\login.dat.
Test Steps	Invoke the M*M application using the Windows 2000 Start menu. In the login dialog box, the Tester should: • left click into the "User Name" field and enter "testuser" • left click into the "Password" field and enter "password" • left click on the "OK" button.
Expected Result	On completing the above steps, the M*M application should startup. Once started, the M*M "Start Up" screen should be displayed (Title Bar contains the legend - "M*M Start Up Screen."
	Page 1 of 1 Page

E1 Completed Example Test Script

Test Result Record Form Template

F1 Introduction

This appendix contains a test result record form template that may be copied and used to record the result of the individual *test cases* comprising a particular test phase. An electronic version of the template can be obtained using the following link: http://www.cambridge.org/9780521148016/.

The test result record form contains the following sections:

▶ Project ID – the unique project identifier
▶ AUT title – the definitive title of the *application under test* (front sheet only)
▶ AUT version – the definitive version information for the AUT (front sheet only)
▶ Testing phase – the title of the phase of testing being conducted (e.g., unit test, integration test, system test) (front sheet only)
▶ Date of test – the date on which the test was performed (front sheet only)
▶ The names of the tester and the test observer
▶ Test ID – the unique identifier for the test
▶ Time of test – the time at which each individual test case was started
▶ Observed test result – a brief textual description of the result of the test
▶ Test result category – the *test result category* assigned to this test (as specified from the *test specification* document for this testing phase – see Appendix D)
▶ Test error description – a brief textual description (if appropriate) of the observed *test error*
▶ Tester signature – the signature of the *tester*, recording participation in the test, observation of the result of the test, and agreement to the documented test result
▶ Test observer signature – the signature of the *independent test observer*, recording observation of the result of the test and agreement to the documented test result.

With the exception of the last item, these sections of the test result record form will be completed by the tester in consultation with the independent test observer and any other staff attending the testing phase in an official capacity (such as the *user representative* in *user acceptance testing*).

Where text appears in angle brackets ($<$ $>$), this denotes a place marker, which must be replaced with the appropriate information for a particular testing phase. For example $<$Client$>$ should be replaced by the name of your own company or organization.

Where the template provided in this appendix does not precisely match the requirements of a particular testing project (e.g., where it may be necessary to include other signatures on the test result record form), the test team leader should obtain an electronic copy of this template and modify it as required.

<Client> Test Result Record Form		(front sheet)
Project ID		
AUT Title	**AUT Version**	
Testing Phase	**Date of Test**	

Test ID		**Time of Test**	
Observed Test Result			
Test Result Category			
Test Error Description			
Tester Signature			
Test Observer Signature			
			Page 1 of Pages

<Client> Test Result Record Form	*(continuation sheet)*
Project ID	

Test ID		**Time of Test**	
Observed Test Result			
Test Result Category			
Test Error Description			
Tester Signature			
Test Observer Signature			
		Page of Pages	

Test Log Template

G1 Introduction

This appendix contains a template for a *test log*, which may be copied and used to record the activities and events comprising a particular test phase. An electronic version of the template can be obtained using the following link: http://www.cambridge.org/9780521148016.

The purpose of a test log is to document the chronological record of all relevant details of a testing project (in effect, a test log is a diary of all relevant events that have occurred during the testing project).

The test log forms part of the formal documentation associated with the testing project and will be filed at the completion of the testing project.

The test log template presented on the following pages is based on that found in (1) with additional information from (15), plus extensive feedback obtained in implementing testing frameworks for a number of clients (see the case study section of this book).

Two different test log pages are presented on successive pages:

▶ Test log front sheet
▶ Test log continuation sheet.

The information that needs to be filled in on the test log front sheet includes:

▶ Project ID – the unique project identifier
▶ AUT title – the definitive title of the application under test (front sheet only)
▶ AUT version – the definitive version information for the AUT (front sheet only)
▶ Testing phase – the title of the phase of testing being conducted (e.g., unit test, integration test, system test) (front sheet only)
▶ Date of test – the date on which the testing project was initiated (front sheet only)
▶ Overview – a brief overview of the testing activity, including what is being tested and by who, and any other appropriate details relating to the testing activity (front sheet only)

▶ Activities and event entries, which includes:

   Date – the date on which the activity/event took place

   Time – the time at which the activity/event took place

   Activity/event – a brief description of the testing activity/event being recorded.

Where text appears in angle brackets (< >), this denotes a place marker, which must be replaced with the appropriate information for a particular testing phase. For example <Client> should be replaced by the name of your own company or organization.

Where the template provided in this appendix does not precisely match the requirements of a particular testing project, the test team leader should obtain an electronic copy of this template and modify it as required.

<Client> Test Log			*(front sheet)*
Project ID			
AUT Title		**AUT Version**	
Testing Phase		**Date of Test**	

Overview	

Activities and Event Entries		
Date	**Time**	**Activity/Event**
		Page 1 of Pages

<Client> Test Log		*(continuation sheet)*
Project ID		

Activities and Event Entries		
Date	**Time**	**Activity/Event**
		Page of Pages

Test Certificate Template

H1 Introduction

This appendix contains a specimen test certificate template, which may be customized and used to formally record the successful completion of a specific test phase for a particular *application under test* (*AUT*). An electronic version of the template can be obtained using the following link: http://www.cambridge.org/9780521148016.

Although it is unlikely that a test certificate will be used to formally record the successful completion of the earlier phases of the testing process, in any formal acceptance of an AUT, and in particular from a third-party developer or supplier, the use of such a certificate should be mandatory.

When customizing the specimen test certificate template for a particular AUT under a specific testing phase, the following information should be considered for inclusion within the test certificate:

▶ The title of the AUT
▶ The test phase name
▶ A statement of acceptance describing the circumstances of the test, its date (and optionally, its location), and what the AUT has been tested against
▶ The signature of the member of staff accepting the tested AUT (must be of an appropriate level of seniority, particularly for acceptance of third-party bespoke developed systems or products). The signature should be dated
▶ The signature of the independent test observer (this item may not be appropriate for an acceptance test where the system has been supplied by a third-party organization). The signature should be dated
▶ The signature of the supplier or developer (these need not be the representatives of a third-party organization – for example, the AUT may have been developed in-house, with a suitably senior representative of the development project signing). The signature should be dated.

Where text appears within the body of the certificate in angle brackets (< >), this denotes a place marker, which must be replaced with the appropriate information for a particular testing phase. For example <Own Organization> should be replaced by the name of your own company or organization.

Once the test certificate has been customized, it should be printed on good quality paper (and particularly when a third-party supplier or developer will cosign the certificate). If it is appropriate, company branded or headed paper should be considered.

Where the template provided in this appendix does not precisely match the requirements of a particular testing project, the test team leader should obtain an electronic copy of this template and modify it as required.

\<AUT Title> \<Testing Phase> Test Certificate

It is hereby agreed that:

The delivered \<AUT Title> (version \<version details>) as supplied by \<Name of Supplier or Developer> under contract to \<Own Organization> conforms to its functional specification (\<Definitive Reference to the Functional Specification Document>).

for and on behalf of \<Own Organization>
Signature: ....   Dated: ....
Name: \<Name of Own Organization Representative, e.g., Senior User (see Chapter 4)>
Role: \<Own Organization Representative Job Title>

Optionally, where a quality assurance representative is involved
for and on behalf of \<Own Organization>
Signature: ....   Dated: ....
Name: \<Name of Independent Test Observer, e.g., QA Rep. (see Chapter 4)>
Role: \<Own Organization QA Representative>

for and on behalf of \<Name of Supplier or Developer>
Signature: ....   Dated: ....
Name: \<Name of Supplier or Developer Representative>
Role: \<job title of Supplier or Developer representative>

Reuse Pack Checklist

I1 Introduction

This appendix contains guidance on ensuring that the reuse of tests and testing materials is achieved between testing phases and testing projects. It includes:

► How and when to create a reuse pack
► A list of the typical contents of a reuse pack
► Guidance on using reuse packs.

I2 Creating a Reuse Pack

At the end of any testing phase, the *test team leader* (or *development team leader* during *unit* and *integration testing*) should collect copies of a number of items generated during the testing project into a single file (a simple A4 manila folder is usually sufficient for this purpose). This file is termed a reuse pack.

The reuse pack will be archived with the rest of the project files and can be subsequently retrieved on request from the *testing manager* (or equivalent role).

The contents of the reuse pack can be used by other testing projects to reduce the effort and cost associated with testing and to improve the consistency and quality of testing.

Examples of the use of reuse packs include:

► During subsequent testing phases of the same application under test *(AUT)* (such as reusing some system tests during acceptance testing)
► In regression testing modifications to the same AUT (such as either rerunning a complete system test or selected elements of the system test)
► Where the AUT is similar or related to another AUT (such as employing existing integration test material when an additional module is added to an existing suite of applications).

I3 Contents of a Reuse Pack

A typical reuse pack should contain:

▶ A paper copy of the test specification document
▶ A paper copy of the test log
▶ A paper copy of the test script(s) (and any revised test cases)
▶ A paper copy of the test guide used during the testing
▶ A paper copy of the test summary report document
▶ A floppy disk of the appropriate format containing the previous
▶ A floppy disk copy of the test data, and in particular any "handcrafted" data (if technically feasible) or a reference to an electronically archived copy of the data
▶ General (see Section I.4) and specific instructions (written by the test team leader prior to archival) on using the reuse pack.

I4 How to Use the Reuse Pack

The following steps should be employed in using the reuse pack within the context of a new testing project:

▶ Discuss the availability of existing appropriate testing material with the testing manager and obtain a copy of the reuse pack
▶ Review the contents of the reuse pack for its relevance to the current testing requirement (in particular, read the specific instructions for using the reuse pack)
▶ Identify any tests and testing materials that can be reused for the current testing project
▶ Incorporate these tests and testing materials into the current testing project
▶ Where possible, use the electronic versions of the tests and testing materials to save time and effort
▶ On completion of the testing project, restore the initial state and contents of the reuse pack and return it to the testing manager for storage.

Test Summary Report Template

J1 Introduction

This appendix contains a test summary report template, which may be copied and used as the basis of a test summary report for a particular test phase. The purpose of a test summary report is to summarize the result of a particular testing phase and to provide the basis for subsequent improvement of the testing process. An electronic version of the template can be obtained using the following link: http://www.cambridge.org/9780521148016.

As described in Chapter 4 (The Management and Planning of Testing), each testing project must generate a test summary report as one of the documents produced at the conclusion of any given testing phase.

Where text appears within the body of this template in angle brackets ($< >$), this denotes a place marker, which must be replaced with the appropriate information for a particular testing phase.

Text that appears in italic is provided for information only (such as illustrative examples) and should not appear in the final test summary report.

The principal approach to be used in writing a test summary report is to try to produce a succinct document. Make best use of the supporting information presented in this book (such as the other relevant templates), as well as pertinent material from the appropriate testing phase chapters.

Where the template provided in this appendix does not precisely match the requirements of a particular testing project, the test team leader should obtain an electronic copy of this template and modify it as required.

Test Summary Report Front Sheet

Document Information {to <Client> Doc Standard}	
Project ID:	<Project ID> *the unique ID for this testing project*
Document Ref:	<Doc Ref> *a unique document reference for this document*
Testing Phase:	<Testing Phase> *the testing phase (e.g., unit test)*
AUT Title:	<AUT Title> *the definitive title of the application under test*
Date:	<Date> *the date this document was completed*

Distribution	
Copy Number	**Recipient**
1.	<activity manager> *i.e., the testing manager*
2.	<activity leader> *i.e., development team leader for unit and link testing, test team leader for system test.*
N.	Project File

Review & Approval	
Issue:	<issue status> *issue status of the document, e.g., draft, 1.0.*
R&A Number:	<R&A reference> *the reference to the final approving review*
Author	<name of the author>
Author Signature	<signature of author> *the person who wrote this document*
Approval (PM)	<name of the project manager>
Approval (PM) Signature	<signature of the project manager>
Approval (QA)	<name of the quality assurance representative>
Approval (QA) Signature	<signature of the quality assurance representative>

Contents

1 Introduction

1.1 Background

This document provides the test summary for the <Testing Phase> testing of the <AUT Title>.

This section should contain a brief background and history to this testing project, which should include:

a) a brief description of the purpose of the AUT
b) definitive version information for the AUT
c) any other relevant supporting information.

1.2 Structure of the Report

This report is structured in the following manner:

a) Section 2 Overview provides a high-level overview of the significant events and activities documented during the <Testing Phase> testing of the <AUT Title>
b) Section 3 Variances records any variances of the artifacts from their design specification (as documented in the <Testing Phase> test specification document (Reference <reference number from Section 1.3 of this report>) or as documented within the overall testing process
c) Section 4 Assessment provides a brief assessment of the comprehensiveness of the testing process for the <Testing Phase> testing of the <AUT Title>
d) Section 5 Results provides a summary of the results of the <Testing Phase> testing of the <AUT Title>
e) Section 6 Evaluation provides an overall evaluation of the testing process including any observed problems and/or limitations
f) Section 7 provides a summary of the major testing activities and events for the <Testing Phase> testing of the <AUT Title>.

1.3 References

A numbered list of documents referenced within this document. For example:

   <list of references to overall project documents>

    1) <Project authorization document>
    2) <Overall project plan>
    3) <Quality assurance plan>
    4) <Configuration management plan>
    5) <Relevant policies referenced within this document>
    6) <Relevant standards referenced within this document>

<list of references to items specific to this testing project>

7) <AUT Title> <Testing Phase> Test plan document <Ref> (version N.N), <date>
8) <AUT Title> <Testing Phase> Test specification document <Ref> (version N.N), <date>
9) <AUT Title> <Testing Phase> Test script document <Ref> (version N.N), <date>
10) <AUT Title> <Testing Phase> Test result record forms <Ref> (version N.N), <date>
11) <AUT Title> <Testing Phase> Test log <Ref> (version N.N), <date>

2 Overview

This section provides a high-level overview of the significant events and activities documented during the <Testing Phase> testing of the <AUT Title>.

This section also specifies the scope of the testing (what was and what was not tested) and the test environment details (including the hardware, software, and data used in the testing).

For example:

The acceptance test for the SuperSoft software (v1.1, 2001) was begun on January 4, 2001, and completed on February 12, 2001. During this acceptance test only the customer services module was considered.

The testing was conducted on a Pentium III processor with 64Mbytes of memory running Microsoft Windows 2000 SP1. Data set DS:301 was used to test the AUT.

3 Variances

This section is used to record any variances of the artifacts from their design specification (as documented in the test specification document or as documented within the overall testing process).

For example:

Conditions observed during the course of testing resulted in the design of additional test cases to explore concerns regarding the customer details input routine. A number of additional defects were identified as a result, which were subsequently corrected and successfully retested. The additional test cases were appended to the end test script for the acceptance test and listed as TP12/AT1/TS1/TC:35 to TC:46.

4 Assessment

This section provides a brief assessment of the comprehensiveness of the testing process for the completed testing phase against the test objectives and constraints specified in the test plan document.

Where code coverage measurements have been made, the results should also be included in this section.

This section also identifies any aspects of the AUT that were not tested as thoroughly as planned (due to insufficient time or resources).

For example:

All test cases were executed with the exception of test cases TP12/AT1/TS1/TC:14 to TC:18 (testing the customer database details access routines), which were omitted due to challenging testing timescales combined with the need to further investigate concerns associated with the customer details input routine.

All priority 1 test cases associated with the customer database details access routines were executed successfully, providing sufficient confidence to omit the test cases with lower priority.

5 Results

This section provides a summary of the results of the <Testing Phase> testing of the <AUT Title>. This section identifies all resolved issues and summarizes details of their resolution. This section also lists outstanding issues.

For example:

Three of the test cases TP12/AT1/TS1/TC:06 to TC:08 revealed problems with the logic of the new customer input routine. The developers corrected the observed defects and the amended code passed the retest. However, it was not possible within the timescales of the testing task to regression test the associated add new customer details to database routine. This issue remains outstanding and should be observed following installation and use in the live environment.

6 Evaluation

This section provides an overall evaluation of the testing process including problems and limitations. The evaluation is based on the observed results of testing and how well they matched the evaluation criteria listed in the test specification document for this testing phase.

If available, an assessment of the risk of failure of problem areas of the AUT should be included. This may be qualitative (e.g., following a low, medium, and high scale) or quantitative if it is possible to produce probability of failure values.

For example:

The customer services module of the SuperSoft application (v1.1, 2001) underwent comprehensive testing, with only five defects being observed, and three of these were associated with the new customer input routine.

Additional test cases were designed and executed to explore the customer details input routine, and following correction and retesting it is believed this routine will have a high degree of reliability in use.

Because a number of problems were observed with the new customer input routine and only perfunctory retesting was possible due to challenging testing timescales, it is thought that there will be a medium likelihood of failure in use.

Similarly, the lack of time for regression testing the associated add new customer details to database routine may cause issues in use. However, because of the success of the initial testing of this routine, it is thought that the likelihood of failure of this routine is low.

7 Summary of Activities

This section provides a summary of the major testing activities and events for the testing phase. This section also summarizes testing resource information, such as total staffing levels, total testing time, time spent in analysis and design.

It is useful to include planned and actual data where possible.

The information recorded in this section will depend on what information is collected during the progress of the testing. Such information may well form part of any metrics program used as part of the testing process.

For example:

Test start date: January 4, 2001, test end date: February 12, 2001

Item	Planned	Actual
Staff Levels	5	5
Test Design Effort	2.5	3.0
Test Execution Effort	3.5	3.5
Retest Effort	1.0	1.0
Test Management and Reporting	0.5	0.75
Etc.		

Equivalence Partition Example

K1 Introduction

This appendix contains an example illustrating the testing technique of *equivalence partitioning* described in Chapter 3, which the *test analyst* can use to select specimen data for use in testing the *application under test (AUT)*.

K2 The Testing Problem

The specification for a software system for validating expenses claims for hotel accommodation includes the following requirements:

▶ There is an upper limit of £90 for accommodation expense claims
▶ Any claims above £90 should be rejected and cause an error message to be displayed
▶ All expense amounts should be greater than £0 and an error message should be displayed if this is not the case.

K3 Analyzing the Testing Requirements

To support the process of analyzing the previous requirement, it is useful to graphically show the partitions and their boundaries and to state the ranges of the partitions with respect to the boundary values (see Figure K1).

K4 Designing the Test Cases

The next step is to design the *test cases* by drawing up a table showing the *test case* ID, a typical value drawn from the partition to be input in the test case, the partition it tests, and the expected output or result of the test case (see Table K1).

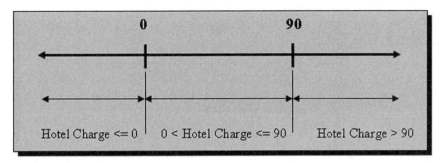

K1 Graphical View of Partitions

This process can be repeated to select further representative data for use within the test cases generated by the test analyst.

Table K1 Test case table

Test case ID	Hotel charge	Partition tested	Expected output
1	50	0 < Hotel Charge <= 90	OK
2	−25	Hotel Charge <= 0	Error Message
3	99	Hotel Charge > 90	Error Message

Boundary Value Analysis Example

L1 Introduction

This appendix contains an example illustrating the testing technique of *boundary value analysis* described in Chapter 3, which the *test analyst* can use to select specimen data for use in testing the *application under test (AUT)*. This example uses the same testing problem as that presented in Appendix K – Equivalence Partition Example.

L2 The Testing Problem

The specification for a software system for validating expenses claims for hotel accommodation includes the following requirements:

▶ There is an upper limit of £90
▶ Any claims above £90 should be rejected and cause an error message to be displayed
▶ All expense amounts should be greater than £0 and an error message should be displayed if this is not the case.

L3 Analyzing the Testing Requirements

To support the process of analyzing the previous requirement, it is of benefit to graphically show the boundaries and to determine the boundary values and significant values either side of the boundaries (see Figure L1).

L4 Designing the Test Cases

The next step is to design the *test cases* by drawing up a table showing the *test case* ID, the values about and on the boundary to be input for the test, the boundary it tests, and the expected output or result of the test case (see Table L1).

Appendix L. Boundary Value Analysis Example

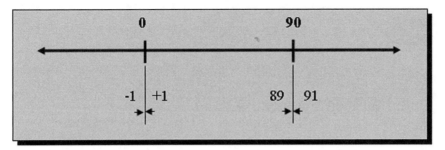

Graphical View of the Boundaries

These values for hotel charge can now be used by the test analyst to design an effective series of test cases to test the boundary values.

Table L1 Test case table

Test case ID	Hotel charge	Boundary tested	Expected output
1	−1		Error Message
2	0	0	Error Message
3	1		OK
4	89		OK
5	90	90	OK
6	91		Error Message

State Transition Example

M1 Introduction

This appendix contains an example illustrating the testing technique of state transition analysis described in Chapter 3, which the *test analyst* can use to select specimen data for use in testing the *application under test (AUT)*. State transition analysis is also termed state transition testing.

M2 The Testing Problem

This example describes part of the specification for the software controlling the operation of a water pump:

▶ The pump can be in one of three states: isolated, ready, or running. The pump cannot start (i.e., move to the running state) if it is isolated

▶ Opening the water valve will move the pump from the isolated into the ready state. Closing the water valve when the pump is ready will return it to the isolated state

▶ Pressing a start button when the pump is in the ready state will start the pump and move it into the running state. Pressing a stop button when the pump is running will stop the pump and move it into the ready state.

M3 Analyzing the Testing Requirements

To support the process of analyzing the previous requirement, the test analyst draws a state transition diagram to graphically show the states, their transitions, and the events (see Figure M1).

M4 Designing the Test Cases

By inspecting the state transition diagram it is possible to identify a number of *test cases* to verify the requirements (i.e., *positive testing*) for the pump control software:

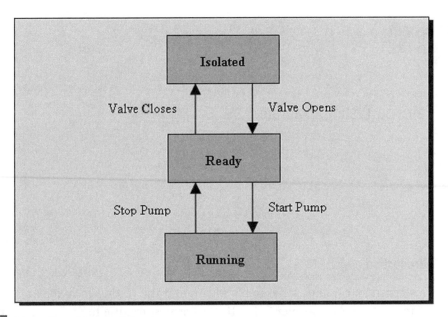

States, Transitions and Events

▶ Test Case 1 – with the pump in the isolated state, does the pump move to ready on opening the valve?
▶ Test Case 2 – with the pump in the ready state, does the pump move to isolated on closing the valve?
▶ Test Case 3 – with the pump in the ready state, does the pump move to running when the start button is pushed?
▶ Test Case 4 – with the pump in the running state, does the pump move to ready when the stop button is pushed?

Similarly, by inspecting the state transition diagram it is also possible to identify a number of test cases to check the operation of the system outside of the stated requirements (i.e., *negative testing*), for example:

▶ Test Case 5 – what happens if the pump is running and an attempt is made to close the valve (typically catastrophic for a real pump)?
▶ Test Case 6 – what happens if the start button is pushed when the pump is in the isolated state?
▶ Test Case 7 – what happens if the start button is pushed when the pump is already in the running state?
▶ Test Case 8 – what happens if both the start and stop buttons are pushed simultaneously when the pump is in the running state?

The ability to visualize the operation of the AUT using the state transition technique is an effective way of identifying test cases and is particularly effective for negative testing purposes.

Pairwise Testing Example

N1 Introduction

This appendix contains an example illustrating the testing technique of pairwise testing described in Chapter 3 that the test analyst can use to select specimen data for use in testing the application under test (AUT).

N2 The Testing Problem

Continuing with the hotel room booking theme, when the employee comes to book a room using an on-line booking system on the hotel Web site, he or she may have to make a selection using radio buttons of whether he or she wants a single, double, or family room. The employee may also have to decide whether he or she would like a bath or a shower in the room and whether he or she needs smoking or nonsmoking accommodation. Table N1 shows the unique combinations of options that the specification will result in:

Table N1 Table of possible combinations

	Room type	Bathroom	Smoking
1	Single	Shower	Smoking
2	Double	Shower	Smoking
3	Family	Shower	Smoking
4	Single	Shower	Nonsmoking
5	Double	Shower	Nonsmoking
6	Family	Shower	Nonsmoking
7	Single	Bath	Smoking
8	Double	Bath	Smoking
9	Family	Bath	Smoking
10	Single	Bath	Nonsmoking
11	Double	Bath	Nonsmoking
12	Family	Bath	Nonsmoking

Table N2   Extended table of possible combinations

	Room type	Bathroom	Smoking
1	Single	Shower	Smoking
2	Double	Shower	Smoking
3	Family	Shower	Smoking
4	Apartment	Shower	Smoking
5	Single	Shower	Nonsmoking
6	Double	Shower	Nonsmoking
7	Family	Shower	Nonsmoking
8	Apartment	Shower	Nonsmoking
9	Single	Bath	Smoking
10	Double	Bath	Smoking
11	Family	Bath	Smoking
12	Apartment	Bath	Smoking
13	Single	Bath	Nonsmoking
14	Double	Bath	Nonsmoking
15	Family	Bath	Nonsmoking
16	Apartment	Bath	Nonsmoking
17	Single	Both	Smoking
18	Double	Both	Smoking
19	Family	Both	Smoking
20	Apartment	Both	Smoking
21	Single	Both	Nonsmoking
22	Double	Both	Nonsmoking
23	Family	Both	Nonsmoking
24	Apartment	Both	Nonsmoking

Even in this simple example, we have generated twelve unique combinations, each of which could be used as the basis of designing a *test case*. Adding an additional room type (perhaps apartment) and a further option of having both a shower and a bath in the room results in twenty-four unique possible combinations (see Table N2).

Adding additional possible options in the existing columns, or even adding an additional column – perhaps "with or without fridge," causes a combinatorial explosion of unique combinations of options, each of which could potentially generate a separate test case. In any realistic testing scenario, the numbers of parameters and possible values quickly means that we have far too many combinations to design individual test cases against. How can we select an effective subset of values to design test cases that will uncover the most defects?

N3   The Pairwise Testing Solution

As discussed in Chapter 3, where there are a number of different parameters that can be in a number of different states in a program, the two most effective approaches for finding defects are to change the state of a single parameter or to change the state of a pair of parameters (75).

To obtain a practical number of effective test cases, the technique of pairwise testing seeks to reduce the need to exhaustively test all combinations of states of the application under test (AUT). The technique achieves this goal by exploiting the observation described previously by selecting pairs of parameters and states to give best coverage of the total set of combinations.

Starting at the bottom of Table N2 and working our way up the table, we pair off parameters. Marking this pair, we now look up the table and cross off any other occurrences of the pair. We repeat this process until we have crossed off all entries in the table.

Table N3 provides typical results produced by this approach:

Table N3 Pairwise analysis results

	Parameter 1	Parameter 2	Parameter 3
1	Family	Shower	Smoking
2	Double	Both	Smoking
3	Family	Bath	Nonsmoking
4	Family	Both	Nonsmoking
5	Apartment	Bath	Smoking
6	Apartment	Both	Nonsmoking
7	Single	Bath	Nonsmoking
8	Apartment	Shower	Nonsmoking
9	Double	Shower	Nonsmoking
10	Single	Both	Smoking
11	Double	Bath	Nonsmoking
12	Single	Shower	Smoking

If each row listed in Table N3 is used to design a test case, then using this technique we have reduced (in this relatively simple example) the number of test cases by half. With increasing complexity of the AUT, there will be increasing savings in time and effort using this technique.

N3 Pairwise Testing in Practice

With increasing complexity of the AUT, and with ever greater pressure on test practitioners to squeeze as much efficiency from the testing process as possible, in practice most examples of pairwise testing are conducted using tool support (e.g., 76). Tools take the mechanical drudge out of identifying the paired values, avoid mistakes in what can be an error-prone exercise, and present the results of the analysis in a simple and usable form.

Automated Testing Tool Selection Criteria

01 Introduction

This appendix contains a list of criteria to be used in evaluating *automated software testing tools* and a suggested approach to conducting the evaluation. A simple scoring scheme with weightings is described, which can be used to score each of the evaluation criteria. The values for weightings and criteria scores may be modified through experience and use.

An evaluation summary checklist can be found at the end of this appendix, which can be copied and used in evaluating testing tools.

An electronic version of this appendix can be obtained using the following link: http://www.cambridge.org/9780521148016 so that the evaluation criteria and template can be customized to more closely match the evaluation requirements of the reader.

02 Scoring Scheme

In conducting a review or evaluation of testing tools, the following approach should be employed:

- ▶ Review the evaluation criteria and assign a weighting to each of them:
  - ▷ 1 for an essential criteria
  - ▷ 0.75 for important criteria
  - ▷ 0.5 for desirable criteria
  - ▷ 0 for nonapplicable criteria
- ▶ When evaluating the tool, consider each criterion and score them as follows:
  - ▷ 1 if the tool satisfies the criteria fully
  - ▷ 0.75 if the tool largely satisfies the criteria
  - ▷ 0.5 if the tool partially satisfies the criteria
  - ▷ 0 if the tool does not satisfy the criteria

▶ On completing the review, multiply the score for each criterion by its weighting and total the scores. The resulting value can be used to compare different automated testing tools.

The following sections list the evaluation criteria, which are grouped under the following high-level headings:

▶ Support for testing phases and techniques
▶ Support for test management
▶ Tool technical issues
▶ Tool defect analysis facilities
▶ Tool documentation issues
▶ Tool integration issues
▶ Tool usability issues
▶ Supplier issues
▶ Training and consultancy issues
▶ Contractual and financial issues
▶ Miscellaneous issues.

03 Support for Testing Phases and Techniques

In selecting a testing tool, it is important that the tool is capable of supporting the key testing phases your organization is involved in.

Does the testing tool provide support for the following testing phases?

▶ Functional testing
▶ Regression testing
▶ Installation testing
▶ Configuration testing
▶ Maintenance testing
▶ Network testing
▶ Performance testing (including load, stress, volume, and scalability testing)
▶ Multiuser testing.

04 Support for Testing Management

Management of the testing process is key to successful, effective, and efficient testing. It is important that any testing tool supports effective management of testing, providing good support for the typical testing management tasks.

Does the testing tool provide the following test management facilities?

▶ Support for multiple users with varying user privileges
▶ The ability to record test plans or integrate seamlessly with a project planning tool

▶ The ability to seamlessly integrate with a requirements management tool to represent and store and manage test requirements

▶ The ability to design test scripts and verification points against requirements (and for this information to automatically be updated when requirements change)

▶ The ability to seamlessly integrate with a defect management and change request tool to allow the creation, monitoring, reporting, and resolution of defects

▶ The ability to run predefined reports on all aspects of the testing process

▶ The ability to customize existing/create new reports.

05 Tool Technical Issues

In selecting a testing tool, you will need to consider how well the tool facilities match your testing requirements (e.g., does the tool support testing against the programming language you are developing in or does the tool perform on your selected operating system?)

Does the tool provide the following technical capabilities?

▶ The ability to record and play back test scripts or procedures

▶ The ability to work with a particular development language or environment (e.g., Java, Eclipse)

▶ Ability to test object container technologies (e.g., OCXs, VBXs, Data Windows)

▶ Ability to test hidden objects (i.e., nonvisual objects)

▶ Ability to test the attributes of objects (visible, focus, grayed)

▶ Object-oriented recording/playback of scripts

▶ The option of using low-level or coordinate based recording/playback of scripts

▶ Clarity/simplicity of the scripting language

▶ Ability to manually edit scripts

▶ Ability to play back scripts in a range of operating systems/browsers without modification

▶ Ability to trap unexpected windows and act on them

▶ Ability to store all information in a single repository

▶ Ability to integrate with other tools (e.g., CASE tools)

▶ Ability to update/maintain test cases/test procedures by example

▶ Cross-platform support (e.g., mainframe and PC testing)

▶ The ability to automatically recover from general protection faults/crashes and continue to test.

06 Tool Defect Analysis Facilities

Does the testing tool provide the facilities for inspecting and analyzing defects?

▶ The ability to view the test log following testing or at a later date

▶ The ability to determine which test scripts and verifications passed or failed

▶ The ability to examine the first failure and subsequent failures

▶ Context-sensitive facilities for viewing defects
▶ The ability to enter a defect into the defect management system
▶ Full traceability from the original requirement the test was based on through to the point of reporting the defect, and on through the defect tracking facilities
▶ Ability to update/maintain test cases/test procedures by example (e.g., to update master data with observed data).

07 Tool Documentation Issues

Irrespective of how technically good the testing tool is, the lack of clear and comprehensive documentation may compromise how successfully you use the tool.

Some manufacturers now provide complete tool documentation on digital optical disk or via a download to save shipping bulky manual sets and to protect the environment. Such on-line documentation can provide a powerful means of accessing information, allowing the user to search for specified information. Also check manuals can be ordered as a free option.

Does the testing tool support the following documentation issues?

▶ Does the testing tool provide adequate installation documentation?
▶ Does the testing tool provide a user manual?
▶ Does the testing tool provide tutorial information?
▶ Does the testing tool provide quick start information (such as "try it" sheets)?
▶ Does the testing tool provide troubleshooting information?
▶ Does the testing tool provide a scripting language manual?
▶ Is the documentation robust, durable, and of good quality?
▶ Is the documentation clear, unambiguous, and usable?
▶ Are additional copies of specified documentation available on request?
▶ Does the documentation provide further references to source material (e.g., definitive testing books, conference proceedings, testing technical reports)?
▶ Does the testing tool provide adequate contact information (e.g., help desk telephone number, Web site address, e-mail address)?

08 Tool Integration Issues

Integration is an increasingly important issue as senior software development managers appreciate the need to provide good communications between all the members of their projects, from analysts, through developers, and onto the testers.

IT professionals are increasingly looking for cross-development lifecycle tool support rather than stand-alone point solutions.

Also, in considering the level of integration a given testing tool supports, beware of clumsy solutions where the user is expected to open the source tool (such as a requirements management tool), save the information held in that system into an intermediate file form, after which they have to run up the target tool (such as the testing tool), and then load the information into that tool. Such solutions are notoriously unreliable, and in practice maintaining the currency of the information such integrations provides is at best difficult. At worst it results in the tester working with out-of-date information, jeopardizing the success of the testing project.

In evaluating a testing tool, the following tool integration issues should be considered:

▶ Does the tool have an integrated requirements management facility to ensure that each of the requirements for the application under test can be verified
▶ Does the tool fully integrate with design/visual modeling tools to allow automatic generation of test scripts based on design information (e.g., automatic generation of code stubs and test harness code for unit test, automatic generation of integration tests from sequence diagrams, automatic generation of boundary and partition test data from design information). For performance testing tools, is it possible to automatically generate test scripts from design information before any code has been written and execute them against the server logic to test the architecture and scalability of the proposed software
▶ Does the tool have an integrated defect management facility to ensure that defects are automatically reported to the staff that need to know about them (such as the developer, project manager, QA manager). Does the defect management facility provide traceability of the original requirement the defect is associated with
▶ If the testing tool is a functional testing product, does it have a seamless integration to other testing tools, such as:
  ▷ reliability testing tools
  ▷ code coverage tools
  ▷ low-level performance testing tools (to identify code bottlenecks)
  ▷ high-level performance testing tools (such as load, stress, volume, scalability testing tools)
▶ Does the tool provide seamless integration with a complete cross-lifecycle software development and testing process, where requests for help within the tool take the user directly to context-sensitive process information, and where the process provides explicit advice on how to perform specified tasks within the testing tool
▶ Does the tool provide seamless integration with configuration management tools, allowing each artifact generated during testing (such as test scripts, verification points, reports) to be under rigorous configuration management?

09 Tool Usability Issues

Any testing tool should provide facilities that directly support the process by which testers typically test software in a natural and intuitive manner. The tool may be very powerful, but if the user interface to the tool is poor, the user may not be able to realize the full potential of the tool.

This section considers the usability/learnability issues associated with the testing tool (it is important to note that the criteria presented here represent only a sample of the usability issues that would need to be addressed in a full usability review):

▶ Does the tool adhere to user interface standards (e.g., Windows on PC platforms). For example, does the tool use a standard "File, Edit, <tool specific menus>, Help" menu structure?

▶ Is the tool consistent in its use of menus and toolbar buttons? For example, is the "Open" toolbar button icon standard – or is it some form of custom icon? Consistency is key in ensuring rapid familiarization with the GUI?

▶ Where other tools integrate with the tool, do the other tools employ the same style of menu and toolbar buttons (or identical toolbar buttons where the function is the same), and is the look and feel the same (e.g., try comparing the "Open" toolbar button icons between "integrated" tools to see if they are the same)?

▶ Are the toolbar button icons standard and easily understood?

▶ Does the tool provide consistent short cut key access to its facilities?

▶ Is the tool simple, intuitive, and easy to understand and use (i.e., can you easily guess what action to take next in most situations)? Beware tools that have "modal" menus – i.e., menus where the menu items change with the state of the tool – such tools will be difficult to learn how to use

▶ Does the tool provide good user help facilities?
  ▷ Is there a help menu providing help topics?
  ▷ Is there a help button on the toolbar?
  ▷ Do the toolbar buttons have tooltips (the MS yellow pop up help labels)?
  ▷ Are there help buttons providing context-sensitive help in dialog boxes?
  ▷ Does pressing the F1 key provide context-sensitive help?
  ▷ Is there a "point and click" help button? As a test of "attention to detail," find out what happens if you click on this button and then select the button again (i.e., help on point and click help)

▶ Where text is used in the tool, is it legible and free of technical terms or jargon?

▶ Does the tool allow the user to customize its look and feel?

▶ Does the tool allow the user to configure its facilities to match user preferences?

▶ Does the tool have good choice of color for background and text (i.e., is there good contrast)?

▶ Is the tool attractive and enjoyable to use?

010   Supplier Issues

It is essential that you assure yourself about the size and financial stability of the tool vendor. The best tool in the world will be worthless if the supplier business fails. Similarly, small-sized suppliers with few technical consultants may be unable to provide you with adequate technical support, mentoring, consultancy, or training.

Small-sized vendors with poor finances may also have difficulties in performing adequate R&D, have problems keeping to promised release schedules, and suffer quality problems with releases. Another problem facing such organizations is the threat of takeover, with no guarantees that the new owners will continue to support the old product range.

Think carefully before adopting tools from point solution vendors as you may experience integration issues if you need to use other tools in your software analysis, design, and testing process. Consult with the other stakeholders in your organization to find out what tools they use for analysis, design, change management, and configuration management to determine if the suppliers of those tools also provide integrated testing tools before making a decision.

In evaluating a testing tool, the following supplier issues should be considered:

▶ Is the supplier financially and commercially sound?
▶ Is the supplier part of a larger IT company providing a range of IT services?
▶ Have you dealt successfully with the supplier in the past?
▶ Does the supplier have a Web site that provides:
  ▷ company information
  ▷ product release news
  ▷ technical papers on the testing tool
  ▷ help and tips on the testing tool use
  ▷ sample/reusable scripts?
▶ Help desk issues:
  ▷ Is there a help desk available for user support calls?
  ▷ Is the help desk U.K.-based/European-based/U.S. East Coast-based/U.S. West Coast-based (this may affect availability of the service)?
  ▷ Does the help desk provide twenty-four-hour support?
  ▷ Is there an e-mail address for support information?
  ▷ When you need support, how quickly does the help desk respond?
  ▷ When you need support, does the help desk understand your problem?
  ▷ When you receive support, is the help correct and useful?
▶ Does the company have multinational reach and coverage (e.g., if your project is cross-geography/off-shored, can you get universal support from the vendor)?

011 Training and Consultancy Issues

Despite what some vendors may tell you, no competent testing tool can be used without some level of user training. Even if you purchase a tool that has comprehensive on-line tutorial material, the users will still have to find the time and free resources to make use of the tutorial. In practice, training of staff is essential, otherwise lack of investment in training will cause a greater loss of investment when the staff struggle to use the tool effectively.

Similarly, it can be cost effective to put budget aside for mentoring and consultancy to show staff how to best use the tools, and to allow regular "health checks" to ensure continued effective use.

For these reasons, the following testing tool training and consultancy issues should be considered:

- ▶ Will the supplier install the testing tool at your site and provide introductory information (such as a half day walkthrough of the tool)?
- ▶ Does the supplier offer introductory training, and if so?
  - ▷ Can you obtain a copy of the prospectus?
  - ▷ What is the cost (per person/per day)?
  - ▷ Is there a minimum number of attendees?
  - ▷ Can the training be performed at your site?
- ▶ Does the supplier offer advanced training (this is often a good discriminator)?
- ▶ Does the supplier offer testing fundamentals training (another good discriminator of the depth and quality of the training available)?
- ▶ Does the supplier offer software development and testing process training (a particularly important criteria for organizations with a mature approach to development and testing)?
- ▶ Does the supplier offer mentoring and skills transfer consultancy?
- ▶ Does the supplier offer tool consultancy?
- ▶ Are there third-party organizations offering tool training/consultancy and are they certified by the supplier before they are able to provide training (this is a very good criterion to show widespread use and acceptance of a particular tool)?

012 Contractual and Financial Issues

This section addresses a number of financial and contractual issues that must be considered. Some of these issues may be difficult to resolve but must be considered in evaluating a particular tool (such as estimating the value of the tool in terms of the benefits of using or not using the tool).

Although it makes good business sense to inquire about discounts, be careful not to let testosterone get in the way of obtaining a product that will be of benefit to your organization. As incredible as it may seem, there have been many occasions where staff involved in the purchase of tools have walked away from a purchase just because the supplier is unable to reduce the purchase price by, in some cases, tens of dollars!

On the other hand, you should also be wary of suppliers who will suddenly slash the price of their product as soon as they hear that one of their competitors is involved. You will have to work with the supplier following your purchase (perhaps for training and mentoring, as well as ongoing support), so it is worth considering the business ethics of any supplier who was perfectly happy to charge you £X one day and then charge you half that amount a few days later for exactly the same product (while presumably still making a profit). This is not a good basis for a successful continuing business relationship, and suppliers who indulge in such activities are almost certain to find ways to recoup the discount at a later stage, otherwise their business would be unsustainable.

The following contractual and financial issues should be considered:

▶ Does the price/pricing structure for the testing tool represent good value (this issue may require cost benefit analysis to be resolved)?
▶ Is the testing tool priced on a per license basis?
▶ Are there any discounts for purchasing multiple licenses?
▶ Are fixed or floating licenses available?
▶ Does all of the tool functionality come in the "basic package," or do additional facilities cost extra (e.g., does the basic tool support network testing or is this a separate additional purchase)?
▶ How is multiuser testing priced (e.g. is it based on the number of "virtual users" required)?
▶ What is the cost of maintenance and does it include upgrades?
▶ What does maintenance provide?
▶ If priced separately, what is the cost of upgrades?
▶ How expensive is training (basic and advanced)?
▶ What is the cost benefit of purchasing and using the tool (this issue may require cost benefit analysis to be resolved)?

013 Miscellaneous Issues

The following issues are associated with obtaining further information on the testing tool and its use:

▶ Is there a user group for the tool?
▶ Is the user group independent of the supplier?
▶ How vigorous is the user group?
  ▷ How often does it meet?
  ▷ Does it publish proceedings?
  ▷ Does it hold seminars? Is there a mailing list?
  ▷ Does it have a point of contact for testing tool issues/advice?
  ▷ Does it have a Web page?
▶ Is there any independent documentary support for the testing tool?
  ▷ Are there textbooks available on the tool?
  ▷ Technical reports/journal papers?
▶ Annual conference:
  ▷ Is there an annual tool-specific conference?
  ▷ Where is it held?
  ▷ Are the proceedings available?

Testing Tool	Version	Date of Evaluation	Evaluator Name

Criteria	Weighting (0–1)	Score (0–1)	Result
Support for Testing Types			
Functional Testing			
Regression Testing			
Installation Testing			
Configuration Testing			
Maintenance Testing			
Network Testing			
Performance Testing (Load, Volume, Scalability)			
Multiuser Testing			
		Subtotal	
Support for Test Management			
Support for Multipleusers			
Test Planning Facilities			
Test Requirements Facilities			
Design of Test Procedures/Test Cases			
Defect Management			
Predefined Reports			
Customization/Creation of New Reports			
		Subtotal	
Tool Technical Issues			
Record and Playback Facilities			
Required Language/Environment			
Object Container Technology Testing			
Testing of "Hidden Objects"			
Testing Attributes of Objects			
OO Recording and Playback			
Low-Level/Coordinate Recording & Playback			
Clarity/Simplicity of Scripting Language			
Manual Editing of Scripts			
Playback in Different Operating Systems/Browsers			
Trap Unexpected Windows			
Repository-Based			
Integration with Other Tools			
Update/Maintenance of Tests			
Cross-Platform Testing – Mainframe/PC			
Automatic Recovery from GPF/Crashes			
		Subtotal	

Tool Defect Analysis Facilities			
Viewing the Test Log			
Determine Test Procedure/Test Case Failure			
Examine Failures			
Context-Sensitive Defect Analysis			
Entering Defect Reports			
Full Traceability of Original Requirements			
Update/Maintenance of Tests			
	Subtotal		
Tool Documentation Issues			
Installation Documentation			
User Manual			
Tutorial Information			
Quick Start Information			
Troubleshooting Information			
Scripting Language Manual			
Robust, Durable, and Good Quality Documentation			
Clear, Unambiguous, and Usable Documentation			
Additional Copies of Documentation			
References to Source Material			
Adequate Contact Information			
	Subtotal		
Tool Integration Issues			
Fully Integrated Requirements Management			
Fully Integrated with Visual Modeling Tool			
Fully Integrated Defect Tracking			
Full Integration with Other Testing Tools			
Integration with Development & Testing Process			
Integration with Configuration Management Tool			
	Subtotal		
Tool Usability Issues			
User Interface Standards			
Consistent Menus and Toolbar Buttons			
Standard Toolbar Icons between Integrated Tools			
Standard Toolbar Buttons Used within the Tool			
Consistent Shortcut Key Access			
Simple, Intuitive, and Easy to Use			
Help Facilities			
Legible and Jargon-Free Text			
Customise Look and Feel			
Configurable User Preferences			
Good Choice of Colour and Contrast			
Attractive and Enjoyable to Use			
	Subtotal		

Supplier Issues			
Financially and Commercially Sound			
Part of Larger IT Company			
Dealt Successfully with Supplier in Past			
Supplier Web Site			
Help Desk			
Multinational/Off-Shored Presence and Support			
		Subtotal	
Training and Consultancy Issues			
Install and Introduce Tool			
Introductory Training			
Advanced Training			
Testing Fundamentals Training			
Software Development & Testing Process Training			
Mentoring and Skills Transfer			
Tool Consultancy			
Third-Party Training/Consultancy			
		Subtotal	
Contractual and Financial Issues			
Estimated Value of Tool			
Pricing Scheme			
Multiple Licence Discount			
Fixed/Floating Licences			
Packaged Functionality			
Multiuser Pricing			
Cost of Maintenance			
Maintenance Features			
Cost of Upgrades			
Cost of Training			
Cost Benefits			
		Subtotal	
Miscellaneous Issues			
User Group			
User Group Independence			
Vigorous User Group			
Documentary Support			
Tool Conference(s)			
		Subtotal	
		Total Score	

Usability Testing Overview

P1 Introduction

This appendix provides a brief overview of the process of usability testing.[1] For a comprehensive treatment of this topic see (9).

Specifically, this appendix describes the roles and responsibilities, test design, test and post-test activities, and provides a graphical view of the organization of a typical usability test.

P2 Roles and Responsibilities

The following roles are applicable to usability testing:

▶ *Test team leader* – the usability testing project is managed on a day-to-day basis by the test team leader, who is also responsible for liaising with all other staff involved in testing
▶ *Test analyst* – the usability testing scenarios are devised by the test analyst with reference to available usability requirements for the application under test (AUT) and in close collaboration with the development team leader. This collaboration is essential for identifying specific areas of concern within the AUT user interface (UI) that may need to be investigated
▶ *User representative(s)* – Usability testing is conducted by a number of user representatives (users). For the purposes of obtaining accurate statistical results, the more users that can be persuaded to get involved, the better. As a general rule, ten users is the minimum number that should be involved in a testing project
▶ *Test observer* – the testing is remotely monitored by a test observer, who monitors all sources of information from the test (video, audio, and captured AUT UI images) and who has computer-aided support for subsequent analysis of the information

---

[1] This appendix does not discuss the role of psychometric usability tests (11) or expert review of graphical user interfaces (9).

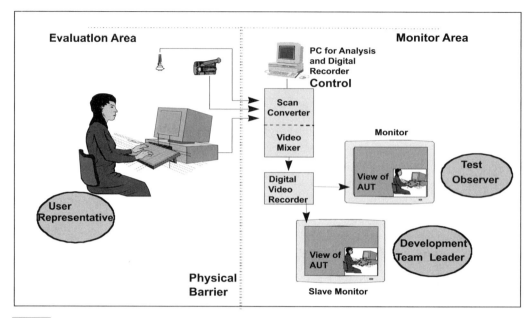

Evaluation Area

Monitor Area

PC for Analysis
and Digital
Recorder
Control

Scan
Converter

Video
Mixer

Monitor

Digital
Video
Recorder

View of
AUT

**Test
Observer**

**User
Representative**

View of
AUT

**Development
Team Leader**

**Physical
Barrier**

Slave Monitor

P1 Organization of a Typical Usability Test

▶ *Development team leader* – the development team leader may optionally sit with the test observer to observe the test
▶ *Independent test observer* – it is important that the testing process (and particularly the analysis and conclusions) is monitored by an independent test observer who is involved in formally witnessing the usability test.

In practice, it is likely that one person will take on the test team leader, test analyst, and test observer roles. However, the user representative, development team leader, and independent test observer must be distinct roles.

P3 Usability Test Design

The aim of usability testing is to confirm that the AUT meets its usability requirements as stated in the functional specification for the application.

The test analyst is responsible for inspecting the usability requirements and designing the individual test cases that will comprise the usability test. The test analyst will also liaise with the development team leader and may base a number of tests on usability issues raised during these discussions.

P4 Usability Testing

Usability testing is conducted in a formal manner under controlled conditions. All information from the test, including video footage of the user representative interacting with the AUT, the image of the AUT itself, and any audio information – such as user representative comments, is captured on video tape for subsequent review and analysis. Figure P1 shows the typical organization of a usability test.

The usability test is organized and managed by the test observer, who during the usability test will observe and monitor the test remotely.

During the usability test, the user representative will be expected to follow the test script generated by the test analyst. The only assistance provided to the user representative will be on-line help (if the AUT supports such a facility), or user manual or help documentation (if available). Depending on the usability requirements for the AUT, the on-line help or paper-based documentation itself may be the focus of the usability test.

For the purposes of statistical analysis, at least ten user representatives should perform the usability test. The user representatives should be drawn from the same user group (i.e., they should have broadly similar IT experience and should all have similar business skills and experience appropriate to the AUT that is the focus of the usability test).

P5 Post-test Activities

Following usability testing the test observer will review the information collected during the usability test to determine if the AUT meets its usability requirements.

Computer-aided statistical techniques are used to analyze video footage of the usability test, which may be recorded on sophisticated professional videocassette recorder equipment or using digital recording technology.

The usability test results are documented in a report, which summarizes the results of the usability test and highlights any usability issues. A brief summary video, which highlights the usability issues documented in the report, may also be produced to provide visual feedback to the developers.

The usability report (and summary video, where available) is presented to the development team leader at a post usability test meeting. The test team leader will also present a summary of the results of the usability test and any usability issues to the development team leader.

Testing Process Health Check

Q1 Introduction

This appendix contains a list of criteria to be used in performing a testing process health check and a suggested approach to conducting the task.

The testing process health check could be used in a number of ways:

▶ To baseline the current state of testing within an organization prior to introducing a formal testing process
▶ To monitor the progress of the adoption of a formal testing process, and to identify areas that were satisfactory and areas capable of improvement
▶ As part of a process improvement program (see Chapter 13 – Improving the Testing Process).

The criteria used in the testing process health check are grouped under the following high-level headings:

▶ Testing and the software development process
▶ Testing process
▶ Roles and responsibilities
▶ Testing phases.

These groups and their individual criteria are described in full in the following sections respectively. Section Q7 contains an optional scheme for scoring the various criteria if a more quantitative approach is required.

A checklist is provided at the end of this appendix that can be copied and used as an aide-memoir during the testing process health check. This checklist is also available to download using the following link: http://www.cambridge.org/9780521148016/.

Q2 Terminology

The term "subject" is used to denote the person, project, department, or organization that is the target of the testing process health check. The term subject could refer to a third-party organization whose testing process needs to be assessed, or internally within the host organization.

The term "auditor" is used to denote the person performing the testing process health check.

Q3 Testing and the Software Development Process

This section contains criteria addressing high-level software development and testing issues:

▶ Does the client have a formally documented process for software development, which incorporates testing issues?

▶ Does the client consider test requirements during all phases of the software development process (e.g., are the system requirements reviewed to verify that they can be tested easily?)

▶ Does the client have plans for software development projects, and can he or she show you examples of such plans? Do the plans explicitly show the points in the development at which testing will take place (i.e., is testing performed at all stages of the development and is adequate time assigned to testing)?

▶ Does the client organization have a quality system (such as ISO9001 or TickIT), and is this integrated with the software development and testing process?

▶ Does the client have a formally documented process improvement scheme (such as CMM or TMMi)?

▶ Does the client make use of software metrics (i.e., does he or she collect and use metrics)? Are metrics collected with regard to testing and used to improve the process (e.g., improved estimating of testing timescales)

▶ Who is responsible for ensuring that software development and testing standards are adhered to (e.g., does the client have a QA group or a testing group with a QA manager or testing manager)?

▶ How does the client manage requests for change/enhancement/defect (bug) fixes? How are these requests tracked, how are they verified, and how are they signed off (e.g., is there some form of tool support for this process)?

▶ Does the client develop and test software under rigorous configuration management?

Q4 Testing Process

This section contains criteria addressing client testing process issues:

▶ Does the client have a formally documented testing process (such as a testing strategy or a testing framework document)?

▶ Does the client have formally documented detailed plans for testing (such as a test plan document), and do the plans incorporate contingency for retesting defects?

- ▶ Does the client understand and make use of the V Model in planning the various testing phases (see Chapter 4)?
- ▶ Does the client have reusable templates for standard testing documentation that all testing projects must use, including:
  - ▷ A test plan document
  - ▷ A test specification document
  - ▷ Test scripts
  - ▷ Test result record forms
  - ▷ Test logs
  - ▷ Test certificates
  - ▷ A test summary report
  - ▷ Other documentation defined within the client process
- ▶ Does the client make reusable templates for standard testing documentation widely available to all projects/groups engaged in testing within the organization in an easily usable form (e.g., as photocopyable sheets in a manual, on digital optical disk, via an intranet system, etc.)?
- ▶ Does the client enforce the use of templates for standard testing documentation within projects/groups engaged in testing within the organization?
- ▶ Does the client have reproducibility of testing (i.e., is the client confident that a given test environment could be recreated and the test rerun with the same result)?
- ▶ Does the client conduct the testing process under rigorous configuration management?
- ▶ Does the client have formally documented test result categories and acceptable frequencies for defects?
- ▶ Does the client testing process formally support reuse (e.g., are testing projects responsible for compiling reuse packs, and for making use of reuse packs compiled by previous testing projects)?
- ▶ Does the client make use of *automated testing tools* within his or her testing process to reduce timescales and save effort?
- ▶ Does the client ensure adequate test coverage (i.e., does the client ensure that all parts of the application under test (AUT) are tested)?
- ▶ Does the client follow a process improvement program within the testing process?
- ▶ Does the client collect and use metrics within his or her testing process? If so, what metrics does the client collect, and how are they used in the testing process?

Q5   Roles and Responsibilities

This section contains criteria addressing the issues of staff roles and responsibilities within the client testing process:

- ▶ Does the client have formally documented roles and responsibilities for the staff involved in the testing process, such as:

> ▷ Testing manager
> ▷ Test team leader
> ▷ Test analyst
> ▷ Tester
> ▷ Independent test observer
- ► Are the reporting/liaison lines clearly defined for each role?
- ► Who is responsible for ensuring that testing is managed correctly:
  > ▷ within the client organization
  > ▷ within each project
- ► Who has responsibility for ensuring independent observation of testing (such as a quality assurance (QA) representative or member of staff not directly involved in the software development and testing)?

Q6 Testing Phases

This section contains criteria addressing the issues of testing phases within the client testing process:

- ► What formally documented testing phases does the client software development and testing process contain, and for each phase is there a specification of:
  > ▷ What is tested within that phase?
  > ▷ Who is responsible for managing that phase?
  > ▷ Who is responsible for performing the testing?
  > ▷ Who is responsible for independently observing the testing?
  > ▷ Which testing techniques should be used?
  > ▷ The test result categories?
  > ▷ The starting and halting criteria?
  > ▷ The formal documentation needed (e.g., test scripts, test logs)
  > ▷ The inputs to and outputs from the phase?
- ► Does the client consider obtaining reuse packs (see Appendix I) from previous testing phases to save time and effort within the current testing phase?
- ► Does the client consider the requirements for, and plan a testing phase during the corresponding phase of the software lifecycle (e.g., does the client plan acceptance testing during the requirements phase)?
- ► Does the client consider reuse at the end of each testing phase (e.g., by compiling a reuse pack of the materials created during the testing phase – see Appendix I)?

Q7 Optional Evaluation Scheme

Although the overall result of conducting a testing process health check is to provide a qualitative view of the suitability of the testing process employed by the client, it may be useful under certain circumstances to take a quantitative approach to the evaluation.

For example, the auditor conducting the evaluation may find it useful to flag certain criteria or results that he or she feels need emphasis, or the client may specify the use of such an approach in conducting the project.

Under such circumstances, the following scheme can be employed:

▶ Review the criteria and assign each a weighting, placing this value in the appropriate cell of the checklist provided at the end of this appendix:
  ▷ 1 for an essential criteria
  ▷ 0.75 for important criteria
  ▷ 0.5 for desirable criteria
  ▷ 0 for nonapplicable criteria
▶ When evaluating the client testing process, consider each criterion and score as follows:
  ▷ 1 if the testing process fully satisfies the criteria
  ▷ 0.75 if the testing process largely satisfies the criteria
  ▷ 0.5 if the testing process partially satisfies the criteria
  ▷ 0 if the testing process does not satisfy the criteria
▶ On completing the evaluation, multiply the score for each criterion by its weighting and total the scores.

This scheme must be used with some caution because it may be difficult to interpret the precise meaning of any particular score a given client testing process may achieve.

Client	Department	Date of Testing Audit	Auditor Name

Criteria	Weighting (0–1)	Score (0–1)	Result
Testing and the Software Development Process			
Formally Documented S/W Development Process			
Test Requirements at all Phases of S/W Development			
Integrated S/W Development & Testing Plans			
Quality System in S/W Development & Testing			
Process Improvement in S/W Development & Testing			
Use of Metrics in the Development Process			
Responsibility for S/W and Testing Standards			
Management of Change Requests			
Use of CM in S/W Development			
		Subtotal	
The Testing Process			
Formally Documented Testing Process			
Formally Documented Testing Plans			
Understanding and Use of the V Model in Planning			
Standard Testing Documentation			
Availability of Standard Testing Documentation			
Reproducibility of Testing			
Use of Rigorous CM in Testing			
Formally Documented Test Result Categories			
Support for Reuse			
Use of Automated Testing Tools			
Adequate Test Coverage			
Use of a Testing Process Improvement Programme			
Use of Metrics in the Testing Process			
		Subtotal	
Roles and Responsibilities			
Formally Documented Roles and Responsibilities			
Clearly Defined Reporting/Liaison Lines			
Management Responsibility for Client Organization			
Management Responsibility within Testing Project			
Responsibility for Independent Test Observation			
		Subtotal	
Testing Phases			
Formally Documented Test Phases			
Access to Reuse Packs from Previous Testing Phases			
Test Planning at all Phases of S/W Development			
Reuse of Testing Materials			
		Subtotal	
Miscellaneous Issues			
		Subtotal	
		Total Score	

The Testing of Object-Oriented Software

R1 Introduction

Irrespective of the technology employed in the development of a software system, any testing process will involve a number of common activities that must be performed by staff with appropriate skills and completed in a particular order to ensure successful testing – this is the essence of a repeatable, predictable, reusable process.

Where an organization has a requirement to test a number of different applications, each of which may have been developed using different tools, techniques, and languages, rather than emphasizing the differences between the applications and their implementation technologies, it is much more beneficial to look for the similarities.

Where differences that impact on the testing process are observed, these exceptions should be documented, and the testing solutions that are adopted to address them incorporated into the process as supplementary activities for future use.

Thus the starting point for determining how to approach the testing of any new or novel technology should be to assume that the testing will fit into the currently used process, and not throw current best practice away in favor of creating a new process from first principles.

This appendix discusses the particular issues involved in testing object-oriented (OO) software systems (36) and makes a number of proposals for how to approach this activity. Specifically, Section R2 briefly reviews the process of object-oriented software development, Section R3 discusses the impact of OO on the management and planning of testing, and Section R4 examines the impact of OO on the design of tests.

R2 Object-Oriented Development

Object-orientation is one of many approaches available for developing computer applications. In the same way that high-level procedural programming languages provided developers with significant benefits over assembler-based approaches, object-oriented programming (OOP) provides further benefits over procedural programming (see, e.g., 36).

OO is fundamentally different to procedural programming in the way it views process and data. In a procedural application, data and process are separate elements; data is passed to procedures that manipulate the data and pass it back when the processing is complete. In an object-oriented language, data and process are associated in programming entities termed objects, which are responsible for controlling access to and manipulation of their own data. When developing an application, OO provides a simple, "one-to-one" mapping between the entities that are to be modeled or represented in the domain of interest and their programming counterparts – the objects.

Another significant difference between OO and a procedural style of development is that of reuse (see, e.g., 37). In writing OO applications, developers are encouraged to reuse previously created objects to save time, effort, and cost. This approach can also improve the quality of the delivered software by allowing developers to reuse tried and tested objects, whose modular nature combined with their well-defined formal interface make it a straightforward task to integrate the objects into the application.

OO includes not just the implementation technology required to support objects, but also encompasses the philosophy of object-oriented development, which incorporates particular techniques for requirements capture, analysis, and design (see, e.g., 6). The particular approach to application development employed in OO software projects is one of the main areas of impact that OO has on the testing process.

The Unified Modeling Language (6) or UML is the foremost of the OO analysis and design methods and has largely achieved de facto standard status. UML includes a number of processes and notations for obtaining and representing information about the domain of interest. Use cases (7), for example, provide a concise approach to obtaining and agreeing the requirements of the AUT by supporting a formal dialog between user representative and analyst. The result is one or more simple diagrams and some associated text, which succinctly describes some specific interaction between the user and the system.

A number of software development processes, such as the iterative techniques (e.g., 39) and rapid prototyping methods (12), are particularly well suited to use with object orientation and further enhance the claimed productivity of OO development. Iteration breaks the traditional waterfall development model typically associated with procedural programming down into smaller steps – termed iterations (e.g., 39). The result of each iteration is a complete deliverable, which can be tested to ensure it meets the particular requirements for that iteration. In this way, testing begins earlier in the development process, and a higher volume of testing can be performed during the course of the overall project.

The next section discusses the impact of object orientation on the process of test management and planning.

R3 Impact of OO Development on Test Management & Planning

Although an effective means of improving the productivity of developers (36), object orientation, in combination with iterative development techniques (39), rapid prototyping (12), and object reuse (37), provide a massive challenge to quality assurance staff in terms of a significantly larger testing load as compared with more traditional development techniques.[1]

This increased testing load presents the biggest impact of OO on the management and planning of testing. Although test management must always be as efficient as possible, the relatively higher volumes of OO code produced in shorter timescales means that test managers must focus on the means of increasing testing effectiveness.

Iterative Development

An iterative approach to development and testing can be viewed in a very positive light because it brings testing further forward into the development process and permits more testing to be completed. The result of this process is to help manage risk and ensure a higher-quality deliverable.

However, in addition to earlier and more frequent testing, iterative development also means that there will also be a significantly higher regression testing requirement. At the completion of each iteration it will be necessary to verify that the changes made during the current iteration have not had an adverse effect on the functionality implemented during earlier iterations. Furthermore, the amount of time and effort spent on regression testing will grow with each iteration as there is progressively more of the AUT to regression test.

Under such circumstances, it is essential that as much reuse of previously developed test scripts and test cases is employed. Test analysts and testers must be made aware of the need to ensure test scripts are developed with reuse in mind, and that these test scripts are rigorously copied and filed for future use. Reuse packs are one means of helping to administer such an approach (see Appendix I).

Automated testing tools should also be considered to improve reuse in testing OO software, as well as to save testing time and effort, and to increase confidence in the quality of the software. The so-called record-playback or capture-replay testing tools (e.g., 22) are well tailored to testing object-oriented software, and use "object recognition" or "object mapping" techniques to identify objects in the AUT and to interrogate their properties. At the end of each iteration, the test analyst designs the set of test scripts to be used to verify that the requirements have been met for that iteration. As these test scripts are executed, the automated testing tool is used to record the process, allowing the tests to be replayed in regression testing subsequent

---

[1] Many advocates of OO would argue that object reuse assists the tester by allowing the developer to reuse tried and trusted objects and components. However, for complete confidence in the software, it is still necessary to ensure thorough testing.

iterations. As the project proceeds, a comprehensive regression testing suite is built up that can be run overnight or across the weekend to perform unattended testing of the AUT.

Although a powerful technique for saving time, effort, and cost, some caution must be employed in introducing automated testing tools, because their use will suffer from an initial learning curve. Their introduction and adoption must be planned and managed, and organizations must persevere with their use to gain the benefits that an automated approach can bring. Although there are reported cases of organizations gaining benefits (i.e., providing savings in time, effort, and cost over equivalent manual testing) after just two uses of such tools (17), typically organizations will need to use such tools three to four times to recoup their investment and to begin to save time, effort, and money.

Chapters 17 and 19 (the Crown and ADP case studies) provide examples of how an automated testing approach can be used successfully to reduce the testing load and to improve the quality of the AUT.

Rapid Prototyping

Rapid prototyping techniques provide users with an opportunity to see and use early trial versions of the AUT. This is a powerful approach to managing the user expectations of the AUT and to obtain rapid feedback regarding any mismatch between the user requirement and the implementation of the AUT. The difficulty for the testing process is that such approaches make it much easier for users to ask for enhancements or changes to the AUT following exposure to the proto-type software, with the concomitant issues of the need to update the requirements appropriately.

Where the AUT is being developed using rapid prototyping techniques, it is particularly important that test managers and test analysts have complete and full access to the most up-to-date requirements and that they are able to assess the implications of changes to the requirements to the testing activity. To ensure rigor and efficiency, a formal process for managing change requests and documenting and maintaining requirements must be followed.

Tool support for managing the requirements in an OO development and testing project must be considered (e.g., 19). Furthermore, the tool must be shared by analysts, developers, and testers, and any changes to the requirements information must be automatically communicated to each of the roles involved in development and testing.

A key means of increasing efficiency will be to ensure the requirements man-agement tool integrates with the testing tool to allow the test managers and test analysts to view the requirements for the AUT within the test tool, and to plan and design appropriate tests against those requirements. The new generation of develop-ment and testing tools that seamlessly integrate requirements, analysis, design, and testing facilities provide a powerful means of unifying the different roles involved in development while optimizing the performance of the individual roles such as the tester (see 23 and 25).

If correctly integrated into the development and testing process, rapid prototyping can be an effective means of managing the expectations of the users, preventing unexpected complaints at acceptance testing from users who are unhappy with the look and feel of the AUT or who are dissatisfied with its behavior or performance.

Object Reuse

The philosophy of reuse that object orientation promotes allows applications to be quickly built from libraries of existing objects. In addition to the benefits of reduced time and effort in development, the use of objects that are "tried and tested" means that the developer has higher confidence in the quality of the resulting AUT. Although the majority of these objects will be available from commercial object libraries, many organizations are becoming increasingly aware of the benefits of encouraging developers to write software with reuse in mind.

The increase in reuse of existing objects and modules that OO promotes provides both benefits and difficulties to testers. Although reuse means that more complex applications can be created more quickly by reusing libraries of predefined objects, the tester is faced with the challenge of how to manage the testing of the much higher volumes of code produced by such an approach. On the other hand, the opportunity for developing the AUT from trusted library objects should result in a product of higher quality.

As with any testing issue, the tester should be looking to exploit the benefits of OO while carefully managing its challenges. Automated testing has already been discussed in the previous section as an effective means of managing the higher productivity that OO brings.

The introduction and use of effective configuration management (e.g., 20) is a powerful approach to managing the testing of reusable objects. Using such an approach, it is possible to associated reusable tests with the reusable objects, allowing efficient testing of such objects by automatically incorporating those tests into the existing test suite.

As particular objects are used more frequently in the development of applications, it becomes possible to have increasing confidence in their quality as they become trusted objects. In such cases, it may only be necessary to test the integration of such objects or modules with other objects or modules when they are incorporated into the AUT, rather than having to test the functionality of the object itself.

R4 Impact of OO on Test Design

Those aspects of the testing process that employ Black Box testing techniques are largely unaffected by the use of object-oriented programming because test cases designed using such techniques are constructed with no knowledge of the internal structure of the AUT or its components. Thus the main area of testing that OO impacts on is unit testing where the programmer will design test cases based on their knowledge of the structure and function of the code, and to a lesser extent, integration testing.

Where developers have followed a UML approach in designing and implementing the AUT, this process can also be exploited by test analysts in designing effective and efficient tests. For example, use cases employed in requirements capture can be exploited in the design of realistic and effective thread tests for acceptance testing.

The impact of OO in the testing phases is described in the following sections.

Unit Testing

The modularity and encapsulation of objects combined with their well-defined interfaces means that the process of unit testing an object is more straightforward than testing a corresponding unit in a procedural language.[2] In effect, the object acts as its own test harness – allowing the tester to invoke its functionality or inspect its state by making the appropriate message calls to the object.

Where UML is being used in the development of the AUT, supplementary information, such as that provided by the OCL (object constraint language – see 38) may also be used by the test analyst in boundary value analysis and partition design techniques

The code generation facilities of some of the OO design (or CASE – computer-aided software engineering) tools (such as 34), can also be used to simplify the process of unit testing by allowing the objects that the unit under test interacts with to be created (albeit in a very basic form) so that the interactions between the adjacent objects can also be verified.

Where an integration exists between an OO design tool and an automated testing tool (such as that provided by 25), it may also be possible to automatically generate unit tests based on the design information providing significant benefits in terms of time, effort, cost, and quality.

Integration Testing

The greatest impact of object-oriented development on the process of integration testing is obtained from the design process, where various UML diagrams (such as the collaboration diagrams) can be used by the test analyst to support the process of test design. Such diagrams describe the interactions between well-defined aggregations

---

[2] Although "experienced programmers" have always striven to write well-encapsulated modular code with well-defined interfaces whatever language or technology they have used, OO helps enforce these principles on all developers. It is of course still possible to abuse the technology and produce poor code using OO.

of objects (analogous to modules in an integration testing sense), and can form the basis of tests to verify:

▶ The correct invocation of one module from another interoperating module
▶ The correct transmission of data between modules
▶ Nonfunctional issues, such as the reliability of the interfaces between modules.

As with unit testing, where an integration exists between an OO design tool and an automated testing tool, it may also be possible to automatically generate integration tests based on the design information.

Acceptance Testing

Use cases have a major benefit of helping to ensure that there is no misunderstanding between the user and analyst regarding the requirements for the AUT – in essence bridging the understanding gap between users who are expert about their domain of interest but are typically IT naive and analysts who are IT experts but likely to be unfamiliar with the domain.

The resulting use cases provide a succinct description of the interaction between the user and the AUT and include not just the "correct" use of the system, but also the alternate courses of action (such as actions leading to failure or error conditions).

Thus use cases can provide a rich source of information for the design of acceptance tests, describing both the navigational aspects of the test script (what the user does when interacting with the system) as well as the specific verifications needed in the test cases (what the user expects to see as a result of his or her actions).

Acceptance tests can frequently be directly derived by inspection of relevant use cases, and often much of the language used in the use case can be copied into the test script (particularly where an OO CASE tool is being used).

Alternate flows (such as error conditions) can also be quickly produced by simply copying the test script describing the typical interaction of user and AUT, and customizing it to reflect the steps involved in the alternate flow.

As with unit testing and integration testing, where the project team is using an integrated support tool for development and testing (such as that provided by 25), it may be possible to automatically view the use cases from within the testing tool so that tests can be planned, designed, and executed against those use cases.

Pragmatic Test Process Adoption – a Real-World Example

S1 Introduction

It is often the case that test practitioners have been tasked with delivering quality improvements in their projects or organization, but do not have the luxury of sufficient time, resources, or budget to devise, design, implement, and roll out a fully formed and working testing process. This appendix provides a real-world example describing how it is still possible to adopt a subset of the best practices described in this book to gain immediate, "quick win," quality improvements.

S2 Test Process Adoption – a Real-World Example

Introduction

As a testing practitioner who has been tasked with improving the quality of the software delivered by your project or by your organization, where do you start the process of adopting and using quality management best practices?

What you have read so far may appear extremely virtuous, but if you do not have sufficient time, resource, or budget, it may appear to be too much change to bring about in too short a time. Grabbing a few users, with no plan and no goal, however busy everyone appears to be, is no substitute for deliberate acts of testing.

If you are able to recognize your predicament as being near the bottom of a waterfall development (69), with a delivery that is in danger of missing the deadline, your testing resource appears scant and the implementation date cannot be moved, then you are not alone!

From past experience of such projects, the typical characteristics include being over budget, way beyond the start testing deadline, and riddled with uncertainties, but with the direction from above that the software must go out on time. Under such circumstances, to initiate all of the best practices in this book will most probably require too great a change in corporate understanding and motivation and, anyway, you have established that time just does not allow for such a revolutionary approach, however sound the reasoning. So don't try!

Instead, adopt an experienced-based approach, where we believe in at least making a start on the adoption of good process and making whatever amount of difference that can be made this time around. This approach is backed up by more than a decade of helping organizations under such conditions significantly improve their software quality.

The Testing Challenge

Your starting point is that you have a system development to test, which most likely contains the accumulation of all sorts of uncertainties introduced during the waterfall process. As discussed in Chapter 13, there is a significant likelihood that the cause of many quality issues will reside in specification materials that have failed to be confirmed as representing what the project sponsor actually wants from the delivered software.

Just for a moment, ditch the word "testing" and make a stock take of your situation. You need to prove that the system development is doing what it is supposed to do, and you know it is going to contain flaws that are already sitting there in the software you are setting out to test. Some of the flaws will be intolerable to the safe working of the system, and some will be tolerable. One short step from recognizing this is to accept that a "fitness for use" notion would be a "good enough to go live but not perfect" approach to adopt.

This can be illustrated by an example I frequently encounter: an insurance company will have decided that a new product will be delivered on a plethora of software-based systems, which will be deciding, on that insurer's behalf, whether a particular risk is acceptable and, if so, at what price and terms.

The software will have been designed to collect answers to all manner of questions and process the answers through the rules for scores of insurers' products. There are many millions of input and processing permutations, and the needs of any two insurers' products are rarely the same. This is further complicated as it is imperative that in such a competitive market, the premium quoted is accurate; otherwise too little or too much business will be attracted. Even worse, if a quotation is erroneously given for an unacceptable risk, this can wreak havoc for a book of insurance business, and not quoting when it should is nearly as bad. This is as business critical an environment as can be found anywhere. There is another layer to consider; as part of the process of fulfilling a quotation that has been accepted, a message containing all of the details of the business done is transmitted to the insurance company. If it is erroneous data, or the wrong kind of business, or at the wrong premium – it is TOO LATE, and there will be serious implications in terms of clerical effort required to correct the situation.

Day one of my involvement establishes that there are any number of anecdotal tales of previous failures and that this must be avoided this time, especially as there are expected to be of the order of 100,000 quotations hitting the system every day. It is supposed to be as automated a process as possible, without the clerical infrastructure for sweeping up errors. Inevitably, there is the desire to be error free, but neither the appetite nor the organization in place to adopt an effective but expensive and slow to implement test process.

Making a Start

First, establish that this is an exercise in quality management and that the testing pursuit is to be delivered to some concept of fitness for use. The testing process will be the minimum necessary stretching of the resources to gain maximum necessary benefit.

Can we capture and document the quality management approach to be followed? Because time does not allow for weeks or even hours of deliberation, we need to keep it simple; how about – "It is important to the business (underwriting and pricing managers) that this system quotes when it should, does not quote when it shouldn't, and when it does, the correct premium and terms are offered?" This doesn't sound like much, but if it is written down it will form the basis of all testing pursuits and provide a datum about which all parties can be orchestrated. So, write it down and have it agreed by all parties.

Having used the term "all parties," have we established who they are? If not, this is the next step. In our example, there will be a:

▶ Business change manager/analyst
▶ Underwriting manager
▶ Marketing manager
▶ Business support manager (clerical and errors)
▶ IT manager (receipt and processing of messages and data)
▶ Systems/programming analyst (or specification writer)

All of these people, possibly their next level up directors and definitely their immediate subordinates (the ones doing the work) should all be invited (and coerced where necessary) to attend a workshop. It amazes me how often when such a workshop is convened to discover that it is the first time they will have all been in the same room. Ensure they understand that the purpose of the meeting is to establish a common understanding that:

▶ This is a quality management exercise requiring quality assurance (testing) and that it must deliver to a universally agreed and understood set of notions:
   ▷ A quality manifesto – to be enshrined as step one of the brave new world of testing properly within the organization
   ▷ That it is not possible to test for everything and so there is no point making the assumption that it is

> ▷ That most of the problems encountered will be as a direct consequence of the waterfall development that has taken place thus far
> ▷ That a radical change of approach is required to prevent the past faults reoc-curring
▶ All testing pursuits are required to be deliberate acts with the sole purpose of delivering to the newly declared quality manifesto. All activity will be:
> ▷ Purposeful
> ▷ Documented
> ▷ Measured
> ▷ Expected to be the start of a new process of evolution within the organization
▶ That it is the responsibility of the entire organization to participate in the testing pursuit, but that it is the responsibility of the testing process to orchestrate the activity of all concerned. To this end there will be:
> ▷ A test strategy – a sequence of "will do this," "won't do that," statements that answer to the directive of the quality manifesto and inform the next step
> ▷ Test plans – A list of deliberately selected scenarios that when they pass, provide confidence that the quality manifesto is being met, and when they fail are a call to arms to decide what corrective action may be required on no account, are a set of scenarios devised to break a process or find errors, we just left that particular playground behind
▶ When a test plan or set of plans has been created, they will be reviewed by all parties in the room, together with any other parties who may be identified, as being the first steps toward a deliberate set of testing pursuits
▶ Last, but by no stretch of the imagination least, topped by the quality manifesto, there will also be a universally accepted definition of "a test": "A reasoned and documented input to the system, where a successful outcome has been prescribed (documented). When the desired outcome is demonstrated, the result provides meaningful confidence, and when not demonstrated, the result allows a measure of the impact to be evaluated."

The test process for this organization should have as its first two or three pages:

▶ Quality management manifesto
▶ Test strategy, the definition of a test and where/when they are to be applied
▶ List of participating subject authorities

Not much, but it is a start, and from beginning to end is about one afternoon's work; one afternoon, to bring about considerable organizational change but not so radical as to be an impossible task.

As a final thought in this section, in making a start, be cautious about placing too much reliance on automated testing solutions to save the day; automation is about repetitively executing something that is known to be good, and you don't have that yet. Keep automation in the testing tool bag for possible later use.

Test Planning

Next, a plan for testing needs to be documented (see Appendix C for guidance), and a series of test cases designed and implemented as test scripts; the techniques to be used are very dependent upon the circumstances of use. In the example of the insurance product, there is a definite split in terms of the sheer number of permutations of quotation input and the relatively limited number of messaging tests (which include printed documents).

Within the quotation testing, it does not take too long to define a set of test cases that typify the important aspects of "quotes when it should," "does not quote when it shouldn't." Irrespective of the potentially vague specification materials, something of the order of 1,000 tests are usually typical. Your own process may render greater or fewer numbers of tests, but the main point is to create them and write them down.

Save time and effort in this process by employing the test case design techniques described in Chapter 3 and the testing documentation templates (including test plan and test script templates) provided in the appendices, and also on-line at the following link: http://www.cambridge.org/9780521148016/.

The power of a test plan as an organ of communication can never be underestimated. In the insurance company example, once all of the tests are scheduled out, it is entirely possible to ask all other participants for their opinion of the content.

This is usually the first time such a group of people have been presented with such order, and it makes it easy for them all to proactively review what has been set out; this is the main purpose of the test plan at this stage.

The testing process needs the participants to rank the importance of each test from their own perspective as a subject authority, and to add any tests of their own. The way to go about making this a success is to present the stakeholders with a copy of the plan and the test cases and ask each participant to assess the test cases from their perspective and to rank them (perhaps using a simple scoring system, such as high, medium, and low), as a measure of how important that test is to them. It is essential that the scoring scheme be understood by all, and for a "high," this translates to "this test passing gives me much confidence and, should it fail, the impact on my responsibilities will be significant."

The job of the testing process at this point is to turn all aspects of the proposed test activity into tangible, measured, and meaningful effort.

When all participants have performed their ranking of importance and, hopefully, added "high" scoring cases of their own, all responses need to be merged together into a single document. Once this has been done and recirculated to all, the test plan represents the measurements that will need to be taken to satisfy all concerned that the test process will provide meaningful quality measures.

As a by-product of this process, there is now clear guidance as to the priority of tests to be executed. One inevitable truth is time will run short; having ranked the tests, we now have a means of deciding the order in which tests should be executed.

In the event that too many people have assigned high priority to too many cases, encourage the participants to take another look at the ranking, with the advice that there may be times where it will only be possible to execute 30% of the test cases. Based upon this, a fresh assessment and agreement of priorities has to be drawn up.

Our orderly, structured, and referenced test plan, written in language understandable to all participants, has acted as the glue that binds the needs of all parties impacted by the development. The first time this happens, it can come as a bit of a shock, as it will inevitably demonstrate how little time has been set aside for such an important aspect of the development. All the while, it is the effort expended on creating a test plan that has acted as a significant medium for communicating the scale, detail, and purposefulness of the impending testing task.

In terms of elapsed time, the previous activities should take about a week of effort to produce the initial test plan and a few hours on the part of each participant.

Test Scripts

The next piece of work is to create the test scripts and, in the case of the insurance product, the step-by-step premium calculation for those cases that quote.

It is not the purpose of this section to teach how to test insurance products, and so the finer detail of the test script will not be labored here. Suffice it to say you will have your own needs in terms of test script input data and setting out expected outcomes if they are more complex than Pass/Fail.

With our completed test scripts to hand, we are now ready to execute some tests.

Test Execution

Step 1. ANTICIPATE, that the system under test will inevitably require some nursing into life. In thirty years, I have never had a new system run end to end the first time. Typically, there will be all manner of "set up vagaries" and security issues to be resolved before testing proper can begin.

With this in mind, and at the time of setting out test cases, create a benchmark[1] set of navigation and inputs, and run these against the test version of the system immediately as it becomes available. In the insurance product example, the benchmark scenario is something that would be agreed with all participants as representing a "clean pass." If the benchmark test cannot be executed, there is no point proceeding. Have this benchmark clearly set out and understood by all. When this test execution has cleared, you have "thrown a six" to start properly.

Bugs, Defects, and Problems

As soon as tests are executed, problems will arise. These could be termed bugs or defects, but it may be more useful in the initial stages of testing to call them

---

[1] Also often termed a smoke test or a crash test (see glossary for further detail).

problems – an unexpected outcome at the early stages has about a 50% chance of having been caused as a result of a test script error, an execution error, or even a cocktail of both. The prudent tester goes back over the ground to be certain that the input correctly reflected the script AND that the script correctly depicted the test requirement.

When these aspects have been discounted, the unexpected outcome has only two potential causes, a bad test or a flaw in the processing. Either way, it is now time to make a defect report.

What we do next is critically important to the testing process. Do we continue execution? Probably, the answer is yes, we need to harvest the outcomes of the largest amount of test coverage that we can. Apart from anything else, we will need to know how long it takes to execute all of the tests, as we will need this information at our disposal when estimating later test phases.

If circumstances have not allowed the purchase of a dedicated defect management tool (e.g., 20), all is not lost; make use of the defect result record form template (Appendix F), and ensure you document the following information:

▶ Problem log reference number
▶ Test number(s)
▶ Descriptive "Input X"
▶ Descriptive "Expected Y" (reference the specification definitive if necessary)
▶ Descriptive "Got Z"
▶ Allow spaces for:
  ▷ The tester ID (and independent test observer – if present)
  ▷ Response
  ▷ Severity
  ▷ Impact

At appropriate points, the most authoritative of the participants must be the person who deliberates over a reported problem, and that individual will have been identified in the earliest of group meetings. This is the point where, if we get it right, we make the biggest impact in terms of how our quality management activities improve the overall process of testing within the organization as a whole. First, by identifying the most appropriate authority, we will have identified the person highest up the waterfall who prescribed the development. They must be the body qualified to deliberate on the certainty of the problem reported as being a deviation from expected behavior.

In the case of the insurance product example, it may be the underwriting manager, the pricing manager, or any one of the other specialists who require certain types of behavior to be upheld.

When all problems have been reported, adjudicated by the appropriate authority, and measured in terms of their severity and impact, there is another important piece of work for the testing activity: communication.

Managing Stakeholder Expectations

The entire purpose of asking for a measure of the severity of a defect is a hard-nosed way of getting the business to understand that all problems may not be solved in time for implementation. If, as they have a habit of doing, the subject authorities have assigned a maximum severity value to every defect, they must be asked to take another look. As testers, we have to create the understanding among the authorities that there never has been and probably never will be such a thing as a "quick one line fix" and that with every fix there is a high risk of collateral damage being caused to the code. This is a simple fact of life.

A defect assessed as falling into the maximum severity category translates to the reasonable expectation that a fix will be applied by the next possible safe release of code. "Safe" means that the fix can be tested, together with all of the other essential tests being executed in time before implementation. This is hard for business authorities to understand, and it is the job of the tester to set out the rules to minimize risks of subsequent collateral damage to code.

With this in mind, we have not yet let the developers see the test log (Appendix G). It is important that we share with them a reasoned list of fixes, being careful to listen to what they have to say in terms of the time and risk associated with bringing them about. The reasons we have not kept the developers up to date with problems found as they have been found is threefold:

▶ First, it is the business authority that holds the decision on the severity, impact, and urgency of a fix, and not the tester or the developer
▶ Second, developers are genetically hard-wired to fix defects immediately, and possess a delusional indifference to the risks of collateral damage. This genetic wiring is vital to the developer or he or she would never get anything completed. It is a known trait and not by any means an insult
▶ Third, the business authority may well need to redefine requirements when faced with a problem. The metrics distilled from many years of experience are as follows:
  ▷ 75% of problems found have their root cause in less than unequivocal requirement definitions/specification materials
  ▷ Of these, where our testing process is supposed to be verifying that the product has been built correctly, up to 50% demonstrate that we are validating that the wrong product has been built
  ▷ These are blood-curdling facts, but they are facts, and everything we can do to nip this in the bud is a worthwhile effort (and exactly why we need to engage our subject authorities).

Because of the previous, we need to dissuade the developers from making any unplanned changes yet.

Ultimately, from this first test phase, there will be some problems recorded together with clarification as to how they are to be fixed and with what urgency.

Relative priorities may require that only the most important are given to the developers, with clear prescription of the fix requirements.

Then it all starts over again with the next phase of test execution.

As time presses on, there will be an ever-increasing need to rely on the prioritization of tests and problems, to enable the focus of all effort onto the elements most necessary to arrive at an implementation that is "good enough" in response to the quality manifesto. There will then be a load of sweeping up of lower priority problems, possibly more intricate problems to solve, test, and deploy in subsequent releases.

Summary

By following the previously described process, the essence of testing discipline has been brought to bear on the job in hand, which is a quality management exercise.

The essential parties have become involved in determining the relevant aspects of "fit for use" or "safe enough," and their bidding has been facilitated and focused by the testing discipline. In my experience, this is often a complete "first" for most parties involved.

It will not be perfect but it will have been deliberate, purposeful, documented, and capable of being used to demonstrate that this time was better than last time. Take account of live errors, post-implementation, gather the authorities and show them how their worst fears were demonstrably averted.

Show the authorities how many of the issues found in testing were corrected by applying the V Model approach for planning testing and dealing with problems, and that most of them could well have been averted if a V Model approach is adopted in the future. Demonstrate that any number of test phases, time, and money spent in re-development were caused as a direct consequence of the waterfall delivery, and that there are clear ways of avoiding this in the future.

In short:

- Everything becomes
  - ▷ Deliberate
  - ▷ Communicable
  - ▷ Measured
- Starts with a quality manifesto
- Tests are planned and clearly understood
- Test executions are phased ~ NO EXCUSES
- Problems are solved by authorities within a recursive V Model process
- The minimum of metrics are retained to demonstrate the worth of good process
- It really does not take much time or money
- It is a start

By following all of the previous, it is possible to become involved in the most chaotic of projects, where temperatures are running high and make a real difference.

So far, this approach has worked in every engagement I have been involved in.

The next step is to decide how to enhance this initial starter set of best practices; which additional aspects of the testing process described in this book should be used in the next project, to further refine the process.

Great oaks from little acorns grow.

References

1. "The Complete Guide to Software Testing – Second Edition," Hetzel, B., QED Information Sciences Inc., Massachusetts, 1988. ISBN: 0-89435-242-3.
2. "The Art of Software Testing," Myers, G. J., John Wiley, New York, 1979.
3. "PRINCE 2: Project Management for Business," 4th edition, CCTA, 1996. ISBN: 0-11-330685-7.
4. "British Library Testing Course," Ref: P6188A/T0, AMSL, 1997.
5. "IT Infrastructure Library," CCTA, Gildengate House, Norwich, December 1993.
6. "Unified Method for Object-Oriented Development," Booch, G., and Rumbaugh, J., Documentation Set v0.8, Rational Software Corporation, Santa Clara, 1995.
7. "Getting Started: Using Use Cases to Capture Requirements," Journal of Object-Oriented Programming, September 1994.
8. "The Rational Unified Process," Krushten, P., Addison-Wesley, 1998.
9. "Human Computer Interaction," Preece, J. et al., Addison-Wesley, 1994. ISBN: Q-201-62769-8.
10. "The Essential Guide to User Interface Design: An Introduction to GUI Design Principles and Techniques," Galitz, W. O., John Wiley & Sons, 3rd edition, 2007. ISBN: 0470053429.
11. "The Software Usability Measurement Inventory: Background and Usage," Kirakowsky, J., in *Usability Evaluation in Industry*, Taylor & Francis, U.K., 1996.
12. "DSDM Atern Pocketbook," DSDM Consortium, White Horse Press, June 2008. ISBN: 0-9544832-1–9.
13. "IBM Rational Functional Tester System Documentation," IBM, New York, 2010.
14. "ISO 9001" & "ISO 9003," International Standards Organization.
15. "Software Testing – Part 1: Vocabulary," BS 7925-1:1998, BSI, August 1998.
16. "IEEE Standard for Software Test Documentation," IEEE Standard 829-1998, IEEE, December 1998.
17. "Automating Software Testing," Graham, D., and Fewster, M., Addison-Wesley, 1999.
18. "Principles of Software Engineering Management," Gilb, T., Addison-Wesley, 1988.
19. "IBM Rational RequisitePro Documentation," IBM, New York, 2010.
20. "IBM Rational ClearCase Documentation," IBM, New York, 2010.
21. "IBM Rational ClearQuest Documentation," IBM, New York, 2010.
22. "IBM Rational Robot Documentation," IBM, New York, 2010.
23. "IBM Rational Performance Tester Documentation," IBM, New York, 2010.

24. "Software Systems and Their Development," Reference: M301, The Open University, Milton Keynes, U.K., 2000.

25. "IBM Rational Team Unifying Platform Documentation," IBM, New York, 2010.

26. "Software Engineering Economics," Boehm, B., Englewood Cliffs, NJ: Prentice Hall, 1981.

27. "European Systems and Software Initiative Process Improvement Experiment," Project 27581, www.cordis.lu/esprit/src/stessi.htm.

28. "James Bach on Risk-Based Testing," Bach, J., *Software Testing and Quality Engineering Magazine*, Vol. 1, No. 6, Nov./Dec. 1999.

29. "CRAMM User Guide," Insight Consulting, Walton-on-Thames, U.K., 1998.

30. "Ris3: Professional Risk Management Software," Line International Ltd, Bristol, U.K., 2000.

31. "Software Metrics," Grady, B. R., and Caswell, D. L., Prentice-Hall, 1987.

32. "Organizational Psychology," Schein, E., 2nd edition, Prentice-Hall, 1970.

33. Complexity Estimating Software," McCabe Associates, Maryland, USA.

34. "Visual Modeling with Rational Rose and UML," Quatrani, T., Addison Wesley Longman, 1998.

35. "Key Practices of the Capability Maturity Model – Version 1.1," Paulk, M. C., et al., Software Engineering Institute – Carnegie Mellon University.

36. "Object-Oriented Programming," Rentsch, T., SIGPLAN Notices, Vol. 17, No. 9, September 1982.

37. "Reusability: The Case for Object-Oriented Design," Meyer, B., *IEEE Software*, March 1987.

38. "Instant UML," Muller, P-A, Wrox Press Ltd., Birmingham, U.K., 1997.

39. "A Spiral Model of Software Development and Enhancement," Boehm, B. W., *Computer*, IEEE, May 1988.

40. "IEEE Standard for Software Test Documentation," IEEE Std. 828-2008, IEEE, 2008.

41. "Software Inspection," Gilb, T., and Graham, D., Addison-Wesley, 1993.

42. "Software Testing in the Real World," Kit, E., Addison-Wesley, 1995.

43. "Software Testing Techniques," Beizer, B., Van Nostrand Reinhold, 1990.

44. "IBM Rational Purify Plus Documentation," IBM, New York, 2010.

45. "British Telecommunications Verification, Validation & Testing Handbook," British Telecommunications plc, Issue 3, 1997.

46. "IBM Rational Unified Process Documentation," IBM, New York, 2010.

47. "VisualTest Documentation," IBM, New York, 2010.

48. "The Chaos Report," Standish Group, www.standishgroup.com.

49. "HP Mercury Quick Test Professional Documentation," HP Mercury, 2010.

50. "Extreme Programming Explained: Embrace Change," Kent, B., Addison-Wesley, 2000.

51. "The New New Product Development Game," Takeuchi, H., and Nonaka, I., Harvard Business Review, January-February 1986.

52. "RAD, Rapid Application Development," Martin, J., MacMillan Publishing Co., New York, 1990.

53. "Agile Retrospectives: Making Good Teams Great," Derby, E., et al., Pragmatic Bookshelf, 2006.

54. "Agile Testing – How to Succeed in an Extreme Test Environment," Watkins, J., Cambridge University Press, 2010.

55. "Six Thinking Hats," De Bono, E., London: Penguin Books, 1999.

56. "Achieving Software Quality Through Teamwork," Evans, I., Artech, 2004.

57. "Problem Solving – Tools and Techniques," TQMI, 2001.

58. http://en.wikipedia.org/wiki/Continuous_integration.

59. "IBM Rational Build Forge Documentation," IBM, New York, 2010.

60. "IBM Rational Software Analyser Documentation," IBM, New York, 2010.
61. "IBM Rational Quality Manager Documentation," IBM, New York, 2010.
62. "Second Life for Dummies," Robbins, S., and Bell, M., John Wiley & Sons, 2008.
63. "IBM Rational Team Concert Documentation," IBM, New York, 2010.
64. "The Eclipse Way: Processes That Adapt," Wiegand, J., and Gamma, E., *EclipseCon* 2005.
65. "Exploratory Testing," Bach, J., http://www.satisfice.com/articles.shtml.
66. http://www.slideshare.net/ravindra2109/enterprise-agile-process.
67. "Evolutionary Project Management and Product Development," Gilb, K., and Gilb, T., pre-publication-draft-work-in-progress, May 2007. http://www.gilb.com/community/tiki-page.php?pageName=Books.
68. "SaaS – The Complete Cornerstone Guide to Software as a Service Best Practices Concepts, Terms, and Techniques for Successfully Planning, Implementing and Managing SaaS Solutions," Menken, I., Emereo Pty. Limited, 2008.
69. "Managing the Development of Large Software Systems," Royce, W., Proceedings of IEEE, WESCON, August 1970.
70. http://www.nunit.org.
71. "IBM Rational AppScan Documentation," IBM, New York, 2010.
72. The International Software Testing Qualifications Board, http://www.istqb.org/.
73. "A Practitioner's Guide to Software Test Design," Lee Copeland, Artech House Computing Library, 2003.
74. "Software Testing: A Craftsman's Approach – 3rd Edition," Jorgensen, P., Auerbach Publications, 2008.
75. "The Combinatorial Design Approach to Automatic Test Generation," Cohen, D., et al., IEEE Software, September 1996.
76. "All-Pairs Test Case Generation Tool V1.2.1," Bach, J., www.satisfice.com/tools.shtml.

Glossary

Introduction

The glossary contains those terms or phrases used within this document that require further explanation or definition.

The definitions presented in this glossary conform to standard testing terms as specified in testing standards documents (see References 15, 16, and 40).

Acceptance Test Certificate a document (typically one-page long), which is used to formally record the successful completion of the *acceptance test* for a particular *application under test* (*AUT*). The certificate is signed by a senior representative of the organization accepting the AUT and the organization delivering the AUT (see Appendix H).

Acceptance Testing Formal testing conducted to enable a user, customer, or other authorized entity to determine whether to accept a system or component. This testing phase is used to test the system as a whole to ensure that it meets its stated business requirements and that it performs within defined constraints. This testing phase takes place after *system testing* has been completed (also see *user acceptance testing* and *operations acceptance testing*).

All-pairs Testing see *pairwise testing*.

Application Under Test The application or program that is the focus of the testing process. Application under test is abbreviated as *AUT*, and is synonymous with *system under test* (*SUT*) in this document.

AUT The abbreviation of *application under test* (i.e., the application or program that is the focus of the testing process). AUT is synonymous with *system under test* (*SUT*) in this document.

Automated Testing The use of software to control the execution of tests, the comparison of their observed results to predicted results, the setting up of test preconditions, and other test control and test reporting functions.

Automated Testing Tools Software tools (such as IBM Rational Functional Tester [Reference 13]) that automate the testing process in order to reduce effort, timescales, and cost in the testing of software.

Automated Test Script A series of instructions in a computer readable form, which allows an automated testing tool to reproduce the navigation and *verification points* programmed into the tool to perform testing of the *AUT*. An automated test script is analogous to a manual *test script*, with verification points analogous to manual *test cases*.

Behavioral Testing See *black box testing*.

Black Box Testing *Test case* selection that is based on an analysis of the *specification* of the *component* without reference to its internal workings. That is, testing where the test cases are designed without any knowledge of how the *AUT* is constructed. The test cases are derived from a knowledge of the AUT's external behavior only.

Boundary Value An input value or output value that is on the boundary between *equivalence classes*, or at an incremental distance either side of the value.

Boundary Analysis See *boundary value analysis*.

Boundary Value Analysis A *test case* design technique for a component in which test cases are designed that include representatives of *boundary values*.

Build Verification Testing A testing technique that verifies the navigational structure of the *AUT*. Typically performed depth first, each menu and its component menu items (and submenus) are invoked to verify that they run some specific aspect of the AUT's functionality or open a dialog box. In the latter case, further navigation is performed to verify that dialog box buttons invoke AUT functionality or open further dialog boxes. Build verification testing is synonymous with *smoke testing*.

Business Process Testing A testing technique that verifies a typical business use of the *AUT* (e.g., the process of setting up a new user account in a banking system). Business process testing takes a typical scenario involving user interaction with the AUT and implements this as a test. Use cases (7) are often cited as being a particularly good source of business process tests.

Business Scenario The combination of navigation through the *AUT* and the invocation of specific functionality to support a particular business use of the AUT. For example, in a banking application, the collection of steps involved in creating a new account could be considered a business thread.

Business Threads See *business scenario*.

Configuration Testing See *installation testing*.

Commercial Off-the-Shelf (COTS) Commercially available software products/tools that can be purchased from vendors. For example, Microsoft Word and IBM Rational Quality Manager (61) are examples of COTS products.

Compatibility Testing Compatibility testing verifies that when the *AUT* runs in the live environment its operation does not impact adversely on other systems and vice versa. Also see *interoperability testing*.

Crash Testing A testing technique used to determine the fitness of a new build or release of an *AUT* to undergo more thorough testing. Crash testing seeks to discover if the AUT is reliable and robust, or if it "crashes" during routine use. In essence, crash testing is a "pre-test" activity that could form one of the acceptance criteria for receiving the AUT for testing. Also see *skim testing*.

Development Environment The IT environment (including the hardware, software, data, and support infrastructure) used by the *development team* to support the development of the *AUT*. Typically, the early phases of testing (such as *unit testing*) are conducted on the development environment. Also see *live environment* and *test environment*.

Development Team The project team with responsibility for developing the *AUT*.

Development Team Leader The member of staff responsible for leading the team developing the *AUT*. Liaises with the *test team leader* to report on the progress of the development of the AUT and likely dates for delivery of AUT for testing purposes.

Domain Testing See *equivalence class testing*.

End Users The members of staff who will use the delivered AUT in support of their work. Also see *operations users*.

Equivalence Class A set of the *component's* input or output domains for which the component's behavior is assumed to be the same from the component's *specification*. An equivalence class may also be termed an *equivalence partition*.

Equivalence Class Testing A *test case* design technique for a *component* in which test cases are designed to execute representatives from *equivalence classes*. This form of testing may also be termed *domain* or *partition testing*.

Equivalence Partition See *equivalence class*.

Equivalence Partition Testing See *equivalence class testing*.

Error Guessing A *test case* design technique where the experience of the tester is used to postulate what faults might be present in a *component* or *AUT*, and to design tests specifically to expose them.

Experienced Based Testing See *error guessing*.

Fault Recovery Testing This form of testing verifies that following an error or exception, the *AUT* is restored to a "normal" state, such as the initial state of the AUT when it is first executed. This form of testing may also be used to verify the successful rollback and recovery of the data used or manipulated by the AUT.

Functional Requirements Traditionally, those requirements for the *AUT* that have been specified within the functional specification document for the AUT. Also see *nonfunctional requirements*.

Functional Specification A document that describes in detail the characteristics of the *AUT* with regard to its intended capability.

Functional Testing The process of testing the *AUT* to verify that it meets its *functional requirements*. These requirements are typically recorded in a *requirements specification* document. (Also see *nonfunctional testing*.)

Glass Box Testing See *White Box testing*.

Incremental Testing A testing technique used in *integration testing*, where untested modules are combined with the module under test incrementally, with the functionality of the module (plus the added modules) being tested (retested) as each module is added.

Independent Test Observer A member of staff, who is independent from the development and testing teams, who observes the testing process and is involved in signing off the *test result record forms* for each *test case*.

Installation Testing ... aka configuration testing...

Integration Testing Testing performed to expose faults in the interfaces and in the interaction between integrated components. This testing phase is used to identify problems with communications between modules or units, resource contention, and to verify the system design. This testing phase takes place after *unit testing* but before *system testing* and may also be termed *link* or *module testing*.

Interoperability Testing Interoperability testing verifies that when the *AUT* is operating in the live environment it is able to communicate successfully with other specified systems (such as invoking, passing data to, or receiving data from another system). Also see *compatibility testing*.

IT An acronym for the computing term information technology.

IT Systems Administrator The member of staff within an organization with responsibility for administering the corporate IT facilities and for performing the day-to-day operations of the system (such as installation of software, upgrade of operating system software, back-up and archive, and preventive maintenance).

IT Systems Manager This term is synonymous with the term *IT systems administrator*.

Link Testing A testing phase that is used to identify problems with communications between modules or units, resource contention, and to verify the system design. This testing phase takes place after *unit testing* but before *system testing*, and may also be termed *integration* or *module testing*.

Live Data The actual data used by an organization to support its business activities. This is distinct from any test data that may have been generated to represent the live data for the purposes of testing.

Live Environment The actual IT environment (including the hardware, software, data, and support infrastructure) used by an organization to support its business activities. This is distinct from any testing environment that may have been set up to represent the live environment for the purposes of testing. Also see *development environment* and *test environment*.

Load Testing A *nonfunctional testing* technique that determines the *AUT*'s ability to cope with sudden instantaneous peaks loads (such as the sudden attempt by all users of a system to log on simultaneously) (as opposed to the sample operating conditions likely to have been used during development of the AUT). See also *performance, stress, volume*, and *usability testing*, and Chapter 3 – Testing Techniques).

Millennium Testing A testing activity used to identify and test applications to assess their capacity to operate and restart without disruption resulting from the processing of times/dates from before the year 2000 date change until 29th February 2000 and beyond, and where necessary, to modify systems to support the above objective. Millennium testing is synonymous with Year 2000, Y2K, and Date 2000 testing.

Module Testing A testing phase that is used to identify problems with communications between modules or units, resource contention, and to verify the system design. This testing phase takes place after *unit testing* but before *system testing*, and may also be termed *integration* or *link testing*.

Negative Testing Testing aimed at demonstrating that the software does not behave in a manner prohibited in its *specification*.

Nonfunctional Requirements Within the context of testing, the term nonfunctional requirements refers to the testing of those aspects of the *AUT* not specified within the functional specification document for the AUT. For example, *performance, volume, stress,* and *usability testing* are examples of nonfunctional testing. (Also see Chapter 3 – Testing Techniques, for further details of these nonfunctional testing techniques.)

Nonfunctional Testing The testing of those requirements that do not relate to functionality. Literally, the testing of those aspects of the *AUT* that are not explicitly specified in the functional specification document (although in practice, issues of performance and usability may be well defined in exemplary examples of such documents). Nonfunctional testing includes: *performance, stress, volume,* and *usability testing*. (Also see *functional testing*.)

Operations Acceptance Testing This is a form of *acceptance testing* conducted from the operations perspective (i.e., involving representatives from the operations staff). (Also see *acceptance testing*.)

Operations Representative A nominated member of the operations community for the *AUT* who will be expected to participate in or to nominate other operations staff to participate in the *operations acceptance testing* of the system (it is important that the operations representative be a genuine user of the system, and not, for example, a manager who manages *operations users* of the system).

Operations Users The members of staff who will execute the administrative aspects of the delivered software system in support of the *end users*. For example, typical tasks performed by the operations users include setting up user access and privileges, back-up and archive of system data, and system recovery.

Pairwise Testing A *test case* design technique that seeks to select a subset of all possible pairs of parameters and combinations of values, to provide the most effective test coverage, and in combination with the other test design techniques discussed within Section 3.3, will provide good test results. Also known as all-pairs testing.

Partition Testing See *equivalence class testing*.

Performance Testing Testing conducted to evaluate the compliance of a *component* or *AUT* with specified performance requirements. Performance testing is a particular type of *nonfunctional testing* that measures the speed of execution and response of the *AUT* under typical working conditions with the intention of determining that these characteristics will meet the users requirements (expectations) for the AUT. See also *stress*, *volume*, and *usability testing*, and Chapter 3 – Testing Techniques).

Pseudocode A form of structured English used by programmers in developing the program code to represent the functionality, structure, and flow of the application. Frequently used in *static testing* techniques (such as code review or walkthrough. See Chapter 3 – Testing Techniques).

QA An acronym for the term quality assurance.

Rapid Application Development A software development approach that emphasizes the rapid delivery of the software under development. Such approaches typically engage the end users in the development process as early as possible by the use of prototypes and mock-ups of the system, and employ stringent planning and management using an iterative development style with strictly observed milestones and budgets. See Reference 12 for example.

RAD See rapid application development.

Regression Testing A testing technique in which the *AUT* is tested following modifications or extensions to ensure that the overall functionality of the system has not been compromised. Regression testing may also take place following changes to the environment in which the system is resident (e.g., changes to the operating system or to hardware).

Reliability Testing A *nonfunctional test*ing requirement that verifies that the *AUT* is robust and reliable in normal use, ensuring for example, that the AUT does not suffer from catastrophic failures (such as GPFs on Windows platforms) or from memory leak problems.

Requirements Specification A document that records the requirements for a particular application or software system. These are traditionally obtained from the intended user(s) of the system by an analyst using some form of requirements capture method (such as use case modeling – [7]). The requirements specification is synonymous with the *software requirements specification* document.

Reuse Packs These are documents that allow testers to quickly and easily rerun some or all the tests performed during an earlier testing phase. Where modifications have been made to a system, reuse packs can speed up the process of *regression testing*. Similarly, reuse packs can enable selected tests to be rerun in later testing phases should they be required. (See also Appendix I – Reuse Pack Checklist.)

Safety Testing A testing technique intended to validate that the AUT or SUT meets its requirements in terms of safety of operation. This technique is particularly appropriate for the testing of safety critical systems.

Security Testing Security testing is focused on ensuring the *AUT* and/or its data is accessible to only authorized users. Security tests can be designed, implemented, and executed within any testing phase, but are typically conducted at system test.

Simulation The representation of selected behavioral characteristics of one physical or abstract system by another system. In testing terms, that is the use of a computer program to represent elements of the testing environment that are not available during testing. For example, if the *AUT* is being developed and tested on a standalone workstation but will be delivered on a networked system, it may be necessary to simulate typical network traffic during testing. (Also see *test harness*.)

Simulator A software system or computer program responsible for providing *simulation* services in support of the testing of an *AUT*.

Skim Testing A testing technique used to determine the fitness of a new build or release of an *AUT* to undergo further more thorough testing. In essence, a "pretest" activity that could form one of the acceptance criteria for receiving the AUT for testing. Also see *crash testing*.

Smoke Testing A testing technique that verifies the navigational structure of the *AUT*. Typically performed depth first, each menu and its component menu items (and submenus) are invoked to verify that they run some specific aspect of the AUT's functionality or open a dialog box. In the latter case, further navigation is performed to verify that dialog box buttons invoke AUT functionality or open further dialog boxes. Smoke testing is synonymous with *build verification testing*.

Specification See *requirements specification*.

SRS Common abbreviation of *software requirements specification*.

State Transition Analysis A *test case* design technique in which the analysis of the various states the *AUT* can be in, and the transitions between those states supports the creation of a series of both positive and negative tests.

State Transition Testing See *state transition analysis*.

Static Testing Static testing deals with the inspection of the *AUT* in isolation (i.e., not in a running state). Static testing typically takes place early in the development of the AUT and involves techniques such as code review and code walkthrough. (Also see Chapter 3 – Testing Techniques.)

Stress Testing Testing conducted to evaluate a system or *component* at or beyond the limits of its specified requirements. That is, a particular type of *nonfunctional testing* that examines the ability of the *AUT* to cope with instantaneous peak loads with the aim of identifying defects that only appear under such adverse conditions. Also see *performance, volume* and *usability testing*, and Chapter 3 – Testing Techniques).

Structural Testing See *White Box testing*.

Systems Integration Testing An optional testing phase (typically for those software systems that have a significant requirement to work or interoperate with other software systems) that is used to ensure that the *AUT* can interoperate successfully with any other software systems with which it needs to communicate, and to ensure that the AUT is compatible with other systems that may be running in the same environment. Systems integration testing takes place before *acceptance* *testing* and after *system testing* (under certain circumstance, system integration and system testing may be performed together).

System Testing The process of testing an integrated system to verify that it meets specified requirements. That is, a testing phase that is used to test the *AUT* as a complete system to identify any functional problems not found in *unit testing*, assess *nonfunctional* requirements such as *performance* and *usability*, and establish confidence that the system will be accepted by the users. System testing takes place after *integration testing* and before *acceptance testing*.

System Under Test The application or program that is the focus of the testing process. System under test is abbreviated as *SUT*, and is synonymous with *application under test (AUT)* in this document.

SUT The abbreviation of *system under test* (i.e., the application or program that is the focus of the testing process). SUT is synonymous with *application under test (AUT)* in this document.

Test Analyst A member of the testing team responsible for inspecting the requirements document for the *AUT*, analyzing the test requirements, designing the *test cases*, and drafting the *test scripts* (see Appendix A for complete *TORs* of the members of staff involved in the testing process).

Test Automation See *automated testing*.

Test Case A specific test intended to verify one particular aspect or requirement of the *AUT*, and which will contain a set of input values, execution preconditions, predicted outcome and objective for the test. A *test script* may contain one or more test cases.

Test Data The data used during testing to exercise the *AUT*. To provide complete confidence in the results of testing, the test data should be *live data*, however, there are many reasons why it may not be appropriate to use live data (e.g., where the data contains confidential data or information relating to security issues, or where the testing may threaten the integrity of the live data). Under these circumstances, it may be possible to use a copy of the live data. If neither of these options is available, it may be necessary to generate handcrafted data. Handcrafted data can also be introduced into the live or copied data in order to explicitly test some boundary or error condition in the AUT. Also see *live data*.

Tester A member of the testing team responsible for conducting testing of the *AUT* by following a *test script*. (See Appendix A for complete *TORs* of the members of staff involved in the testing process).

Test Error A specific *test result category*. The test error result indicates that the associated *test case* failed, but that the *AUT* performed correctly, that is, the test case itself was in error (e.g., a typographical error in the test case).

Test Harness A program used to test a portion of the *AUT* (such as a module or unit) by representing other interoperating elements of the AUT. For example, during *unit testing*, it may be necessary to represent other units that provide or receive data from the unit under test (also see *simulation*).

Testing The process consisting of all lifecycle activities, both static and dynamic, concerned with planning, preparation, and evaluation of software products and related work products to determine that they satisfy specified requirements, to demonstrate that they are fit for purpose, and to detect defects.

Testing Environment The IT environment (including the hardware, software, data, and support infrastructure) used by the *test team* to support the testing of the *AUT*. Also see *development environment* and *live environment*.

Testing Manager A member of staff responsible for managing the entire testing process within an organization (see Appendix A for complete *TORs* of the members of staff involved in the testing process).

Testing Programme The complete organizational specification for an organization engaged in performing formal, rigorous testing of software systems. (See Chapter 4 – Management of Testing for further details.)

Testing Project A project whose goal is to verify the suitability of the *AUT* for its intended purpose.

Test/Testing Team A dedicated team responsible for performing the higher phases of testing of the *AUT* (that is, *system testing* and above). The testing team will be managed by a *test team leader* and will contain one or more *test analysts* and one or more *testers*.

Test Log A chronological record of all relevant details of a testing activity (Appendix G provides a template for a test log).

Test Plan document One of the artifacts generated by the *test team leader* during a testing project. The test plan document will be used as the basis of project management control throughout the testing process, and contains information specifying the approach to testing and any constraints, risks, and dependencies, the test assumptions and exclusions, test entry and exit criteria, project controls, and a plan for completing the testing (including contingency for any retest activities). Appendix C contains a test plan document template.

Test Repository The means of organizing all of the testing assets (such as *test cases*, *test logs*) employed by a project using an automated testing tool during a testing project.

Test Result Category A member of a set of results that can be applied to the outcome of a particular *test case*. For example, typical test result categories include:

a) Pass – the observed test result conforms to the expected result
b) Test Error – the observed result is correct, but the expected result is incorrect
c) Acceptable – the observed result indicates that the *AUT* differs from the agreed specification but is acceptable, requiring no change to the system but a change to the functional specification
d) Tolerable – the observed result is incorrect, the AUT is workable and shall be accepted, but the fault must be rectified within an agreed time
e) Intolerable – the observed result is incorrect and the fault must be corrected before the AUT passes this testing phase.

Test Result Record form A form that is used to record the results of executing a particular *test case*. A template copy of a test result record form can be found in Appendix F.

Test Rig A flexible combination of hardware, software, data, and interconnectivity, which can be configured by the *test team* to simulate a variety of different *live environments* on which an *AUT* can be delivered.

Test Script A prescriptive document describing in detail how a test is to be conducted, the inputs, and the expected behavior of the item being tested. A test script will contain a number of *test cases*. In *automated testing* terms, a test script is an automated test procedure used with a *test harness* or tool.

Test Specification document One of the artifacts generated by the *test team leader* during a testing project. The test specification document provides the specification for the testing process required for formal verification of the *AUT*. Appendix D contains a test specification document template.

Test Team The team responsible for conducting the testing process on the *AUT*. (See also Chapter 4 – Management of Testing and Appendix A – Terms of Reference for Testing Staff.)

Test Team Leader A member of the testing team responsible for managing the day-to-day tasks of the testing team. (See Appendix A for complete *TORs* of the members of staff involved in the testing process.)

Thread Testing A testing technique used to test the business functionality or business logic of the *AUT* in an end-to-end manner, in much the same way a user or an operator might interact with the system during its normal use.

Tool Support The use of an automated testing tool (such as IBM Rational Functional Tester (13) to support the testing process in order to reduce effort, timescales, and cost in software testing.

TOR Terms of reference (see Appendix A – Terms of Reference for Testing Staff).

Usability Testing A particular type of *nonfunctional testing* that focuses on the ease of use of the *AUT* from the perspective of the *end user*. Issues to be considered in usability testing include the intuitiveness, consistency, and clarity or understandability of the user interface. See also *performance*, *stress*, and *volume testing*.

User See *end user*.

User Acceptance Testing This is a form of acceptance testing conducted from the user perspective (i.e., involving user representatives). (Also see *acceptance testing*.)

User Representative A nominated member of the user community for the *AUT* who will be expected to participate in or to nominate other users to participate in *user acceptance testing* of the system (it is important that the user representative be a genuine user of the system, and not, for example, a manager who manages users of the system).

V&V An abbreviation of *verification* and *validation*. This is the process of confirming that the *AUT* meets its requirements and has been developed using best practice/formal process.

Validation "Are we building the product right?" The process by which it is confirmed that the *AUT* has been developed in line with best practice and applicable standards. Also see *verification*.

> The International Software Testing Qualifications Board (ISQTB – [72]) definition of validation is as follows. Confirmation by examination and through provision of objective evidence that the requirements for a specific intended use or application have been fulfilled.

Verification "Are we building the right product?" The process by which it is confirmed that the *AUT* meets its requirements. Also see *validation*.

> The ISQTB definition of verification is as follows. Confirmation by examination and through provision of objective evidence that specified requirements have been fulfilled.

Verification Point A verification point is an element of an automated *test script* (i.e., a script that can be run using an *automated testing tool*), which verifies some aspect of the functionality of the *AUT*. A verification point in an automated test script is analogous to a *test case* in a manual *test script*.

Volume Testing A *nonfunctional testing* technique that determines the *AUT's* ability to cope with large volumes of data (as opposed to the sample data likely to have been used during development of the AUT). See also *performance*, *stress*, and *usability testing*, and Chapter 3 – Testing Techniques.

Waterfall Development A particular approach to software development that views the process as a series of linear steps each of which (in the strictest sense of the term) must be completed before the following step can begin. The steps traditionally include requirements, specification, design, and implementation.

White Box Testing Testing where the *test cases* are designed with the knowledge of how the AUT is constructed. White Box testing may also be termed *glass box testing*. (also see *Black Box testing*).

Index